Presence
A JOURNAL OF CATHOLIC POETRY

Presence: A Journal of Catholic Poetry is published annually, each spring, with generous help from the Department of English, Caldwell University, Caldwell, New Jersey.

Subscription rates:
Single Issues—$12 (Back Issues—$8)
Two-year subscription—$22
Three-year subscription—$30

Please see www.catholicpoetryjournal.com
for mission statement, submission guidelines, rights, advertising rates and purchase information.

Printed by
Craftsman Printers, Inc., 535 32nd Street, Lubbock, TX 79404
www.craftsmanprinters.com

Cover Design: Deborah Mercer
Cover Art: Rick Mullin
Behind the Choir (Cathedral Basilica of the Sacred Heart, Newark)
Oil on pine board, 34" x 24"
Photographer: Steven Wesche

Published by
Mary Ann B. Miller
Department of English
Caldwell University
120 Bloomfield Ave.
Caldwell, NJ 07006

copyright (c) 2019 by Mary Ann B. Miller
ISBN: 978-0-9988095-2-6
ISSN: 2573-900X

Presence: A Journal of Catholic Poetry
2019

Editor-in-Chief
Mary Ann B. Miller

Associate Editor
Lois Roma-Deeley

Assistant Editor
Marjorie Maddox

Translations Editor
Gregory Orfalea

Advisory Board
Susanne Paola Antonetta
William Baer
Paul J. Contino
Kate Daniels
Dana Gioia
Paul Mariani
Angela Alaimo O'Donnell
Judith Valente

Promotions Assistant
Regina Montano

Undergraduate Readers
Adam Criaris
Manley Dorme
Jamie Giaquinto
Aimee Jimenez
Devin Lattuga
Chelsea Martinez-Casiano
Connie Naturale
Gisselle Negrete
Nathaniel Parrish

Contents

Mary Ann B. Miller	Editor's Statement	10

ARTIST'S STATEMENT

Rick Mullin	on *Behind the Choir*	11

FEATURED POET

Daniel Tobin	from *This Broken Symmetry*	
	(Rue du Paradis)	13
	(Font)	14
	(Riverside)	15

TRANSLATIONS & ADAPTATIONS

Sharif S. Elmusa & Gregory Orfalea	The Life of Photos by Ibrahim Qa'duni	16
	from *Dark Images* by 'Abboud Sam'u	17
	A Door That Does Not Slap by Wael al-Nassir	18
	Like a Bull Going Left & Right by 'Abır Abd al-Wahid	18
	Life is Flight by Lena 'Atfa	19
Katie Farris & Ilya Kaminsky	The Beginning of a Beautiful Day (A Symphony) by Daniil Kharms	22
	A Man Falls Asleep by Daniil Kharms	23
	A Fairytale from the North by Daniil Kharms	23
Andrew Frisardi	Dante to Guido Cavalcanti	24
Garrett Hongo	from the *Shinkokinshū* by Saigyō, Jakuren, Shunzei, and Fujiwara Toshinari no Musume	25

Garrett Hongo	from Japanese American interment camps by Muin Ozaki and Sojin Takei	27
Susan McLean	Autumn by Rainer Maria Rilke	29
	Saint Sebastian by Rainer Maria Rilke	29
Pablo Medina	Cardboard Dream by Rafael Alcides	30
	Farewell by Rafael Alcides	31
Christine Valters Paintner	You Are Here after Rilke	32
Jeannine M. Pitas	I'm alone in the night by Selva Casal	33
	Like a shipwreck by Selva Casal	34
Jon M. Sweeney	Inhere after Meister Eckhart	36
Wally Swist	Of the Wedding at Cana after Rilke	37
	Consolation of Mary with the Resurrected Christ after Rilke	38

IN MEMORIAM

Maryann Corbett	Funeral Road Trip	39
Rick Mullin	Third Sancerre for Timothy Murphy	40
Gail White	For Timothy Murphy	41
James Matthew Wilson	At Middle Age	42
Marjorie Maddox	Photo with Bald Heads	43
Susan L. Miller	*Et In Arcadia Ego*	45
Julie L. Moore	Hummingbird	47

POETRY

Joseph Bathanti	CiCi's	48
Jill Peláez Baumgaertner	Magdalene	49
Alan Berecka	Note to my Future Self,	51
Tim Bete, OCDS	Lost Things	53

Kathleen Bradley	The Catholics	54
Pat Brisson	Response to Today's Gospel	55
Debra Bruce	Sister Edward's Lunchroom Blessing	57
Mary Buchinger	A Broken Sonnet for the Sparrow Trapped in the Interfaith Center on the 3rd Floor of the McCormick Building at UMass Boston Overlooking the Harbor	58
Roxana L. Cazan	This Is How To Paint Icons At Agapia Monastery, Neamț County, Romania	59
Yuan Changming	Light vs. Shadow: A Recursive Poem	61
Erica Charis-Molling	Lena Waithe speaks to her cape of many colors	62
Richard Cole	Manifest Destiny	63
Barbara Crooker	Petite Marie	64
Joanna Currey	Sunday, Gratuitous	65
Jim Daniels	Gospel	66
P. S. Dean	Lent	67
Jessica G. de Koninck	Crazy Eights	68
Lynn Domina	A Failure of Imagination	70
Sharif S. Elmusa	Companions, Or Clouds	71
Stephen Gibson	On the Everyday Blindness of Mortality	73
Dominic Gideon	The Savior in Starbucks	74
Maria Mazziotti Gillan	Apparitions	75
Ed Granger	Nickel Mines, PA	76
Maryanne Hannan	Beleaguered Church Hears the Call for Apology	77
Jerry Harp	Book of Hours 3 and 6	78
Lois Marie Harrod	Three Sisters	79
Anne M. Higgins, DC	The End of Daylight Savings Time	80
Fr. Thomas Holahan	The Cabin with a View of the Mountains	81
Siham Karami	Angels	82
Elaine Kehoe	Moon Illusion	83
George Klawitter, CSC	Hand in Hand	84
Dean Kostos	The Coat That Wore a Man	85
Leonard Kress	The Relic	86
Michelle Maher	Caravaggio's *The Death of the Virgin*	87

Paul Mariani	What the Waves Kept Telling Me	88
D. S. Martin	How To Listen For God	89
Michael Angel Martín	Adoration Chapel Near Me	90
Pablo Medina	Canticle of the Deer	91
Orlando Ricardo Menes	Ode	92
Philip Metres	Zoo Windows	93
Rhonda Miska, OP	La Guadalupana	94
Robin Amelia Morris	If you cannot pray as yourself	95
Susan Signe Morrison	The Third Plague	96
Elisabeth Murawski	Psalm	97
Stella Nesanovich	Dwelling Among Tombs	98
Matthew C. Nickel	Harvesting Potatoes Under Solar Eclipse 2017	99
Gregory Orfalea	California Rain	100
Barry Peters	Surveillance	101
Daye Phillippo	Thunderhead	102
Mia Pohlman	A Man Who is a Stranger Comes to Visit	103
Christopher Poore	Léon Morin, Priest	105
Dennis Rhodes	Our Housemate	106
Michael D. Riley	Halo	107
Margaret Rozga	Full of Grace	108
Lisa Toth Salinas	To the New Girl at the Women's Shelter	109
Nicholas Samaras	Afterlife	111
Janna Schledorn	Daniel the Prophet Talks to a Psychologist	112
Martha Silano	The hands of all my mistakes	113
Rita A. Simmonds	You Can't Take the Dead	114
Richard Spilman	Finding God	115
Sofia M. Starnes	Dizain 11: Miracle	116
Sheryl St. Germain	Prayer for One in Recovery	117
Sophia Stid	Notes on the Burghers of Calais: Stanford Memorial Church	119
Carole Stone	Looking for a Cure	120
Jacob Stratman	watching Mark Twain's *Is He Dead?* with my son	121
Maxine Susman	Yom Kippur in the Mountains	122
Maria Terrone	A Theft	123
Brian Volck	Emmaus	124
Mark C. Watney	Church Going Under a Jacaranda Tree	125
R. Bratten Weiss	Sunday Worship	126
Paul Willis	McKinley Springs	127

Aliesa Zoecklein   Bible Scholar's Lecture   128

INTERVIEWS

Jerry Harp	Tinkering, Texts, and Divine Excess: An Interview with Kimberly Johnson	129
Mark C. Burrows	"Hungering for the Emptied God": An Interview with Daniel Tobin on a New Collection Exploring the Person and Work of Simone Weil	137

BOOK REVIEWS

Lynn Domina	*We Became Summer* by Amy Barone	147
Cydnee Devereaux	*The Virginia State Colony for Epileptics and Feebleminded* Molly McCully Brown	150
Paul Mariani	*The Chance of Home* by Mark S. Burrows	152
Margaret Rozga	*Night Unto Night* by Martha Collins	155
Jake Oresick	*Street Calligraphy* by Jim Daniels	157
Michael P. Murphy	*Dear Pilgrims* by John F. Deane	160
Ned Balbo	*Single Bound: Krypton Nights / Amazon Days* by Bryan D. Dietrich	166
CX Dillhunt	*Stichomythia* by Tyler Farrell	170
Mary Ladany	*The Lake Michigan Mermaid* by Linda Nemec Foster & Anne-Marie Oomen	175
Ned Balbo	*The Best American Poetry 2018* ed. by Dana Gioia	177
Luke William	*Magdalene* by Marie Howe	181
Angela Alaimo O'Donnell	*Tropic of Squalor* by Mary Karr	183

Susanne Paola Antonetta	*The Night's Magician: Poems about the Moon* ed. by Philip C. Kolin & Sue Brannan Walker	188
Juditha Dowd	*Cures for Hysteria* by MaryAnn L. Miller	190
Shanna Powlus Wheeler	*Full Worm Moon* by Julie L. Moore	193
Jeremiah Webster	*The Five Quintets* by Micheal O'Siadhail	196
Michael Angel Martín	*Before the Burning Bush* by Brian G. Phipps	198
Tyler Farrell	*A Stone to Carry Home* by Andrea Potos	200
Mia Schilling Grogan	*What Will Soon Take Place* by Tania Runyan	203
Kim Bridgford	*Beyond All Bearing* Susan Delaney Spear	206
Maryanne Hannan	*The Consequence of Moonlight* by Sofia Starnes	209
Jim Daniels	*Gloved Against Blood* by Cindy Veach	212
Mike Aquilina	*The Stranger World* by Ryan Wilson	216

LIFE'S WORK

Joshua Hren	"Faith's Ardor in [an] Air-Conditioned Tomb": Dana Gioia's Sights of the Unseen in a Secular Age	219
Susan L. Miller	Extraordinary Spirit: The Poems of Anya Krugovoy Silver	228
Kathleen Marks	The Charlotte Poems of Richard Wilbur and the Shape of a Marriage	239

POETS' BIOGRAPHIES   248

Editor's Statement

    A look back at my previous statements in the first two issues of *Presence*, which considered the roles of the poet and reader respectively in the sacred act of writing, suggests that I had begun, perhaps unconsciously at the time, a trajectory that would eventually lead to considering the relationship of the poem to the world that shapes and yet is shaped by the written word. Quite consciously, with the addition of a translations editor in our third year, we have created a more pronounced commitment to attempting to understand the meaning that poets from other parts of the world are creating through their writing. Our growing section of poems translated from a variety of languages shows our desire to explore what it means to be a "universal" Church, "catholic" with a small "c," by reading the work of others around the world in light of our desire to speak as "one Body."

    A caveat or disclaimer, however, remains. While poems can be prayers and while they are sacramental in giving physical form to the spiritual and in the possibility of God's grace working through them, they cannot be said to be sacraments themselves, not in the same way that the Eucharist is a sacrament, part of the unbroken continuum from Christ's own "take and eat." Nor is this journal the same *kind* of gathering at Table as the Mass, but instead creates a cultural space for dialogue and is created by this dialogue as well.

    As editor, I have found much joy in the way that poets themselves are shaping each issue, finding *Presence* to be a venue for certain kinds of poems. In the second issue, we received so many hymns of praise for other poets that we created the *Encomia* section. This year, we received a number of elegies for two specific poets who are part of the community that we have been building through this journal, Timothy Murphy and Anya Krugovoy Silver, and so we created the *In Memoriam* section. This statement is written with gratitude for the way our contributors are nurturing our praise of the divine in others and our hope in the renewed life of our beloved deceased. What kind of grace will our submissions bring us next?

Artist's Statement

on *Behind the Choir (Cathedral Basilica of the Sacred Heart, Newark)*

The Cathedral of the Sacred Heart at Newark was elevated to a basilica in 1995 when Pope John Paul II entered and celebrated evening prayer. I was not in attendance, but I did marvel at the great irony of his televised motorcade from Newark International Airport to the cathedral. As the Pontiff's entourage entered the neighborhood, the neighborhood disappeared behind white canvas barriers along both sides of the route, placed to keep the hardscrabble landscape of Newark out of the picture. Surely the erection of barriers illustrated a profound misunderstanding of Christianity, cathedrals, and landscape.

I painted the basilica from the sidewalk four times in 2017, coming at it from a different perspective each time. My objective was to capture the spirit of a French Neo Gothic style cathedral nestled against Branch Brook Park, a landscape known for its riotous cherry blossoms in the spring, and the Lower Broadway neighborhood of Newark, a diverse, working class community served by the Archdiocese. What I remember most from each outing was the life around me. The greenery, the people, the city street, the houses, the weather. I joyfully worked with an unobstructed view of something bigger than the most magnificent church in all of North America.

Rick Mullin is largely a self-taught painter, though he benefited from working across the street from the Art Student's League of New York in the 1990s, where he took weekly night classes in the studios of Ernest Crichlow and Hananiah Harari. He is a former member of Viridian Artists, the oldest co-op gallery in New York City, and has exhibited in juried shows at the Salmagundi Club in Manhattan and the National Art League in Douglaston, Queens. He frequently exhibited at the fabled (now shuttered) Cornelia Street Cafe, and his work is in private collections in the U.S., Canada, the British Virgin Islands, Europe, and Tasmania. Paintings can be seen at his website, Only of Objects, https://onlyofobjects.wordpress.com/

Poetry

Daniel Tobin

from *This Broken Symmetry*
(Simone Weil, 1909-1943)

(Rue du Paradis)

"I am giving birth to something," she'll declare, though now
She is midway on from that single sphere Plato had devised—
Here, in Grandmother Weil's apartment on Rue du Paradis

Where the family gathers, called by her who still keeps faith—
Prayers they will chant at sunset to One Who Is Everywhere.
Her son, the doctor, has brought wife and son, called *L'enfant*

As though he were the world's one child, has brought them
With tact, not wanting to chide his mother's piety: *Praise You,*
Your command brings dark to evening… You order the cycles of
    time…

You order the stars on their rounds,,, You create day, You create
    night,
Rolling away light before darkness… Praise You for the evening
    dusk.
A piano begins—Mime Weil? Her mother?—its risen notes.

"When we listen to Bach the soul's powers turn tense, silent,
To apprehend this thing of perfect beauty…." But the one
Who speaks has barely begun beginning, like all, in scales:

Blood rivering its circuits to light the womb's cave—one
From two, single cell, two from one, three, four, so one
Ascends descending, bridge to bridge, until there is Simone:

What do you want in life? The teacher will ask her. *Do not*
    forget
Plants grow out, not only up. And she years later nearing
    death:
"Fruits, leaves are wastes of life if one wants to go higher."

For to leave the cave is to be cut off, is to fasten on hunger.
For there is silence in the universe like noise compared to
    God's.
For even now the keys go quiet, quiet, like a sun standing still.

(Font)

New York bound, a reek of diesel from its pluming stacks,
The *Serpa-Pinto* churns ahead through weeks of rolling swells,
In its hold a cache of refugees, in its cabins the affluent—

All escapees in passage from the muzzle of naked force.
Sickened from her lower berth, she stretches out on deck,
Daughter of the Chosen who has chosen contumacy...

Here, in a middle vastness, with other "wretched mortals"
Pressing themselves to the rail, wordless as in a desert,
Will this be the evening all suddenly refracts and shines?

"What could be more beautiful than the fugitive folds
Of waves, the near eternal folds of mountains? This world,
To us, is the only reality available, and we must love it

In all its terror, or love the imagined with its self-deceits...
Oh if we are torpedoed what a beautiful baptismal font!"
She looks out into the ocean, the boat, herself, the planet,

Infinitely tiny specks in an infinite web of necessity,
And matter the measure of distance to her emptied God.
Osiris, Melchisedech, Krishna, incarnations of the Word

Before the Word-Made-Flesh—how can the emptied God
Be with us if not in our imagining? Through a porthole
The hall mills with voyagers, father, mother, the hold below.

Like so many currents of water rushing headlong for the sea,
Or like moths ablaze for the flame, so the heroes of this world,
And the even the teeming worlds run to their deaths in your
        mouths.

(Riverside)
Andre Weil

"Below the brownstone solid bulwark of the Palisades,
Flowing and flown, this river appears a living manifold,
Infinitely transmutable, congruent to us only by its will.

My sister watches, it seems, for hours from our window
As if she saw another window open to, maybe beyond
The scene, a vision captivating but foreign to everything…

When we were young during the War, we'd hike a hill
To that summer house in the Alps above our lone resort,
The garden grown half-wild with its panoply of blooms,

And the mountains snow-covered against the bluest sky,
Like something from Friedrich—her laughter at our reciting
Cyrano together, her obstinacy at the prospect of leaving…

Indomitable Simone—how do I save her from herself?
Sundays she goes to Mass at Corpus Christi, and again
To worship at that church in Harlem, loving as she does

The singing and shouting, the florid dancing in the aisles—
She who drabs herself in breeches and refuses baptism;
But, still, she nestles my newborn, Sylvie—her "Patapon"—

In her arms, and tells Eveline the child should be baptized:
Daughter of agnostic Jews whose faith her aunt refuses,
Her counsel practical, regardless of what faith or none

The child comes to choose. I take mine, if any, from Arjuna:
I see you everywhere, Lord of the Universe—faces, bellies, arms,
    eyes,
I see you, Manifold One, who have no beginning, no middle, no
    end.

TRANSLATIONS & ADAPTATIONS

Sharif S. Elmusa & Gregory Orfalea, trans.

[The following five poems by Syrian refugees were found on a website, posted by `Imad al-Din Mousa: "Syriadha: Syrian Poetry in the 'Diaspora'." Syriadha is a composite of "Syria" and "Iliadha," the Arabic for "Iliad."]

The Life of Photos

The photos were rare, dear.
We knew by heart their spot on the wall,
Gazing down at us, ancestors
With silent love. In a town next door,
Lifting weapons, they seemed far away!

Photos adorned with plastic flowers by the Koran
Old as the wedding night on the bedroom dresser.
They were young! It was a "night of a lifetime!"
Others were thrust in the guts of albums few ever saw.
Or in wallets parents opened, like brittle secrets.
We were proud of our school pictures, innocent
Down the years.

The photos were alive and spoke
Straight, in black and white.
We touched them, read the old writing on the back.
In time, we repaired their frayed corners with black tape
And began to ignore them, avoiding their glow, their stories.

Still, these photos told us who we were, cherished
More now than when we were young,
Until we saw them strewn in rubble in pictures of war
Their frames amputated
Corpses of memory in our ruined homes.

As if they had been expelled from Paradise,
Ciphers hardly seen by strangers, on cold screens.

                Ibrahim Qa'duni
                (Syrian)

Ibrahim Qa'duni is a writer and translator residing in Britain. He won second place for al-Hussein al-`Awdat Prize for Arab Journalism from the Harmon Center for Contemporary Studies, established by Syrian intellectuals in Istanbul. He is a contributor to a number of print newspaper and magazines and electronic websites.

from **Dark Images**

We don't call the old elderly
They don't forsake their houses
They stay
They guard their memories
And die defending them
The sniper's bullet
That settled in our neighbor's thigh
As much as it bled
Was a distraction from agony
That bullet
Lived without company

                'Abboud Sam'u
                (Syrian, b. 1992)

`Abboud Sam`u was born in Manbij, a city northeast of Aleppo, in 1992. He published a book of poetry, *al-barid al-tasi'* ("*The Ninth Post Office*"). Sam`u resides in Lebanon.

A Door That Does Not Slap

When a strange door slaps you
You stop for a moment
Feel the place where you were slapped
Without daring a return slap
And you move on
Lugging the stranger's abuse
The act repeats
You stop again to feel the smarting
And move on
To another door
And another slap
And so on and so forth
Till a country with doors
That don't slap strangers
Takes you in

     Wael al-Nassir
     (Syrian)

Wael al-Nassir is a poet and writer with a degree in philosophy. He has published two books of poems: *al-qadam al-yusra li-tilka al-hadiqa* ("*The Left Foot of That Garden*" [dar al-takwin, Damascus, 2013]) and *shawari' la tasil al-hayat biba`diha* ("*Streets That Don't Connect the Districts of Life Together*"). He writes for several periodicals and websites. Al-Nassir was born in the city of Hamaa and now lives in Germany.

Like a Bull Going Left and Right

Even the small things let me down
The things that were close
The tune that once gripped
The prized pen
The plant in its pot on the desk

The idea of a let-down itself lets you down
For how can you blame them for being distant
For letting you down
When you yourself got there before them

And emptied the word of its core
The homeland lets you down
You stage love rituals for her
In memory of pain

The homeland lets you down
The stranger asks you about which country
You hail from
And you swallow your bitterness
When you whisper its name

Hope puckers its lips
And says it has oversold itself
That it is provisional
And that you pinned yourself to it
More than it could deliver

Hope is a gift of pain
Trying to shed its sins
The world savors letting you down
And you savor complaint and alibis
And let-down goes left and right
Like a bull with a scarf around his eyes

      'Abir Abd al-Wahid
      (Syrian)

Abir Abd al-Wahid is the author of two books of poems, *untha al-hub wa al-harb*, ("*Female of Love and War*"); and *washm mukhmaliyyu al-jamar* ("*A Tattoo With Velvet Coals*"). She lives in Saudi Arabia.

Life Is Flight

The road is a march to a waterway. Passage?
No, a void. Are we going to float?
We followed the scam till the very end.
We were neither prophets nor gods nor fish—we sank.
O sea! Give us back what you seized!
O civilized world! Thank you for dressing our tale,
For making it a spectacle in the museums of the post-modern.

The tired road is a march to despair.
We thought the trucks would take us. They did—to solitary
        cells.
Where the ghosts we fought groaned.   Try suffocation.
We traversed the road and we became the road.
The road is all those stranded at the border.

To the killers: You will miss us one day.
To the war: Do you grant heroism or safety?
To the one who counts the foreheads of victims: What's your
number?

We were shaded by trees that don't rustle
And wept for the roses in the courtyard.
There wasn't enough gravel to spread to get home.
Our numbers shrank and identity cards scattered in the wild.
And yet there are people who envy us!
Who are infected by the same wound
To immigrate to enlightened lands.

Here we doze before the mirrors. We cut
Ourselves—that's our end.

I haven't memorized the name of the new place
But keep repeating: *My house stood by a park*
And the fresh spring. In the strange land
I don't believe the color of the trees.
My spirit is a dry cloud.
I hallucinate: Take me back to the desert!

I am now in first grade. I ask for a glass of water
Or cup of tea. The teacher is happy
And my friends clap for me.
And I cry—*but in my language I am a poet!*
I don't want to go to school,
I don't want to learn by force. My wound
Bites salts. Languages are a luxury.
I am here, someone who didn't die.
I ask this country who gave us haven: Who am I?

In a street back home I heard a cry that toppled my heart
Like an overripe apricot.
I've become only a sound, hardly a shout,
Lost as if I were the echo of a shout,
A string off a seam on a shirt.

Yes, I survived along with others who gathered
By land, air, or sea to this remote corner.
Run like fugitives through borders
And capitals, as if maps were unreal.

Friend, family, my lost people—
Life is flight.

> Lena 'Atfa
> (Syrian, b. 1989)

**Lena `Atfa** is the author of the poetry collection, `*ala Hamish al-najat* ("*On the Margins of Escape*"). She was born in the town of al-Salamiyya in 1989 and now lives in Germany.

Katie Farris & Ilya Kaminsky, trans.

The Beginning of a Beautiful Day (A Symphony)

As soon as the rooster had crowed when Timofey jumped out of the window and onto the roof and frightened all of us in the streets. The peasant Khariton paused, picked up a stone, and threw it at Timofey.
    Timofey disappeared.
"That is a clever one!" the herd of people shouted, and Zubov ran full speed and rammed his head into a wall.
    "Oh!" shouted a woman with a swollen cheek.
    But Komarov punched up the woman, and she ran away, howling through the doorway.
    Fetelyushin walked past and giggled at them.
    Komarov walked up to him, "Hey, you bacon," and smashed Fetelyushin in the gut.
    Fetelyushin leaned against the wall and started to hiccup.
    Romashkin spat from the top-story window, aiming at Fetelyushin.
And not far from there, a big-nosed gal was beating up her infant with an iron plate.
And next to her a lovely, a slightly fat young mother rubbed a pretty little girl's face against the brick wall.
    A tiny dog having broken its thin leg lay flat on the asphalt.
    A little boy ate something shitty out of a spittoon.
At the grocery store there was a long line of neighbors waiting for sugar to arrive. The old shouted, spat and pushed one another with bags.
    The peasant Klariton having drunk vodka too early this morning, stood in front of the old women, unbuttoned his trousers and said bad words.

Thus began a beautiful summer day.

                      Daniil Kharms
                      (Russian, 1905-1942)

A Man Falls Asleep

One man falls sleep as a believer but wakes up an atheist.

Happily, this fellow keeps medical scales in each room, and has a marvelous habit of weighing himself each morning and each night. And, so, he weighs himself at nights he finds he is 175 lb. And in the morning, having woken up an atheist he weighs himself again and discovers he only weighs 173 lb.

"Therefore," he gleefuly announces, "my faith weighs nearly 2lb."

> Daniil Kharms
> (Russian, 1905-1942)

A Fairytale from the North

Imagine yourself an old man. What does an old man do? He walks into the forest of course. Why? Who knows why.
    He keeps walking.
    Then he turns back looks at us, and says:
    Hey, an old woman, you!
And, the old woman falls straight down from the tree. Since then, rabbits are white in winter.

> Daniil Kharms
> (Russian, 1905-1942)

Daniil Kharms was born Daniil Yuvachev in 1905 in St. Petersburg to a family whose father had been imprisoned for acts against the Tsar. As a poet, he took the name "Kharms," some thought as a combination of the English words "charm" and "harm," but also, perhaps, as a nod to his beloved Arthur Conan Doyle's Sherlock "Holmes." Kharms experimented with absurdity before the Theatre of the Absurd was born in Beckett and Ionesco. Known as a children's writer, only two of his adult poems were ever published in his short life. He suffered, as had his father, in a government prison, though this time under the Communist system his father had fought to establish, and died of starvation in 1942 at the age of 36.

Andrew Frisardi, trans.

Dante to Guido Cavalcanti

Guido, I think it would be great if you,
Lapo, and I were seized by magic, placed
together in a little boat that raced
the breeze to go where we all wanted to;
so neither storm nor throes of fate could do
a thing to interrupt our steady-paced
advance, and all of us had so embraced
one goal, that our affection always grew.

And Lapo's Lucy and your Vanna now,
along of course with her whose beauty blows
away the thirty best, appear somehow;
and we discuss—guess what? (it starts with *L*).
And they would be delighted with us beaux,
and I believe that we'd be pleased as well.

Garrett Hongo, trans.

from the *Shinkokinshū* (13th century)

[The Shinkokinshū *is a 13th century anthology of about 2,000 Japanese poems, the eighth in a series of 21 anthologies of classical poetry begun with Volume One in the 10th century and ending in the 15th century. Scholars debate whether the* Shinkokinshū *(translated as "New Collection of Ancient and Modern Poems") is a return to origins or a renewal with new experiences treated in a miscellany that falls outside the traditional groupings of the four seasons, felicitations, mourning, parting, travel, and love.]*

    This bitter sorrow a song
Heard even by my own heartlessness—
  Over the shallow waters of the marsh,
    In the autumnal light of evening,
      A snipe breaks into flight.

        —Saigyō

      The fullness of sorrow
Comes neither from emptiness nor completion.
  It is the black pine of the mountains
    Against autumn's evening light.

        —Jakuren

At midnight the wind sighs through the pines
    The same as ten years ago.
    But she hears it forever
  Under the moss, year after year. . .

        —Shunzei

      All has withered
On the grassy path he took to meet me.
      No trace of his steps . . .
    Frost clutching my house,
      Clutching me.

           —Fujiwara Toshinari no Musume

The classical Japanese poets presented here include **Saigyō** ("Western journey"), a 12th century former guard to the emperor who became a Buddhist monk, retired alone in turbulent times to several mountain retreats on the northern island of Honshu. Saigyō was taken as a model by the famous poet Basho, before dying at 72. **Jakuren**, 68, an orphan adopted by the well-known poet Shunzei, became a Buddhist monk himself after losing out in inheritance to Shunzei's natural born sons. **Shunzei**, a low-ranking chamberlain to a dowager princess came from a famous 12th century line of poets; he also was known as a chief exponent of the *Tale of the Genji*, considered one of the earliest novels in world literature. Shunzei said of a good poem, "it will possess a kind of atmosphere distinct from its words." **Fujiwara Toshinari no Musume** was known as "Shunzei's daughter" but was in fact his granddaughter. Little is known of her except that she, too, was a successful poet.

Garrett Hongo, trans.

poetry from Japanese American interment camps (20th century)

To the faces of my children sleeping,
I will not say goodbye nor will I forget . . .
   Taken prisoner by the furious
   On this dark night of endless rain.

—Muin Ozaki

Fort Sill Interment Camp

   The number "111"
A nameless wretch of fear
   Carved in red paint
   On my naked chest.

—Muin Ozaki

Volcano Interment Camp

I look around at the darkness without stars,
   My new home near the volcano
   And hear a voice I know . . .

—Muin Ozaki

Lordsburg Interment Camp

   The sky's horizon
Has no fences for the crows
Who fly up, who disappear
   Into the Everlasting.

—Sojin Takei

In the raining dark, I calm myself.
    It's my turn to be arrested.
    Heavy shoes, heavy boots . . .

        —Sojin Takei

    Even while we eat our meals,
The soldiers stand guard with bayonets,
      Their eyes, their guns . . .

        —Sojin Takei

More than fifty of us
Prisoners gathered
Around an empty sardine can,
Burning incense, chanting
For the departed to reach Paradise.

        —Sojin Takei

Of the interment camp poets, no biographical information is available. For his translations, Hongo used *Poets Behind Barbed Wire*, edited and translated by Jiro Nakano and Kay Nakano, reprinted in 1983. The original poems appeared in camp magazines, letters, or other ephemeral places.

Susan McLean, trans.

Autumn

The leaves are falling, falling from on high,
as if far gardens withered in the sky.
They're falling down with gestures that say no.

And in the nights, the heavy earth falls, too,
from all the stars down into loneliness.

We all are falling. Here this hand is falling.
And look at others: it is in them all.

And yet there's one whose hands hold all this falling
with infinitely gentle tenderness.

>   Rainer Maria Rilke
>   (German, 1875-1926)

Saint Sebastian

He's standing there like one who's lying down,
held upright wholly by his will's great force.
He's far removed, like mothers when they nurse,
and bound up in himself like a floral crown.

Now and now, the arrows penetrate
as if they sprang from his own loins, like steel,
quivering at the outer ends. And still
he's darkly smiling and inviolate.

Just one time is his sorrow magnified,
his eyes laid naked in distress. At last,
they cast something, as trivial, aside,
as if they were forsaking in disgust
the ones who lay a lovely thing to waste.

>   Rainer Maria Rilke
>   (German, 1875-1926)

Pablo Medina, trans.

[Cuban poet and writer Rafael Alcides (Barrancas, Cuba, 1933) was the author of numerous works of poetry and fiction. An early and enthusiastic supporter of the Cuban Revolution, his disillusionment with the Cuban regime began in 1968 when Castro supported the Soviet invasion of Czechoslovakia. For many years the Cuban cultural apparatus refused to publish his work. He withdrew from the island's literary scene and entered a self-imposed internal exile (what Cubans call insilio*). He died in Havana in 2018 and is considered one of the greatest poets of the revolutionary period. His work includes* Conversaciones con Dios *(2014), from which these two poems are taken, and the posthumously published novel* Contracastro*.]*

from *Conversations with God*

Cardboard Dream

The city is being eaten by termites.

The great dream was a cardboard house.

There is a hole
where love and hope should be,

and another
where the Hero's statue once stood
with his fist raised to the sky.

And lots of solitude.

Between the horror and the tears
of waking, I am speaking to you, Lord,
under the sawdust.

Rafael Alcides
(Cuban, 1933-2018)

Farewell

Here, Lord, is the portrait,
the image of the hero who led us astray,
who kept us from finding a new world
possible among men. Perhaps
he didn't do it out of malice.
Perhaps he couldn't see that with so
many padlocks and stern commands
and threats of execution
he undermined the road in whose name
he marched off, barefoot at times.

And here we are, Lord,
the barefoot ones, who gave our lives
for each meter of conquered land,
without roads for going
or roads for coming back, darkly
seated at the edge of all those lost years,
tearing up the portrait
as if saying goodbye to a dream,
an age,
an Atlantis sinking.

                              Rafael Alcides
                              (Cuban, 1933-2018)

Christine Valters Paintner

You Are Here
        after Rainer Maria Rilke's *Book of Hours II, 22*

You are the now and not-yet, the darkened dawn just before
the first rays rise and you are the rays that pierce and prod.

You are the siren screeching through city streets
dropping me to my knees in prayer.

You are the lilac and the dust,
the refugee's body found on shore with empty pockets.

You are the wound that does not heal, the salve,
the bandage, and the raised scar that remains.

You are the dandelion growing through concrete cracks,
the mirror smashed into pieces, the mosaic created.

You are the vigil for my mother dying, you are the steady beep
of the heartrate monitor and the long tone that makes me wail.

You are the ash from the burning towers
the great gashed tree felled by storm, now moss-coated, silent,

You are the grey headstone and the red bird that lands and
        sings,
the gaunt face I ignore while rushing down the street.

You are the old man's spectacles
and the love letters from his wife now gone.

Jeannine M. Pitas, trans.

[Born in 1930 in Montevideo, award-winning writer Selva Casal is the author of fifteen collections of poetry and one book-length essay on her father, Julio Casal, who was also a poet. A former penal lawyer, Casal writes from a deep concern for justice, denunciation of violence, and compassion for society's most vulnerable. Her publication of No vivimos en vano *in 1974, read as a denunciation of Uruguay's then-dictatorial government, led to the loss of her position as Professor of Sociology at the University of the Republic. She resides with her husband in Montevideo, and she continues to write and paint each day. "Everything in life nourishes poetry," she says. "Everything."]*

I'm alone in the night

I'm alone in the night
awake at this entreaty
as certain and stubborn as death
which persists which strikes
makes us suffer smile
one day when you're dead
when you've forgotten
all this love
a gorgeous summer night
will come to raise you up
and all the leaves will be raised
and you'll do whatever you want
drinking glass after glass
night after night
one day when you're far away
looking at the sea that was there
the parade of kings and presidents
hearing the cries of the drowned
and the newly born
and the terrible truths in the corners
when shoes fall
and I strike you again and again
when the world resounds in your memory
shrieking like a wounded beast
this love alone on its own
saying nothing

doing nothing
though we don't recognize each other
it will be in the place where you were
wherever you are
this love will come looking for you

>					Selva Casal
>					(Uruguayan, b. 1930)

Like a shipwreck

Like a shipwreck
a televised series
a program watched again and again
like a chair
like a dog at midnight
like the way you're stripping me of my skin
and skin is infinite
we're alone
arms nails emptiness
to die I'd throw myself into the sea
to die I'd throw myself into the air
I'd cover myself fully
in dense and dark earth
I wouldn't be able to die
I'm not here no
I walk in the shadows of another life
I hang from the anvils and the scaffolding
I become fire vegetation iron
sometimes I get up at dawn
to listen to the sirens of their voice
their proletarian day
goodbye thanks to the body
thanks to the gaze
only the slap the foam
only nakedness comes for me
I'm the earth and I'm undoing myself
I come in through the windows
I call upon the doors of the houses
I watch the blood run
and feel the earth turn
with its jail cells its mental hospitals
its bosses in their offices
insurance policies are floating
letters where wives abandon husbands

leaves angels
the newspapers denounce sedition
their sources confirmed
I see a murdered man:
he's crying
his blood is filled with flies
his tortured blood rises up
and fills the walls with roses.

                      Selva Casal
                      (Uruguayan, b. 1930)

Jon M. Sweeney

[A poetic rendering in English of the last two paragraphs of Meister Eckhart's German sermon on St. Luke 1:26,28]

Inhere

Has he ever wondered
what it is like to know God is there,
or even, to see if the God his mother
seemed to know so well finds its
way to where he sits
in the darkness?
Inhere, right here, find me,
he would like to say,
but he can't.
I tell you this, if you cannot desire the
Inhere, right here, for
yourself, at least you can desire
to desire it, and that my friend,
is nearly enough.

Wally Swist

after Rainer Maria Rilke's *Marienleben*

Of the Wedding at Cana

How could she not be delighted with him who fashioned
The simplest things beatifically for her?
Was not even the majesty of the night itself upset,
The night inured to so much, when Jesus appeared?

And what about that time when he became lost,
Then strayed, his glory growing exceedingly.
Have not the wisest traded
Mouths for ears? And wasn't always the house refreshed

With his youthful voice? *Oh,* surely,
Inestimable times she'd have to extinguish her rapture
In him, lest it shine all too brightly. And all astonished
She accompany the boy.

But when, beyond all prudence, at that feast,
The wedding guests were bereft of wine,
She looked toward him and her eyes importuned him
For but a gesture, but Jesus did not comprehend such

A sign, since he initially protested. Then, unexpectedly,
Jesus achieved it. Afterward, she realized
How she might compel him to perform the miracles
He worked instantaneously, and the entire sacrifice

Was a temptation predestined. *Yea,*
Even written—but adequately formulated satisfactorily.
Yet she had facilitated it to come to transpire so
In her imperceptible pride.

At the table that bore a plentitude of herbs and fruit,
Celebrating along with the others, she had not comprehended
That her tears, which were watered at the depth of their roots,
Were what had been transmuted to blood from this very wine.

Consolation of Mary with the Resurrected Christ

What they then detected—is it not honeyed,
And above all mysteries;
But such an earthy, human imperfection,
That he, a little wan still from the tomb,
Walked toward her, slowly, absolutely absolved,
Though thoroughly resurrected?
Ah, initially to her. How each of them was
Then healed ineffably.
Yes, all of them were healed. That's it exactly.
There was no need to touch one another tacitly;
Instantaneously
Jesus placed his hand, that of a nascent eternal,
Upon the shapely female shoulder,
And then it was initiated,
In silence, as with trees in springtime,
Immeasurably, at one, together,
This perennial season of their supreme communion.

IN MEMORIAM

Maryann Corbett

Funeral Road Trip
i.m. Timothy Murphy

The whole four hours to Fargo,
our engine bucked and stuttered
in bucketing rain, and we wondered
if a poet's intercession
would help a struggling car go,
when heaven itself remembered
the flash of his drunken passion

and yet we thought it answered:
three booms, distantly muttered—
the poet's clipped concision
but huge now, long now, *largo*.

Rick Mullin

Third Sancerre for Timothy Murphy

You were everything that's good and bad
about sestinas, hunting, and Catholicism.
Redolent of Scotch and Balm of Gilead,
transcendent, gay, and full of catechism,
you conveyed, O Murderer of Birds,
the heavy Canine soul. King David psalms
in Sullivan's English, Protégé of old
Penn Warren. Double barreled Brahms
and cloistered forests were the things you told
us over and again. In other words,
Purveyor of the Kennel Trunk, the sonnet.
With its sonic turn, its orthodox
and crusty bucket list. And you were on it,
captured and released, O Paradox
of Capture. Choir of the Eternal Thirds.

Gail White

For Timothy Murphy
(poet, d. June 30, 2018)

Cancer could not extinguish Tim.
His poems came flooding out of him,
like creatures who, before they die,
seek one more chance to multiply

till aided by the Holy Ghost
as muse, he finally could boast
that he had written (good or bad)
more verse than Thomas Hardy had.

But now Tim Murphy cannot reach
our hearts with living voice and speech.
The busy words, the tongue, the brain
shut down for good and can't complain.

Spirit alone can celebrate
the Beauty that he loved so late.

James Matthew Wilson

At Middle Age

From the ledge of this anniversary
    I see the years ahead,
Obscured by nonexistence still,
    Are fewer than those now fled,

And, with the waking of this day,
    Comes news Tim Murphy's died,
His body worn away by drink,
    But mind sure in its pride.

Even at ten, I stood in dread
    Of how the hours passed
And looked at every season's turn
    With longing it would last.

What sorrow, the midsummer twilight,
    As the mosquitoes neared
And voices called us from our play
    Until the yards had cleared.

What certitude, though, Murphy had
    In his returning home
To those wide flats of prairie grass
    And adding poem to poem.

Little less sure have I been of
    What I've been given and made;
The home we've built and filled with children,
    How little their price paid.

But that just coldly clarifies,
    Whatever we may say
Of living well and making rich,
    Small epics of our day,

That calculus of time's firm passage,
    Relentless, without rite,
Alone is cause of terror, encircled
    By ever-encroaching night.

Marjorie Maddox

Photo with Bald Heads
for Anya and Noah Silver

or nearly; the baby fuzz is hers,
compliments of the cancer we seldom speak,

though she does—loudly and often—but not now.
Instead, on this matte finish, she calmly cradles

the red-faced infant, his small mouth open,
life from the still-living pulsing.

His soft spot already
sprouts strands she'll touch

and touch again. See
how she stares out at us

or at God, just this side of the picture-
perfect smile she owns

in the bright flash
of her dark room. See how

she embraces, with her
sleep-deprived, wide-

awake eyes, much more
than the omniscient

one-eyed camera
could ever claim. Only she

can reveal her "See
this is me there, here, now,

grabbing my own ever after,"
the camera clicks and subtle shifts

that follow: her liturgy not of beginnings
or ends, but persistence, holy continuation

into our space of now, brimming
just so with this immortal moment of joy.

Susan L. Miller

Et In Arcadia Ego
          For Anya Krugovoy Silver

Yesterday a new Tom Waits song
was released, and I thought

of you. In a different world
we would have met up this October,

our heads together over a cafe table,
and we could have sung it

like schoolgirls singing the anthem
of their country--not Russia,

not America, but the country of those
who joke about death and carry

a St. Agatha prayer-card wherever
they go. In April your hair

was growing back, and you wore
red and black earrings that swung

like pendulums over our lunch.
You ordered a giant cup of coffee.

I ordered a giant sugar bomb.
The sun warmed our walk

through Central Park, and we linked arms
talking about how much making out

is okay for a 14-year-old, being moms.
It was and was not an ordinary day.

Now I am the only one
who remembers how slowly we walked,

how I returned you to the apartment
because you feared

getting dizzy alone.
I've been trying to pray more,

reading your poems.
I painted my nails red

because of you, letting the chips show.
I walk through the house, wishing

you would haunt me the way you said
your dead friends would sit with you

during chemo. One more time
I would sing to you *bella ciao, bella ciao,*

bella ciao.

Julie L. Moore

Hummingbird
> *Thy hair soft-lifted by the winnowing wind . . .*
> *John Keats, "To Autumn"*

The hummingbird sips at the feeder, nectar sliding
    down its ruby throat like the last drop
        of a summer shower, one of a million

yet precious as any breath it takes.
    And its wings beat fast as death,
        the way it zips onto a dusk-lit deck,

slips into a door without knocking,
    glides down the hallway, then ascends
        the stairway to reach a higher floor.

There is no warning, no sure-fire sign.
    So when the bird lifts its emerald crown,
        if we were close enough and knew how

to poise our bodies, we'd hear a winnowing wind,
    like words escaping,
        and taste their lemon liqueur.

We'd feel the lift of the small, fragile spine
    and sense, perhaps, in its felicitous flight,
        a generous God of orthodox light.

In memoriam, Anya Krugovoy Silver, 1968-2018

Joseph Bathanti

CiCi's

Cici's door is flung to noon.
Sun spills through its lintel.
The lone bulb sways on its wire
above the scarred cash register,
tacked with a crucifix,
behind which CiCi perches –
Jimmy Durante's silent twin – mute,
a living daguerreotype:
gray cardigan, chipped horn buttons,
striped mourning pants, colossal ears
and nose, fedora snap-brim.
Breath from his blue teeth whistles in *Abbruseze*.
In a glass casket lay penny candy:
Jawbreakers Sugar Daddies,
Sputniks, Kisses, Tootsie Rolls
Mary Janes, Fireballs.
Aquarial urns squat the counter:
pickled eggs in pink brine,
green dills, the size of river carp.
CiCi spreads his arms, palms up,
his way of asking what I desire –
though I wonder what took his tongue.
I arrange three pennies –
Lincoln's profile from his mausoleum.
The store smells of turned earth,
deNobili smoke, the silence
of aged *paesani* and their *spettri* escorts.
In East Liberty, the dead, like the birds,
consort with the living.

Jill Peláez Baumgaertner

Magdalene

i.
Demons, All Seven

She could not say
More than
A pot of claws,
A cruel jag of glass.
Litzangle, mosh, she said,
Chugging bad wine,
Shrugging, flesh squirming.
Scritchel, rolfwangler,
And then,
Jesus Christ.
Was it prayer or curse?

And then the sudden silence,
Sun on breezeless waters.
Her eyes still,
The color of sea.
His eyes calm,
The color of earth.
Evenly spaced
Breaths.

All seven finished,
Collapsed, gone.

ii.
Crucifixion

He seemed far away and not so far away.
How could he be far away?
But suffering took him there.
Beyond her.

She watched as if it
Were someone else's story.
She would say later that her distance
From him brought it all back,

Those times when she had no choice
But to submit to chaos
And darkness chewed her whole.

iii.
Resurrection

Afterwards when she tried
To close her eyes
She heard only his cry
To silence, his God.

So she rose in the dark,
Set out for the grave.

But the startle of its vacancy.
How to explain this, she thought.
Completely gone—
Not even cold flesh
Which was not quite nothing.
And here was—nothing.

But then everything.
His sudden presence
Still distant.
He would not be touched.
This time, however,
Sternum, ear, and breath,
Tongue, flesh.

Praise him.

Alan Berecka

Note to my Future Self,

the next time the universe and time conspire
to bring you back to work in Waco at that library
run by that maniacal director with an iron fist,
the woman who fired your predecessor the day
he closed on his house, the woman who just put
into policy a draconian measure—a ten dollar fine
for each library item that sets off our anti-theft system—
accident or not—please be smart enough to ask
the first kid with accidently bagged books for his id
before you explain the new policy. This simple act
will keep that look of hope from suddenly forming
on his face just before he runs through the giant
loophole you provided and out the front doors.

Note to my future self, if you see
the wily and wispy kid take off,
do not chase after him, or, if
in the white heat of the moment,
you feel you must, please remember
you are now a middle-aged couch potato;
your soccer playing days are long,
long in the past, so do not attempt
to vault over the circulation counter;
it will not work, and your foiled attempt
will give the escaping kid a healthy
and unneeded head start.

Note to my future self, cinch up your belt
before you bolt through the library's doors;
your dress pants have gotten a bit too small
and will work their way down your ample
Lucille Clifton sized hips with each ponderous
stride, so just as you begin to gain on the runaway
and reach the brick stairs near the main fountain
on campus, you won't find yourself running
on the inside of the knees of your falling britches,
so you will not learn that tripping down brick steps
rips skin on knees and elbows and shreds pants,
nor will you learn that pain and the sight of blood
will kick in even more adrenaline as you tumble
out of your literally half-assed Aikido roll.

Note to my future self, do not vocalize
your anger. Yelling at the top of your lungs,
"You better run you son of a bitch,
because if I catch you, by God I'll kill you,"
will not encourage a book thief to stop.
So you will chase him through parking lots,
as he hides and crawls beneath parked cars
in an attempt to get away, until he
in total desperation begins to sprint down
the middle of the busiest street in town.

Note to my future self, you are about to learn
you have exercise induced asthma.
Your past athletic career, poor as it was,
was a minor miracle. It wasn't a lack
of conditioning that kept you winded
during games. You should see a doctor
about your lungs years before this fit sets in,
so the rescue inhaler you so badly need
will be in your pocket when you find yourself
gasping for air miles from campus.

Note to my future self, this time as you find
yourself wallowing in defeat as you limp
and wheeze your way back to campus
and that homeless guy with the concerned look
stops you to say. "Hey pal, I think you need this
more than I do," as he extends a dirt caked hand
that opens to reveal a Halls metho–lyptus cough drop
in a graying wrapper covered in what might be
hair and pocket fuzz, accept his gracious offer.
It will make both of you feel better.

Note to my future self, when you make it back
to campus, do not return to the library,
for you will never be able answer,
"What the hell were you going to do
if you caught him?" and no matter what
you do from that day forward, in Waco
you will forever be known as the psycho
librarian who nearly killed himself chasing
after a couple of cheap paperbacks.
Instead, go straight to your car, drive home,
apologize to your wife and kids,
and contemplate a career change.

Tim Bete, O.C.D.S.

Lost Things

St. Anthony of Lisbon,
patron saint of lost things,
did not answer the prayer
to find my lost youth,

saying it wasn't lost
but rather squandered—
a cruel technicality
I did not wish to hear.

Nor did he help find
my lost patience,
saying I had never really
possessed any to begin with,

and what had not been lost,
could not be found.
When I asked him about
an embarrassing incident

in which I lost my dignity,
all he found for me was a dose
of humility, and a memory
I did not want to recount.

Sure, St. Anthony is great
when something small
has been misplaced,
but give him a difficult issue

and you'll find he is the patron
saint of brutal honesty,
making you wish
your car keys were missing.

Kathleen Bradley

The Catholics
for my father, my brother, and Jackie Gleason

The Catholics are the wide guys with cigarettes
guys at the racetrack
guys with thoughts that do high wire acts
and man the trapeze
The Catholics are humble, in brown suits
with heads a little down
or wide and wise guys with sunglasses
hands in pockets
      smirking

Catholics are fat guys and oily guys
but they smell good
They have big, pounding hearts
dying to dance
their minds glitter and no scene is too wide
for the yearning of their hearts
for the red sun to fall behind the snowy prairie.
Their souls take in the prairie and the park
And they remember every change of sky.

Pat Brisson

Response to Today's Gospel

It's not often that I take issue
with the Lord,
but today's Gospel—
the one about Martha complaining
to Jesus that Mary wasn't helping in the kitchen—
has me shaking my head.
Again.
And today I'm finally speaking up.

You remember how it goes, don't you?
Jesus tells Martha that Mary
has chosen the better part.
Well, anyone can see that—
who wouldn't prefer sitting around
listening to stories
instead of standing out in the hot kitchen
shelling peas and peeling potatoes?

I *know* His mama taught Him better than that.
What He should have said is,
You have a point there, Martha,
why don't we all come out to the kitchen
and help you,
instead of telling her not to be so anxious.
Like that will help—
now she's mad at Mary *and*
upset that Jesus won't stick up for her.
And she's not the only one bothered by that answer—
so is every woman who hears that story
and is tired of being alone in the kitchen
while everyone else
is relaxing in the living room
shooting the breeze.

Lord God Almighty!
You want to eat?
You can at least set the table.
Grab a spoon and stir that pasta.
Go on—You can talk
while You're working.

You, of all people,
should be able to multitask.

Debra Bruce

Sister Edward's Lunchroom Blessing

White bread not yet stubbed with fingerprints.
I took one bite and knew what my mother had done—
turkey sandwich on a meatless Friday—
How could she forget? Sister Edward
appeared by my table as if she'd already heard,
as if my mother had called the school to confess.

I'd seen the man sitting on our piano bench,
arranging all her fingers into a chord
the day before, my father on his way home.
I'd never tell, but Sister Edward's hand
resting on my head was heavy, warm,
as if to let the tight twist of my braids
begin to loosen. I didn't know his name.

She said my sandwich was only a mistake.
My mother had not sinned, and I must eat.

Mary Buchinger

A Broken Sonnet for the Sparrow Trapped in the Interfaith Center on the 3rd Floor of the McCormick Building at UMass Boston Overlooking the Harbor

You dart   no   flit   no   this is not   flying   still   you test   what is   here   the what
this   inside   a building   holding you   up   and
   in   yet   you   rise   and move   try   the spin
the span of   this   closed   space—   I
won't   say   *metaphor*   you   are
   you,   singular   bird,   trapped   flailing
in the   Inter- Faith   Center   where   "All   are Welcome"
Outside   dark-screened   windows   the sky   we
both   seek   holds in its basket a broad city   glittering
and   there below   us,   the belly   of a harbor   blue
blue   harbor   abandons   its banks, catching
in its littered   muddy   mirror,   a silver   airplane
cutting into clouds   its steady mechanical path.

Roxana L. Cazan

This Is How To Paint Icons At Agapia Monastery, Neamţ County, Romania

Like with any job,
you start in prayer:
You ask the stones
to give you back the sun,
Drizzling along an oiled beam,
Sinking mutely in a pond of darkness
In the north corner of your cell
At Agapia Monastery.

Blinded by its resuscitated light,
you're left only with voice.
Your whispers bounce
from wall to wall,
polished shale cast by David's
sling. Your murmurs thin
into the gold leaf,
the sheen of gesso,
the kind that turns any
color into blood
so that the flesh sticks
onto bones in the liquid bole,
the bodies spooling dusk
with spirit from the Him.

And that's when you start painting.
Time stops, curled and heavy,
when you tie the tongues of bells
with blades of green.
A suggestion of God flickers
in a tint of lapis-lazuli
the withered fig tree,
the softened highlights suggesting
the Theocosm
and all around is numb silence
ripening the clayey pigments
into fields of the purest purple.

When you run out of
Voroneț blue
Or Arbora green
You ground new gems
and mix the grits
with perfumed myrrh,
crisp wine,
and egg yolk,
you knead them between your
fingertips, you cup them inside
the nest palms the way
your grandmothers
labored over dough,
gathering their faith in fistfuls
raised above the hard-earned flour,

you press your knuckles
into the ceramic
until you scrape off
their paper-thin skin.

Since birth you've been
crawling into slumber,
that place where we go
to sleep next to our ancestors,
and yet through pain
you are blown into light.
You whisper three times
that God is great,
and you expect His sign
fracking the crisp morning,
when candle light
becomes ocean.

Yuan Changming

Light vs. Shadow: A Recursive Poem

I.
    Was it the shadow?
    Was it the shadow beyond?
    Was it the shadow beyond the shadow?
    Still fell the thick night,
    When the heart blocked the light.

    Yes, it is light!
    It is light within!
    It is light within light!
    Loud sweeps the morning glow,
    Where the mind has no shadow.

II.
    If only there were still 10 suns hanging in the sky
    as in the ancient Chinese mythological universe

    If only all stars were close, close enough to us
    like millions of broken mirrors put back together around
        us

    If, if only every light on earth were much brighter
    or, simply if our eyes were just a bit more insightful

    There would be no shadows moving before or behind us,
    there would be no darkness within or without our
        minds.

III.
    Do not be carried away with so much sunshine
    for shadow is right behind your feet.

    Do not be afraid of shadow in front of you
    for the sun is arising just behind your back.

Erica Charis-Molling

Lena Waithe speaks to her cape of many colors

Genesis 45:5

Don't be another train skimming the carpet. Be glorious
    heavenly
upset, and don't apologize for a single stripe. Let the cappa
    magna
be cross with your spectral divinity. Let it roll off my back.
    Forgive
yourself for wasted years, hanging and flagging. The church
    keeps
selling me to my shame, tossing me down that well. But we
    dreamed
this place. It wrapped each long night in multicolored tiers and
    each tear
was God, who wept. Dry my eyes with your prodigal folds. Each
    step
sent me here, my shoulders carrying your bow like the sky. The
    angel
ahead of you holds no feather to you. But you do not need wings
to preserve this, my body, stitched in the Image. This moment,
    this
your life work. Me, the King's dream, prismatic and mantled at
    last.

Richard Cole

Manifest Destiny

Raise the white flags beautifully,
great flags of shocking silk unfolding,
billowing above our homes
and the homes of all our neighbors,
flags over quiet, hurting towns
and stubborn factories, our last,
heroic cities winding down,
from green fields to silent industries
chilled and unforgiving,
a thousand flags stepping off into darkness,
signals in the wind, surviving
the hard, dividing nights
of a vast, lonely and anxious nation.

History whispers in our ear — *If you even
think about fighting, you've already lost.
If you win, you lose. If you lose
you lose.* So this is my dream — an army
of white flags lifted in overwhelming surrender.
No borders, no walls, no demarcations
scratched in crumbling concrete. This is my dream —
we have won the peace, an enduring republic,
infinitely yielding, falling and rising
again with the wind.

Barbara Crooker

Petite Marie
*small statue on a back road above the village
of Auvillar, France*

Petite Marie, full of grace, you stand
in the midst of a harvested field, stubble at your feet.
Holy Mother, glazed in ceramic, your robes are the same
blue-green of Lot-et-Garonne, the color of shutters and doors.
Your bare feet rest on a stone. Behind you, sunlight
dips the leaves in precious metals, copper and bronze.
Your eyes are cast down, hands folded, lips closed.
Nearby, in a neighboring tillage, someone
in a sunlit vineyard is turning the blood
of ordinary grapes into wine.

Joanna Currey

Sunday, Gratuitous
February 8, University of Virginia Garden X, 71°F

Praise for our ripe bodies napping in the milk-
washed light.

                Praise for the bird trilling triplets—
late Epiphany hymn from the boxwood tree.

Praise for someone's bad country music
clinking over from Garden VIII.

                         Praise for my stack
of used poetry books, schooling and scripture,
inexhaustible gifts.

                Praise for the column
of dust-gold float, and your musky sawdust hair.

Praise for you, smooth-lipped languisher, aimless zeal
in the heave and brick of your chest.

                         Praise for this pleasure
that is close to grief, this lazy breeze
that smells like mulch and lime zest,

            for this day that is worthy
because it will not last, and praise the sun

on your upturned cheek
that burns and burns as you sleep.

Jim Daniels

Gospel

I saw the Great Blue Heron today,
still, above the flat horizon, staring
as I passed on my bike. Some mornings
I admit, I scare it into rising just to see
those wide whispering wings spread
over grape vines clenched into earth
in bright green rows. Nothing is here
for my amusement. The heron fishes
in the small stream where the narrow road
turns. Easy pickings. Today, I don't scare it.

My son dropped sticks off the narrow bridge
into that stream twenty years ago—a man now,
and I'm sad for it on days like this. Thousands
of miles away, he sings songs I've never heard.
Look, I'd say to him, and point. He's not here
for my amusement, getting on with it, screwing up,
muddling through. We used to watch current carry
those twigs till they disappeared. Sometimes
it's so quiet, I can hear wings. The heron, straight,
graceful pin above flatlands along the stream.

To dig our roots deeper, or to fly? How to hide
nests, protect our young? My son is tall somewhere out there. We build nests one thin stick
at a time. The sticks never disappear. I don't
want to live far from water. My amusement
is finite. Leaves on the vines redden
and wither while elsewhere fruit ferments
into wine. It's an old story, I know,
but teach me the words, my son.

P. S. Dean

Lent

She packed a suitcase
on a Wednesday and left
while I was in the shower
took my keys without a word
from the kitchen table
to back down the drive
Later on I saw a blonde
with great legs at the grocery
got a deal on day old sausage
but it made me lonesome
so I packed a duffle bag
and took a cab to a motel on I-10
I opened a warm beer
the stars stayed up with me
my neon heart buzzed slow
with the NO VACANCY sign
Hell I'm sure Christ almighty
undressed Mary Magdalene
with his eyes a time or two
even if only for a moment
not even I can live forever
in the temple of this world

Jessica G. de Koninck

Crazy Eights

> *and He ceased on the seventh day from all the work that He had done*   --Genesis 2:2

And on the eighth day...

No talk about the eighth
day. God finished in seven
threw down the cards and left
in the way that God exits

the story only to enter again,
wreak some havoc and flee.

By the time
we reach chapter eight,
God's cleaning up after
his Big Flood and about to start
over.

In another version
electrons come into being eight seconds
after the Big Bang. For millennia
the universe remains
too hot for light to shine.

Separating light from darkness
is a parlor trick of the Big Magician.

Radio telescopes go back and back and then
at the instant of creation–
nothing.

Before the Big Whatever time
did not exist. Place did not exist.
The rubber band of curved space
and multiple dimensions snaps
when I try to stretch it to fit
around my head.

God took a day off.
Things got complicated.

God sent lice, locusts,
frogs, leveled the Cities of the Plain.

Light takes so long to travel,
people who live at the other
end of the Milky Way
can only see our past.

Ask the Magic 8 Ball:
Will the universe stop expanding?
Will the sun explode?

If I could shuffle time,
I'd fold my cards,
spend an afternoon with Grandma,
take a nap on her soft mattress.

Once upon a time it was
the safest place in all the universe.

Lynn Domina

A Failure of Imagination
Holofernes

If he was vain
of his appearance, if he was indifferent,
if he oiled his hair and felt it
glisten, if he permitted it to descend
into knots, each strand
twisted around another, he never

imagined a woman,
clever as that one was and knowing
more than he knew
of desire, dangling
his head by his black hair,
his black beard drooping, stained
black with blood.

Sharif S. Elmusa

Companions, Or Clouds

No closure. I am here at the cemetery
of Sahab ("Companions," or "Clouds")
in Jordan, returning the countless visits
my parents paid me since they died.
The mass of graves are a grid
of crudely cut, white limestone
mounds and headstones
bleached further by the fierce summer sun.
Same blessings. Built-up wilderness.
Even the intricate Arabic calligraphy is flat.
As if the planner spent the nights watching
moths swarm around blazing lamps.

At first, I feel distressed
by grief's gray ground.
Then I think to myself,
why must the graveyard be pretty,
a picturesque of cut grass and flowers
to bury deeper the buried bones?

My parents— good farmers from the guts
of a country rubbed out from the map—
paid life's slow price, held fast
their handfuls of joy, did their work.
Their genes thrive now in far-flung lands.
I am pulled here by the strange gravity
of the truth, the irrevocable, tucked underground.
No accounts to settle, hatchet to bury,
I only want to thank them
(they who don't hear)
thank them for a love a son can never match.

I stand between their tombs,
pause, and close my eyes.
Only the wind takes questions.
I say prayers that were warm bread
to their mouths. I wish I could beseech the gods,
as an Ancient Egyptian did for his deceased,
that they not die a second time.
My tears assume this is the place to be,

and drop into an invisible puddle
shed by a herd of untethered eyes.

Leaving, I see no wall, no fence
between the here and the hereafter.

Stephen Gibson

On the Everyday Blindness of Mortality
on vacation, Quebec

They found in the latrines of the fort-chateau
women's personal articles, chipped crockery,
broken glass bottles once holding cognac—

what else they would find, they didn't know
but the photographs of the dig let you see,
in situ, such items being unearthed: bric-a-brac,

a man's belt buckle; a jar of skin cream; bricks;
someone's bone toothbrush—memento mori
right underneath the promenade of the Frontenac

where tourists like my wife and me hold selfie-sticks,
look back.

Dominic Gideon

The Savior in Starbucks

With a man-bun, skinny jeans, and a
Paisley button-down, he orders a
Grande Hazelnut Mocha Coconutmilk Macchiato
And a chocolate croissant.

The pretty barista with an ink dragon running
Down her arm looks at him with narrowed eyes:
"Has anybody told you that you look like
Jake Gyllenhaal?"

As he watches another artisan intently craft his
Coffee cocktail, a toddler glues himself
To the street-side window, open-eyed,
Before his mother yanks him back into
The stream of pedestrians.

He sits, sips, and breaks chocolatey bread
Among the patrons who scroll and tap and
click, and he admires his Father's creation until
A few fellows notice his gaze and
return uneasy glances.

Leaving, he waves to the counter,
Unseen by the bustling baristas,
And opens the door to a flutter of birds
Synchronizing a winged dance around
The crown of his head.

Maria Mazziotti Gillan

Apparitions

How many ghosts can gather in one house?
If you had asked me twenty-five years ago,
I would not have known how to answer,
but now too many years crammed with loss,
too many of the people I love gone
to that other country where I cannot touch them.
But some days I swear all of them gather,
one by one, at my table as they did
all those years ago on holidays.
I am glad to see them
though they speak a language I no longer understand.
I want to know about the country they now call home.
I put out small cups of espresso and pastries and anisette and smile.
I know they're happy to see me,
to fill my house again with their presence
and their chirpy voices and their laughter.
I wish they still spoke my language,
but I too am happy to be with them—
my husband, my mother, father, sister,
cousin, aunts, uncles, best friends for years.
They are like a warm breeze on my skin.
Their ghost arms encircle me.
I beg them to stay longer but I understand
they need to go back.
Their bodies gradually vanish
as though they are made of smoke
and they rise up and drift off
though I call and call their names.

Ed Granger

Nickel Mines, PA

Lost between hushed palisades
of ripening corn, I blunder into
Nickel Mines, where hatred was
unable to take root after ten
Amish girls were shot and killed
in a one-room schoolhouse in 2006.
Compass restored, I drive on toward
my need to sow forgiveness, having
glimpsed its green magnetic north.

Maryanne Hannan

Beleaguered Church Hears the Call for Apology

Long history, that word. Socrates' last words
on the false-gods charge. With a little help
from his friends—*a po LO gi a*. How cool

does that sound? Then centuries of Christian
apologists, after we finally figured out
the Really Right god. Using evidence, hard

and fast, and lots of quotes from each other.
Then, Shakespeare, says the dictionary, made
apologies personal, as in the admissions you want

from the legions of annoying people in your life.
If you're still with me, you've noticed
apologizers and apologists have parted ways.

Although, really, don't they still need each other?
Our newly sainted John Paul got on a roll.
Apologies: *Come one and all, you we burned*

*at the stake, sacked with our Crusades, sold
into slavery, stole with laws, converted,
persecuted, ignored when you needed us most.*

We're sorry. Mistakes have been made.
Are we missing anyone? Oh, them. Of course—
Papal apologies come to town regularly

on their honking-big camels, struggling for breath
through gagging halters, nose pegs, buckling
under saddles, weighted down with bags of gold

and Renaissance art. Not everything you'd hoped?
Together again—apologists, there to help them
pass through the eye of an excruciating needle

Jerry Harp

Book of Hours

3

It's an all-around crapshoot this time of year.
Will I fade or go? Depends on the weather,

the ins and outs I'm riding, my pills
a slow incandescence. I could say I'm better,

but why go there when I can just stay politic
and here, where it all comes down to the four

last things pratfalling like a comedy team
come out of retirement? I'm nagging myself

to sleep, wagging into oblivion.
Will you stay with me a minute?

It all comes together,
my cells in separation flashing neon saints.

Book of Hours

6

This whole human thing I'm after, it's
so past tense, I'm sheared, shared out, shut
down to the very parts I'm patterned on.

I'm fraying, or need to be, needling
the heart that is my matter and can
no longer stand or sit, especially at night

when this dear darkness is my only companion.
Hello, friend, your company I keep
under wraps disrupts

the autopsy I once settled on.
That's when the windows close and whatever
thing's left begins, agains, and then.

Lois Marie Harrod

Three Sisters

In at least one folk story
the first is brainy, the second beautiful,
and the third hobbles in last in the sack race,

In Chekhov, the first is headmistress,
the second a slut, the third marries someone
she doesn't love, as my sister says she did.

Elsewhere it's the first who is gorgeous,
black hair and thick lashes, the second wide-eyed
and generous, the third a lamb to the slaughter.

In my family all these and more—
depending on who tell the story:
when I was first, I never spoke

to those who said, *keep quiet
if you don't have anything to say,*
a dictum that disallowed pearls.

When I was second, the blonde parrot,
I chattered like a canary on hemp seed,
adapting myself to the cage.

Third I was the bi-polar moose,
who is to say what went wrong with my life?
My mother was rigid, my father huge,

and my sisters claimed I demented myself
with stories of my own concoction,
none of which, in their experience, was true.

Anne M. Higgins, D.C.

The End of Daylight Savings Time

Random scatter in the paling sky
This All Soul's evening dusk arrives at five.
Each fall the convent graveyard makes me cry.
Random scatter in the paling sky,
The calm before November's migrants fly
By next week , early dark, and cold will drive
Random scatter from the paling sky.
But All Soul's evening dusk arrives at five.

Fr. Thomas Holahan

The Cabin with a View of the Mountains

His face is flickering with
the embers of the TV screen,
his wife, emptied of tears and
prayers and even memories,
holding his hand.
Both are quiet the way the woods are
before the lightning.
Their son paces the cabin,
twenty-four, fascinated to be
witnessing his father's death
and terrified.
He cannot help himself so
he stares out the window at the view,
icy grey mountains and a jet stream
dipping down
close to home.

                Nederland, Colorado

Siham Karami

Angels

They only speak to your pre-earthly sense,
in waves and/or particles
(you will never know which)
of light: but what is light?
Not words. Too earthly, those:
throated, tongued, inflected, toothed, parting lips
and humming through them.
Those were born in mud and in its higher incarnation,
neurons, carriers of electricity.
Angels too are carriers, but
also scintillators, jellyfish of holy spectra
and you feel them in your aura, rippling through, a sigh.
Only pure thought brings them,
thought unsullied by its striving.
A thought of them resides in that same bloody heart
from which they wish to cringe
but to which they prostrate out of reverence
to the One whose name
also forms a heart
intangibly and yet so sensual
only the blind can see its blinding light
and feel the ruddy darkness
of its pulse, abiding peace.

Elaine Kehoe

Moon Illusion

Perception scientists say
> it's just an illusion, the way
>> the horizon moon gapes so huge and orange
>> and fills up the eyes

But someone drove his car off the edge of the highway
> trying to get there,
>> to go through the hole in the sky
>> into heaven.

George Klawitter, C.S.C.

Hand in Hand

To be feathered by the likes of you
and fly beyond the body that is mine
requires the lift of love. I swim in air
too rarified for simple mortal taste.

That's ecstasy. We get it from the brew
that witches stew inside our brain. I sign
the pledge of flight, take off, and even dare
the gods to sing my arm around your waist,

your heart in mine. I wouldn't think to choose
some other way to live. It's angel-life
we find between the farthest stars and earth.

Our secret—this metaphoric cruise—
divinity controls. We get a slice
of God, Who accepts our death for birth.

Dean Kostos

The Coat That Wore a Man
after Top Coat, *a photograph by Sofia Kostos*

A long, black coat contained a man,
wool shielding from blizzards.
The man trudged through fog until he
disappeared. The coat remains, hung
from an empty closet, above

a ruined wall, the adjacent building
razed. The coat waits, as if
the vanished man will return,
slogging through rain & snow.
But no, the man will not come back, the coat

angled toward the future. Because coats know
nothing of time, the wool holds the man's shape,
perspiration, flakes of snow, & the dog-scent
of rain embedded in wool. The garment's arms
flap in wind, as if it longed to rise again.

Leonard Kress

The Relic

Not another end-of-the-year high school party in
the suburbs, circa 1970, and of course
no one danced, though all movement seemed to be solemnized
by the strobe and thick-rolled joints passed around and the keg
in a tub out back—the only rule that was enforced.
My girlfriend had dumped me and though she was invited
didn't show up. And soon I realized I could arise
from my slack, lovesick slumber, enough to try to stroke
the host, who fended me off by introducing me
to her mother, who bade me follow into her bedroom,
to a shelf with nothing but a tiny golden box,
whose etched glass lid revealed, stretched between silver clips,
a single strand of blond hair from Saint Thérèse's scalp.

Michelle Maher

Caravaggio's *The Death of the Virgin*

He shows her stretched on a bed
in a rumpled red dress slightly brighter
than the red canopy hanging
from the ceiling of a shabby room.
The window in the upper left corner
allows a single shaft of light
to fall on the upper body of the Virgin,
whose young face lies beneath
a halo that's a bare gold thread.
Her belly appears swollen,
and her feet are exposed.
Aged apostles, some balding,
bend over her bed, undone by grief.
A few cover their eyes.
A young Mary Magdalene
sits alone in the forefront,
the only other woman present.
Her head is buried in her lap,
her hair woven into braids
atop the crown of her head.
Her supple neck and back glow
in the same light that shines on Mary.
She grieves as if it were her mother
who has died. The Virgin's body
and extended arm seem to float
above her in an embrace,
and Mary Magdalene is so close
we can almost touch her—
but no, even if we could,
she would not move.
It's as if she is being drawn down
to the earth's dark, fiery core,
where bone and dust,
mother and child,
are indistinguishable, one.

Paul Mariani

What the Waves Kept Telling Me

> *Mighty waters cannot quench love*
> *Nor can floods sweep it away.*
>   *(Song of Solomon 8:6-7)*

We were somewhere off the coast of Sweden,
the land my mother's mother's family had sailed from
all those years ago. A cruise. My wife, my oldest son,
myself. Mid-morning, and I kept staring into the sea
below us, mesmerized by the wake the liner made,

how wave after wave after wave kept forming
before each fell back, the luminescent foam
coalescing as if somehow held together,
then breaking up bit by bit by bit,
until each seemed to disappear forever.

I kept thinking of the strange dream I'd had
months before, my body burnt and turned
to ash, how the dust seemed to float now
somewhere in a dark and alien space
as on a wave somehow held together, unlike

the waves I was watching now, for a distant light
seemed there to hover over what was left of me.
And I knew now there was nothing those particles
could do, that if they were ever to coalesce
and rise again, it would have to be by the hand

(hand? yes, hand is what I thought) of the Father
(yes, the one he'd called his Father, his and mine)
who would lift me up and somehow make us whole
again, my family, my wife, my son, smiling now
as I turned to wave at them and they drew nearer.

D. S. Martin

How To Listen For God

Turn off your cell phone   lace up
    a good pair of hiking shoes
        leave everything at the trail head
            except the words of the prophet Isaiah
& set out on your own   Open the book
    of field mouse & shrew   where unseen
        songbirds call from the green   & a hawk
            slowly patrols the cloud-enhanced blue
like an illumination from some
    ancient manuscript so the distractions
        of reports & percentages seem abstractions
            & there's no street noise to normalize
the ugly things you've said   Don't be afraid
    to squirm at your hollow justifications
        to feel far from holy   to wipe your hands
            again & again   You're learning to listen
Soon you may even hear well   the whisper
    some have heard on fiery hillsides
        when you're confined to a room   as narrow
            as Bonhoeffer's cell in Flossenburg

Michael Angel Martín

Adoration Chapel Near Me
John 9:6

The web search yields no results.
I'm surprised there's no diocesan
Database accessible to satellites.
So be it. Prayers work from home.
And there's more to secret devotions
Than listening to the whispered
Novenas of grizzled women
In pre-conciliar veils, prostate
Before the bedazzling monstrance.
I wonder why mud is no dominical
Sacrament. We could just walk out
Into churchyards, cup soil up and spit
Like the savior had. If that batter
Can fill one blind man with sight,
Why not fill a mason jar to the brim
With it, set it on a sill, and kneel?

Pablo Medina

Canticle of the Deer
for Albert Wood

My neighbor comes to the door
with pieces of deer he's shot. He sits
on a plastic chair in the back yard and tells
the story of the hunt--how he went
early into the still, dark cold and crouched
in the yellowing woods and waited--
you have to be willing to wait forever
to get what you want. My neighbor pauses
and whistles a tune from long ago, the *Tantum Ergo*
I heard as a child on Benediction Saturdays.
I smell the incense and hear the Sanctus bells.
Nights, he continues, I spend racking myself,
arguing with angels, faithful and fallen
alike. The next morning I walk into the woods
again, and the deer may come or not
and the leaves fall all around and the trees
go bare, lift their bony branches to the sky
in supplication. Sometimes I hear a rustle
in the undergrowth, a squirrel or a bird.
Maybe it's the Lord come to settle things.
Maybe not. I fall asleep and dream of a girl, frenetic
and beautiful, who loved someone else.
Sometimes the deer appears in the dream.
He lifts his head and stares, black eyes
boring into mine. I raise my gun and the deer
falls. The meat I brought you is from that deer.
The neighbor sits back and closes his eyes.
I listen to the susurrus in the breeze.
Where is the Lord now? I ask.
My neighbor is getting ready to leave.
The dream and the waking come
without a sign, he says, as the Lord does,
in the dark woods and in the sunlight gathering.

Orlando Ricardo Menes

Ode

Having been born in Lima, a desert
By a grey ocean where cold, briny mists smother
Earth & sky half the year, it was in Miami
That my siblings & I saw our first rainfall,
A morning downpour so hard, so quick
That parrots bolted from the mahogany trees
& we flapped our arms as each bead splat on sunburnt skin—
How soft & lukewarm sky's waters can be,
Like those motherly teas—linden & chamomile—
My Cuban Mamá steeped in scoured pots
& left to brood on the stove for all our maladies.
O *lluvia* that soaked our hair, eyes, ears (we almost drowned),
Yet how sweet it was like iron rust—peppery,
Prune-like on our tongues—& earthier than mold
On the bread Mamá orphaned in spare cupboards—
Lluvia that formed creeks, puddles, & bogs in the backyard
Of mangoes & soursops, & we (her sacred brood,
She'd call us, her holy kits, cubs, whelps, tadpoles, too)
Played in *el fango*—the mud, the mire, the muck—
Wearing just Fruit of the Loom briefs, tees, & cowboy boots
(Even the girl) as we rolled, jumped, slid *a lo loco*,
Moon crazy, clutching clods, catching seeds & grasshoppers
In our first deluge—*aguacero tropical*—& then Mamá
Yelled to keep frolicking, mucking, spitting out rainwater
Like dolphins through their blowholes, these creatures
Of God so blessed to have been born free of sin.

Philip Metres

Zoo Windows

How do they get out? my daughter asks,
puzzling over monkeys balancing
on artificial branches, pressing
palms against thick glass windows.

Once, during communion,
my head began to swim—the open
shining stranger faces glided past, all
their names *beloved by someone,*

beloved by someone—as if I'd treaded
ocean swells for hours, staved off
drowning, then, at last, staggered

naked onto the shore.... We drag
our feet along a path that leads to death
and past, trying to escape the glass.

Rhonda Miska, O.P.

La Guadalupana

"The smallest of my sons," she called him. Every time he wondered if it were a childish daydream, if he had imagined her. Every time, the deep orange blooms of *cempasuchiles*, the lilting bird song, and then her soft insistent voice, her benevolent dark eyes.

Today – the December *rosas de castilla*, a brilliant pink against his cloak's dull beige. Harvested carefully around thorns, petals velvety against his *tilma*'s rough weave. The rustle of them as he walked, treasure held to his heart and belly, gestating.

These will become epiphany, revelation, the emblem of the *raza cósmica*. These will become the flag of a hemisphere's holy empress, beloved barefoot *consuelo del mortal*, our snake-conquering *madre mestiza*.

These will be birthed into the pennant of fasting farmworkers and *jornaleros sin papeles*, the matriarch of roadside shrines and living room altars, the omnipresent starry-cloaked Lady stamped on keychains and bumper stickers and inked into human flesh.

But for now the roses are Juanito's alone. Hidden against his body, still cold from the earth. Before the bishop falls on his knees in front of the barefoot *indio*, before the continent shifts, before she is born as a banner without borders, there is the smallest of her sons with this incubating seed, this hidden tabernacle, this concealed grace swelling his belly.

She will cover us all with her mantle, but for now she is veiled within his.

Juan pauses, drops his head in private devotion, and inhales deeply the roses' fragrance.

Robin Amelia Morris

If you cannot pray as yourself

imagine some other person praying.
If you are a man, picture a girl
who repeats as she walks, "Lord Jesus Christ,
Son of God, have mercy on me a sinner."
She does not look like a sinner to you
but no matter. She is walking,
and you are too. Walk along,
imagining her walking, and hearing her recite.
If you are young, make up someone shriveled
because it must be holier to be old.
Do not let his voice lapse into sing song.
Hear the old monk who tastes every word
wrapping his heart around them as he walks,
muttering. Keep doing it. There.
You are praying.

Susan Signe Morrison

The Third Plague

In medieval Montaillou,
the women spread their Word
while daughter delouses mother.
The priest's mistresses remove his lice
as he speaks of Cathars and love.
His mother has her cooties crushed at the inn
as she gossips with the town matrons.
One tiny biting nit determines
the social web of touch and talk.

Even now, even here,
in a kitchen in Brooklyn,
Dalya arms herself with a pencil and wet paper towel.
Her nickname is "the Ladybug."
She slathers a child's head with margarine
and covers the yellow goo with plastic wrap.
The ashamed mother calls her a saviour,
this orthodox Jewish nurse.
She gets no rest.

To delouse someone is intimate.
You hold the head against your belly
in an erotic capitulation.
John Donne knew a flea could contain a world.
The mingled juices of alienated lovers,
a carnal trinity, pulsated in that insect's body,
obliterated in a striking instant.

In deHooch's painting, the mother holds the child's head
in her starched white apron-lap.
The light immobilizes each object in time.
The woven basket stands out as clearly as the dog.
The bed's curtains are draped as crisply
as the girl's dress and hair.
She bends forward in humble trust,
while the mother modestly works,
picking over
the cherished innocent.

Elisabeth Murawski

Psalm

I struggle with the stone
blocking my entrance
to the runway.

Hands and feet go first,
a stadium in crystal.
My God, you're locked in,

the glaze is permanent!
And yet I'm drawn
to your crazy syntax,

honey and ashes like jazz
after midnight, blue
letters on green

hard to read. You whisper
like a charm sliding
on a bracelet, a hive

to come back to. And I
listen, proud as a crocus
parting the snow.

Stella Nesanovich

Dwelling Among Tombs
Gerasene Demonic: Mark 5:1-20

I have lived among these tombs too long,
mourning my dead. How I yearn to live
again in the simmer of sunlight, no
shadows, no dark spirits to restrain hope.

I know great grief, the wounding
of self with stones, the urge to punish,
to torment myself: the agony bred
by hindsight, my lost moments of kindness.

Unclean legions beset me, cast a pall
of sorrow. The swineherd rests amid
his flock on a nearby hill as I dwell
fitfully, await my savior's arrival.

Matthew C. Nickel

Harvesting Potatoes Under Solar Eclipse 2017

Late season, August, for early reds, weed-choked
from summer travel, Paris and Provence,
pilgrimages to villages and sacred places
by the sea, we sang the songs of strange lands,
then home, we wondered when exile ends;

surprised there is anything under soil, at first,
we dig the mounds and find rotten potatoes,
left too long in wet cool summer soil, the coldest
August in years, not even tomatoes have ripened
yet and it's August 21, summer almost gone—

but soil yielded some fine Red Norlands
early harvest, Charles digging the edges
of rows, finding small oval shaped potatoes
here, papa, another one for my bucket, and
suddenly the sky turns red and bees are gone,

when the bees are gone, Charles asks, *where
are they*, above us hangs the silent blossoms
of the sunflower, crickets suddenly in choir,
asking the darkness of daytime while night birds
note the day's contradiction, the world bends,

I have never felt the world bend before
it makes my heart fold in on itself and wonder
who it belongs to, this potato, this boy digging,
the woman finishing her rosary on the porch
trying not to be noticed, but I notice this too

because I have often tried not be to noticed
in most moments for most of my life—until,
that is, I met a woman who wouldn't let me
go without notice—we all feel the sky move
so slow you can hear the earth tilt in the wind

under purple streaks of sky and Charles asking why
and why and why we can't look directly at the sun
but still know it's there, behind the moon, *you can't hide
from me sun*, until light, opening its fingers, brings
back the bees and then there are no more questions.

Gregory Orfalea

California Rain
for my sister

By your old girls' high school by
Accident I half-wondered
If you had nudged the cars
To stop as you once did.
You were that beautiful.
A brown girl probably fresh-
Man coiled her little body
To an older taller friend or sister
In the parking lot as if to say:
"I learned this," or better,
"You learn this." Freshman going
On sophomore. The cars
Moved some and stopped
Again. This time the beauty
Was wild mustard across from the school
So bright and full from California rain
It's visible from space. Imagine!
The Spanish Franciscans thoughtlessly
Or faithfully lofted it three centuries
Ago, knowing what could come
From a mustard seed. You were barely
A seed when you left us. Here
I am, an old man,
Passing where you used to dance,
Not dancing, stopped.
Where are you? Can
You see the mustard
Better than I?

Barry Peters

Surveillance

Cameras on every corner isn't so bad,
I say, remembering fourth-grade
movie day when Sister Regina Marie
lost her temper trying to thread
Jacques Cousteau's *Mysteries of the Ocean*
into the reels of the big metal projector
that heated up so much we could feel
the fire inside. Once she told us
what would happen after we die,
when we would sit with God
in His private theater and watch a movie
expose every single action of our lives
including, heaven forbid, everything
we thought and did when we were alone.
I imagine trying to leave for popcorn and soda
but God puts his hand on mine as if to say
Don't, you'll miss the good part.
Finally the curtain descends, ending
the shame/guilt/embarrassment,
and while the credits roll, a cast of thousands,
I wonder whether God's going to judge
my performance thumbs-up or thumbs-down,
so no, I don't mind cameras on every corner,
it could get a whole lot worse than that.

Daye Phillippo

Thunderhead

Last week, at the supper table I was daydreaming
after the meal, looking and not looking
through the dining room's wavy glass,
glass as old as its farmhouse, which is to say
almost a century older than me.
As I'd been doing all afternoon,
I was mulling the word "radiance,"
how to use its Latinate voluptuousness
in a poem in a way that wouldn't seem cheap,
when my husband said, *Your face. It's glowing,*
and I said, *Well, maybe I'll just sit here in this light forever,*
and he said, *No, it's not that.*
I noticed it earlier, in the kitchen, too.
At my age, I knew it couldn't be youth, so maybe
the word itself was incandescing? I mean, what if,
in choosing words to ponder we choose
our countenance, too, the simple way
switching out a blackened bulb for new
relights the shade, the room, in which case,
You have another think coming,
as my mother was fond of saying, could actually mean
something to look forward to.
The way those thunderheads rolled in
yesterday evening between rains
—white, gray, old lavender rimmed in gold—
cumulous, piled so high they made the sky
into a great Midwestern sea, and thunder
into a great whale sounding its depths,
sights and sounds one might expect
when being born into the next. . .
the setting sun diffusing gold through
the humid air, light pouring over
beanfield and barn, pasture, cat, every tree
and me, summer robe and flipflops, out
in that light, stepping through wet grass
and the aroma of wet grass, searching,
camera in hand, trying to find a way
to capture it all. Giving up, just standing there,
letting Radiance thunder through my head.

Mia Pohlman

A Man Who is a Stranger Comes to Visit

The lines in his dark skin
tell stories
like rivers and ravines
and the last time I saw you
(which might be the last
time I ever see you,
but who ever knows)
and he wears a cowboy hat,
the ten-gallon kind
like a mitre on his head.

He sits on our porch and we
drink lemonade,
water in cubes
floating, frozen.

His legs stretch
out and fold
at the ankles,
hand that covers
the glass of my grandma's crystal.

Once I found myself in a country
where I couldn't read or speak the language.
The loneliness
was like
the noise leftover
from cars passing under interstate overpasses,
until it became
like the reprieve from rain,
that second of silence,
driving under a bridge.

Words, I say, give me words,
and the stranger nods his head.
He is silent as
breath,
as bread rising,

as the way my mama's pretty pink peonies are
all the sudden
balled fists
then all the sudden
blooms,

like God closed his eyes and
blew the fuzz off
a dandelion

and the world's still floating into place

Christopher Poore

Léon Morin, Priest

The priest in the movie is leaving
the town for
the parishes in the country the priest
will feed the lambs with his food which he keeps
in a box food he lifts with his hand so the women
kneeling can see it
their heads are covered they
cover their eyes with their lids because when
they are blind they can see better the prayer
they say with the mouth in their heart please
don't let him go to the country please don't leave
me don't let me go please they go
after mass to see him in his white-washed
room with all the furniture gone now leaving
the ghosts of dust the ghosts of soot
they ask him
where is the piano
it was rented where are the
books they are all packed away who can still
hear the wind moving over the pages who can
hear it but no one knows where it is going
where I am going you cannot come

Dennis Rhodes

Our Housemate

Jesus Christ lives here. Very quietly.
He takes a long time in the bathroom,
but we don't mind. It is his only
shortcoming. We are never out of wine,
and the fridge is always well-stocked with fish.
His personal needs are so modest
it is hard to believe he's a King.
It's grand to see his snow-white tunic
dancing on the clothes line in the spring.
As you might imagine, he gets tons
of mail, and notes are always posted
to the front door. It is an honor
of course to have him in our house. We
have just one rule: no showy miracles.
We are always out when his mom visits.
We have a barbecue every summer
for his disciples. Matthew is by far
my favorite. Likes his burgers well done.

Michael D. Riley

[Poet, professor, husband, father, grandfather, Michael D. Riley, passed away unexpectedly on February 23, 2019. Presence was blessed to have received a poem from him for this issue. We present it with prayers and love and thanks for all his writing.]

Halo

Mine weathered badly.
Base metal dulls through all round
the thinnest of plating—no more than
a warm breath of gold against a cold window.
Chinks, scrapes, ferrules:
the thing weeps without a sound.
I never graduated to the hovering trick,
but the coat-hanger hook
that once kept it a respectful
three inches over my head, is long gone,
so it snugs my hairline just below
my natural tonsure. You would hardly
believe the weight of it by the end
of the day. It's like a perfect thought—
round, complete, sufficient—
become a manacle. I don't mean
to complain. After all, eternity is long
and here it is Tuesday already.
I have time, they all say smiling.
And tonight at vespers, such lovely singing.

Margaret Rozga

Full of Grace

I carry a sack full of my failures.
It is the way I pray. I draw letters
freed from words   pull them back
into words   a line   a poem
a praise song to the faces of courage,
another prayer.
                Some mornings
at the first of sunrise, I look east
which is at a twenty degree angle
from the lay of my misplotted east-west street.
The angle of my face then is also a prayer
unsaid in this holy moment.
                      Sometimes
rote prayers of my childhood rise from deep
memory   In the name of   Hail Mary
is now and ever shall be   a descant
to my day.
            Some evenings all seems impossible
not impossible   difficult   That, too,
my unsayable prayer.

Lisa Toth Salinas

To the New Girl at the Women's Shelter
A Cento

You found your voice, named the fear.
Know that this hour alone is enough to feed us.
The shadows fall. Illumination now
will come like crying in the night
and even when the weeping stops...return –
fragile like a child is fragile –
to the future's gentle healing, to the blooming
as one turns, forgetting, from the past.

You love a man whose footprint leaves
bargains struck, words broken, prayers, promises
to make ourselves forget the drowning river
those who stay in safety cannot know.
Wide-eyed in the dark hours,
changed in ways we can't name,
no word to name what's lost,
but in the ragged edge of a torn photo:
the endless *why* and *why* and *why*.

Here are the stories of how many years
must reinflate spirit and write recovery
by crossing over borders without maps until
She carries herself with grace, they say.

Sometimes the only thing we have left:
what we knew,
       what we thought we knew,
              what we'll never know,
and every aspiration to could-be.

1. Loretta Diane Walker, "After the First Snow" 2. Beverly Monestier, "Waiting for the First Moonrise" 3. Maurice Manning, "Lent" 4. Rowan Williams, "Advent Calendar" 5. Annabelle Moseley, "A Time to Weep" 6. Mary Jo Bang, "You Were You Are Elegy" 7. Susan Maxwell Campbell, "Mending Grief" 8. Natasha Trethewey, "Pilgrimage" 9. Nicole Rollender, "Aleuromancy" 10. Paula Meehan, "The Statue of the Virgin at Granard Speaks" 11. Adam Kirsch, "Outlet Mall in Western

Massachusetts" 12. Nicolas Giese, "Denying Tenure" 13. Marjorie Stelmach, "Canticle of Want" 14. Heather Tosteson, "'Vão ou vazio': Empty" 15. Andrew Collard, "Vital Organs" 16. Kindra McDonald, "What Remains" 17. Natasha Trethewey, "Southern Gothic" 18. Susan Maxwell Campbell, "Dear Dave" 19. Budd Powell Mahan, "Night from the 9th Floor" 20. Rod Jellema, "Why I Never Take My Watch off at Night" 21. Kindra McDonald, "Loss and the Definitions of Carry" 22. Loretta Diane Walker, "After the First Snow" 23, 24, 25. Michael Farry, "Public Records Office, Kew, London" 26. Christine Boldt, "Hic Sunt Serpentes"

Nicholas Samaras

Afterlife

All we brought with ourselves
was nostalgia and regret,

their dark folds and long list of alternate endings.

What was left for us
but consequence of choices,

repentance for some
or stubbornness.

We remain what we became:

a black erasure, a gold embrace.
We became what we embraced back,

steward to the feast or famine,
journeying to Heaven and hell,
voyage the same destination.

Janna Schledorn

Daniel the Prophet Talks to a Psychologist

"You're catastrophizing," my therapist says
when I tell her this slouching beast,
(one king after another in visions)
robs our daughters, leaves lonely mothers
suckling orphans in Mongolian cold.
Fathers paralyzed, hysterical, numb.
Too many armed men on the prowl,
children with no locks on their doors—
naked in the night.

I turn white in my alarm. He sends
his angel edict across time to say
one will come to conquer, satisfy.
"Delusions," she notes. No one believes
in a god who steps off his throne
to take the iron teeth of our decline.

Martha Silano

The hands of all my mistakes

are clapping wildly like aspens in a squall. The blackbird is
flying away from the unappeasable wasp. Everything is
disappearing, especially the reddish egret—no pale blue eyes
on the Tamiami Trail. Science is a magic show, all of us
scurrying through tunnels to appear unharmed at the back of
the room. God, who's always loved a game of chicken, has been
court-ordered into therapy. I know because we sometimes
share the backseat of my grandmother's Buick Riviera, cruise
into Paris where God, being God, falls in love with the Dark
and Stormy at Le Mary Céleste. We end up, as always, at Père
Lachaise, throwing ourselves at Apollinaire's grave. Who says
no one swoons when they walk straight up to death?

Rita A. Simmonds

You Can't Take the Dead
A Villanelle

Photos are memories awakened
with borders for colors that bleed.
The living can only be taken

positioned or snapped in creation
expanding wide angles undreamed.
Photos are memories awakened

recording a life in its making
framing the best that's been seized.
The living can only be taken

through lenses in focus, not shaken
by movement that time guarantees.
Photos are memories awakened.

An image that fades unmistaken
moves out of the frame that we freeze.
The living can only be taken.

No camera can capture what's vacant.
No flash can expose what's deceased.
Photos are memories awakened.
The living can only be taken.

Richard Spilman

Finding God

Begin with lights that swim and whisper
on the ceiling on moonless nights.

Add breaths that creak, twitter and sigh
like the stridor of a sickly child,

a painful crackling of skin, the blush
of hands waking from winter numbness,

and the perfume of loss, the otherness
that bodies seek like deer coming to salt.

Meld them into the brine of dawn
that rankles every waking tongue.

Sofia M. Starnes

Dizain 11: Miracle

A word disperses what a breath has caught,
as crimson bird fraying the autumn mist,
or ruffle in a cloth, a thread, once knot,
now a quiver.   *Tell us*, the crowds insist;

for *telling* means that languages exist
past brokenness—until they taste the salt

of being healed. Far closer now, the fault
that split the girl's lips from her Hebrew tongue.
Talitha koum! Her breath, turned somersault,
pinwheels the distance between gasp and song.

Sheryl St. Germain

Prayer for One in Recovery

may you come to imagine
and believe in another life

may you find strength
to turn from those
who would lead you
back to a labyrinth
of misery

may you stand with those
who have survived

may you learn to see
beauty in small things:
tomatoes as they redden
in sun, the smell of pine
in the woods near your house,
the stunning quiet
that graces the first hours
of each new day, and may you
laugh at the way your face
sometimes looks in the morning,
wounded and proud and full
of nothing but desire for
that first warming taste of day

may you learn to take solace
in the passing of the hours,
in the clarity and richness
of touching the world,
of hearing, seeing, loving,
unclouded by dope,

may you keep company
with those who feed
your soul so that you
in turn can feed others

may you stand tall as
a thousand-year cypress,

may you learn to love
this new life, your feet become roots
that grip hope's dark soil

may your children
and your children's
children find refuge in you
when disaster strikes

and may you blossom with song
and story and poem, beacons
whose truth lights
the blackest nights.

Sophia Stid

Notes on the Burghers of Calais, Stanford Memorial Church

We are twelve. My brother walks the sandstone path
to church on his knees because I say I'll pay him although
I won't. The path scattered with brides & tourists
& the Burghers of Calais. Six sad men, nooses loose—
rough-hewn jewelry demanded by the English king,
who pawned his wife's crown to pay for the siege
he laid to Calais. The people of Calais, cut off, gates
locked, ate dogs & rats that year out of a century
of war, until the streets ran empty, gutters rustling
with nothing but rain & leaves. No more meat. Six old men
carrying the keys. Their bodies the price the King
had Calais pay. His pleasure: their bare feet, roped
necks. Long economy of godding, pouring other bodies
into the shape of our hollowed-out desire, praying *do what I say*

make me complete.

Carole Stone

Looking for a Cure

A pelican dives into the bay.
Vendors hawk popsicles,
women, clay masks
from baskets on their heads.
Noon, they rest under palm trees,
umbrellas of the poor.
Overhead, a flock of gulls
flap their way north
returning to their first nesting place.
How can I find mine, father
embalmed in whiskey,
mother shrouded in a silver sheath.
Not in the sky, on land
or in the sea, they are the ache
that lives in me, no tin *Milagro*
a woman offers, can cure.
Back north, my daughter cares
for her ill husband.
Will he be with her next year?
It's January 6 and the Three Kings
are following the star to bring gold,
myrrh and incense for the infant.
Soon shattered *piñatas* will release
their gifts. Mine, I am alive.

Jacob Stratman

watching Mark Twain's *Is He Dead?* with my son

We know the punch-line is coming. The second Act's tension
is predictably drawing to a sweet, amicable knee-slapping
conclusion, but we are polite and knowing, having read
Shakespeare and seen episodes of MASH, but still waiting to
    see
how these kids—actors, make-up and costume-deep in comic
sincerity, will help us rest statically in our expectations.
Not my son, though, this boy, next to me, dressed in a collared
    shirt
and slacks, prerequisites for a night out together at the
    theater,
unlike church, so immersed and stunned during the first act,
like a raccoon or armadillo in wide oncoming brights,
that he leans just a little too far forward into the homespun
dramatic irony and finds himself standing, like sleep walking,
and has to be led back down to sitting. Now that the punch-
    line
has been delivered, he laughs and laughs, red faced and not
    breathing
well, and claps, not in applause, confined to decorum, but in
    praise.
Cupped, hands clap as an echo claps as response as reaction
as being led, like standing. And, the adults begin to applaud,
not clap, but I smile knowing that he has led all of us
to this place.   Later that evening, I read Updike say
about Winslow Homer that "in his vast space he has his space,
and no more," so I will try, for this moment, to forget
about travel bans and alternative facts, about the enemy
of the enemy of the people, and write these lines that snap
some whip in me—that send that lead that propel me to his
    room
where I kneel in his space to watch him, a calm echo, in
breathy sleep.

Maxine Susman

Yom Kippur in the Mountains

Shots ring out.
Beyond a few acres of woods the neighbors
are at target practice. Old college friends
assembled for Columbus Weekend,
hunting season, peak foliage—and this year
Yom Kippur falls on *Shabbos*, holiest of days.

Volleys keener than *shofar* ricochet
from many hills. Stabs of headache.
I break the fast with milky tea.
Loud music, dogs barking,
the chuk-chuk of extruded shells.

I came to the *shul* of the woods
to inquire of my soul, its false vows,
empty promises. Crest of the ridge
and the pink edge beyond, sky settling
into end of day on the Day of Awe,
a gibbous moon rising behind stars
sharp as bullet holes.

Gates of Repentance, Book of Life,
it's both hateful and useful
to hear guns on Yom Kippur.

Maria Terrone

A Theft

Deep within the tiny shop in Rome, a woman is drawn
to the painting of a child savoring gelato in an outdoor café.
She moves closer to inspect, penetrating the clutter,
and sees her son, two decades earlier, wearing
that blue sweater she bought him there, and she sees
herself seated across the table, a mother watching
her child with indulgent pleasure, ignorant
of being seized. But by whom?
No one stood before an easel, stroking them
into another life across the canvas that she holds now
like a relic. She thinks: no, they were captured
in the era of shutter click, of a bath inside a locked,
darkened room, the stolen scene slowly
emerging. Their photo studied with a voyeur's eye,
and only then painted and framed in gold—
the color surely chosen to reflect the light.
She recalls it was late afternoon,
light soft and beginning to suffuse, before time
brought its changes. After the thief was done
with them both, then what? Yet another life
with strangers, nailed to a wall above a sofa, later sold?
Or abandoned in a storage bin, ending
in this dusty shop for how long, barely visible?
The woman knows she must reclaim the son
taken from her. And she does, not asking the price
as she holds the painting close in both her arms.

Brian Volck

Emmaus
Luke 24: 13-35

He played the stranger well, asking,
as if he didn't know, the source
of our manifest grief, and then –
with words we had thought familiar
rendered most strange in his telling –
breathed new flame, redolent of myrrh,
from banked ashes in our hearts.

There was, to be sure, something
familiar in his trick of speech,
but his face had turned a cypher
and even his hands, disfigured
by fresh wounds gaping like mouths,
commanded less scrutiny
than his body's quickening grace.

I have long since stopped asking
why we failed to recognize him
there, on the road. We knew him then
already two days dead, his tomb
newly desecrated, with nothing
but the ravings of dubious
women to suggest another fate.

There remains, though, one memory
I would better understand: how
at the place where travelers lodged,
while we sat at table, he looked
as though there were more to say –
some present matter he wished us,
in that moment, to apprehend –

yet he held his peace, words proving
perhaps insufficient for such
gravity, and then, with the look
of some great harrowing remembered,
collected himself like one
about to enter the temple
and silently reached for the bread.

Mark C. Watney

Church Going Under a Jacaranda Tree

Someone will forever be surprising
A hunger in himself...
And gravitating with it to this ground...
Wondering what to look for
                    "Church Going" by Phillip Larkin

I too
wondered what to look for
when I saw some Zulus under a Jacaranda tree in a Jo'burg
park.

Robed in white
and sashed in blue;
Eating bread
and sipping a little wine

they saw me (a white boy)
looking.

Come!
they said
and fed me too:

Bread--
tearing off a piece and presenting it
with both hands
into my palms--

and wine.

Christ!
They fed me too--

And surprised a hunger in myself

R. Bratten Weiss

Sunday Worship

The others are all calling for you to come, come
with them to the empty tomb, see how neatly the
linens are folded, it's a miracle, did any dead man
ever leave his room so spare and clean?

But still you are crouched there in the dark, breaking
your nails against the dirt, in the place where years
ago you marked an X to show where it was. Where
you'd planted it. The thing.

Because you're okay with the miracles that make
a mess of everything, all the cups spilling over, green
vines growing out of empty eye sockets, and you want
your own thing, the thing you buried, and they're saying,
come, put your fingers into these clean clean holes, see
this beautiful golden corpse.

But you had your own corpse once, all yours, even if it
couldn't promise to fold its linen once it'd gotten out of hell.
You planted it here, a seed, dark and hard but also beautiful
like a walnut, like sinews in an arm.

You were pretty sure it was a seed, although it lay so silent,
the way bodies of nocturnal animals curl by the roadside.
You were pretty sure it would live.

But now you are bent alone here, and if anyone goes by
they'll say "look at the witch, check out the crazy lady"
when you used to be a goddamn princess, and your
your back is bent like a sickle.

Is it enough to say that once you cheated the sun and once
you walked in the wind with your hair loose, flinging
handfuls of golden wheat like rain?

Paul Willis

McKinley Springs

One for the people, one for the horses,
both for the bears, and all for the oaks,
the bigleaf maples. The water makes

a quiet talk in the deep ravine,
just the words I wanted to hear
on a dry trail, and just the words

I hear in the night for the moonless hours.
So much to say, and said so well
in that ancient Esperanto of tongues:

You who are thirsty. You. Come.

—Los Padres National Forest

Aliesa Zoecklein

Bible Scholar's Lecture

The mistakes, he assures us,
are with us still. The beloved book's
oldest pages like torn wings.
Papyrus, later vellum, discarded,
found in the trash sometimes.
Look there for what's missing—
stained or miscopied by scribes
in a sputtering lamplight.
Follow the spine of knowing
far enough, and you'll touch
the bone of certainty
softened to chalk.

Interviews

Tinkering, Texts, and Divine Excess: An Interview with Kimberly Johnson
by Jerry Harp

JH: In the realm of literary pursuits, which I think of as language work, you are a language worker many times over. Not only do you write poetry, but you also translate (your version of Virgil's *Georgics* appeared in 2009, that of Hesiod's *Theogony* and *Works and Days* in 2017), pursue scholarship (*Made Flesh: Sacrament and Poetics in Post-Reformation England*, your study of Herbert, Taylor, Donne, and Crashaw, appeared in 2014), and edit (you are, for example, the project editor for the electronic archive of John Donne's Sermons at Brigham Young University). When did these pursuits begin for you? How did these multiple interests develop?

KJ: I came to the study of language via a slightly circuitous route. My natural inclination is to rummage around inside of things to see how they work; as a kid I used to spend hours taking apart and putting back together stereo sets or small mechanical devices, trying to learn how all the parts interacted with one another to produce the designed outcome. When I was younger, I fully intended to pursue a career in medicine because the body is one of the many machines that delights me, and I spent some time teaching human anatomy in a cadaver lab—there's something so satisfying about understanding how, say, the contraction of a muscle in the hand produces visible consequences from the fingertips right up the lower arm. This tinkerer's habit expressed itself fairly early in my interest in popping the hood and rummaging around in the engine of English, and I started studying ancient languages as a means of knowing the gears a little bit better. When finally I began to consider seriously that the study of language might make a viable career, which was quite late in my time (or even beyond my time) as an undergraduate, I had long been prepared by habit to approach words on a page—whether as a reader or as a writer—as a kind of mechanical investigation. I really just like to figure out how the constituent pieces of something complicated cooperate together to make some kind of change.

JH: Could you say a little more about how you went from teaching anatomy to devoting yourself to poetry? Is there a conversion narrative, perhaps even a text that was crucial to your vocation as a poet?

KJ: I managed to talk myself into a graduate poetry workshop with the poet who would become my first mentor, Mark Strand. I had no business being in that room, but Mark encouraged me and guided me through a transformative reading list: Calvino, Borges, Bishop, and others…many works that I'd never been directed toward before. Your use of the term "conversion narrative" is just, because my work with Mark changed my view of poetry; I no longer understood it as a kind of Wordsworthian spontaneous overflow of emotion but rather as a deliberate set of language decisions coordinated to produce interpretive effects. Mark taught me, as it were, the nuts and bolts of composition.

JH: As I reread your poems, your description of "rummaging around in the engine of English" leads me to look for the ways that you are tinkering with this engine. For example, I notice that in section 5 of "Wing" (published in *Leviathan with a Hook*, 2002), there is a run of nine words, each of which is composed of the same letters as the previous, though with the addition of one letter:

Concerning lift:

tar	star	tares
stream	steamer	mastered
resonated	stamp-erode	atmosphered

What are some other ways that you tinker with this engine as you write? How important is such tinkering to your writing process?

KJ: One of the "tinkerings" that happens pretty often in my poems is deep etymological puns. I'll often incorporate a string of ideas that play with a single ancient term that never appears in the poem but is present through its derivations. In one of the "Pater Noster" poems in my first book, *Leviathan*, I describe a flower as "the brooding columbine," which makes a submerged nod toward Genesis 1.2 by way of Milton, since the etymological root of the flower called *columbine* is the Latin word for *dove*, a traditional symbol for the spirit of God. In my most recent collection, *Uncommon Prayer,* there's a section of my long poem "Siege Psalter" called "Hotel":

> How hospitable these hired rooms! Their square corners and the assurance thereof, their efficiency! Here is the room in which we first met, years ago, you playing the victim and me on my knees. Here is the room where, Love, you invited me to incline upon the cushions and taste, a night unlike all the other nights. Here is the room where you stand with your knives to prepare a table before me in the presence of mine enemies. My dear host, dear hospitaller, all your rooms have enemies, and all are a sacrifice to leave. In my solitude are many mansions.

Throughout its lines it gestures toward the divergent ancient origins of the contemporary homonym *host.* On one hand, *host* derives (like "hotel" and "hospital") from *hospes,* which means both *host* and *guest* simultaneously. On the other, it derives from *hostis,* meaning *stranger* or *enemy.* Two opposite ideas contained in the same contemporary group of letters! I was playing with that opposition and allowing its implications to register in another word in this little family, the eucharistic *host,* and what kinds of tension that deep pun introduces into the relation between human and divine. There's no reason that a contemporary reader would ever be alert to these puns, but it's one method I use to help determine how the logic of a sentence develops. It's a kind of constraint, a limit that enables creative play and leads to discoveries that I might not arrive at without the introduction of rules external to the semantic meaning of the sentence. Indeed, as I reflect on your question here, I wonder if one alternative term for this kind of "tinkering" might be "poetics"--that is, the marshalling of features of a word that are not exactly part of its dictionary definition to communicate something in addition to the denotative content of a word.

JH: In "The Melancholy of Anatomy" (from *A Metaphorical God,* 2008), the following lines occur: "The anatomist never looks up, / / tries never to think on the lab's humane / piecework—not that the scene's too gruesome / but too stately, in its bloodless displays / / no remembrance of the messy blessed / animal." So I read the poem to be more on the side of the messy animal than the stately lab. How does your experience as a teacher of anatomy speak to your sensibilities as a poet?

KJ: Well, I suppose both activities seek to make order out of....not chaos, precisely, but the potential for it. There is so much of the labeler, the charter, in the poet. So much of the effort in organizing words into sonic structures and visual arrangements on the page has to do with giving shape to something as elusive as thought or sense perception, each of which is messy. The lab, the poetry part, *is* stately, but that stateliness depends upon the mess which gives the organizing impulse its purpose and direction, and likewise the mess remains incomprehensible without the urge toward order. I'm not sure we can have one without the other, and I think this productive tension is at the heart of poetry itself. As it may be at the heart of human experience.

JH: I see this tension between order and mess running through your poetry, as in "Three Bouquets" (from *A Metaphorical God*), where the "U.S. Geological Survey map / grids the haphazard landscape into restrained / / geometries." However, in the map's corner, the cartographer has drawn "a compass rose"— "freehand arabesques" that "transgress the quadrants" of the map. But then, faith in this "compass rose" turns out to be misplaced, as if this "love-knot / could fix beauty." In other words, this free-hand figure transgressing the map's quadrants is itself an attempt to pin down a beauty that will not be contained. It makes me think of your poem "Sweet Incendiary," whose speaker wishes for an angel to "rip / the veil and show me the shining / / undeniable face of God. / No such luck." I take it that your poetry strives to put into words what must always exceed language, so that every poem is in part the story of its own failure. This seems to be quite a fix for a poet to be in; it may be, in some ways, ideal. What do you think?

KJ: I wonder if what you describe here is a tension that inheres not only in my own poetry but in poetry generally. I think it's built into the animating principles of the genre. There's a desire to represent experience in a comprehensible way, through words that can be looked up in the dictionary and through attentive description and so forth. And we yearn to understand, to overcome the distances between human minds that persist even in the most intimate relationships, and to glimpse beyond the *selftaste* that Gerard Manley Hopkins both gloried in and lamented. But language is by definition a generalized medium, blunt and cumbersome and not particular to any single person's perspective. How can it be true that I can use the word *love* to describe either my feeling about my child or my feeling about oranges? The sheer unreliability of language to communicate my singularity feels sometimes like a betrayal. It seems to me that poetry, as a genre, seeks to compensate for betrayals such as this with devices and strategies that communicate *around* semantic meaning. Meter, for example, cannot be said to *mean* in the way that we usually use that term, but the manipulation of attention through cadence and the creation of patterns that emphasize ideas as a line progresses and the textual marking of time does convey something *meaningful*. I turn to poetry, both as a reader and as a writer, for this kind of tension, for the productive groanings of form against content, of matter against spirit, of order against chaos.

JH: In the past, I've emphasized your poems' apophatic theology, a mode of thinking that so stresses the divine excess of human categories and language that it seeks to assert only what the divine is not, for the divine remains beyond human articulation. This procedure reaches something like an outer limit at the end of your poem "Nonesuch" (in *Uncommon Prayer*, 2014): "You are not my _____. I am not your sign." Given that the blank space is the very sign of negation, this poem negates even the mode of apophatic negation. This would seem to leave next to no room for human consciousness to move. What happens after such a moment as this?

KJ: I would say that my own mode of thinking seeks to thread the needle on these points. On one hand, the notion that any divine reality must surely exceed human apprehension leads to the kinds of moves you've identified here in the poem's argument. On the other hand, my participation in the world around me can only be characterized as lavish plenitude—an excess of its own that, even if it doesn't precisely coordinate with the contours of the divine, may nevertheless serve as its analogue. In other words, *My God, the world is full, and that fullness calls me to love it.* To my mind, the thing that happens after a moment of profound unknowing such as the blank space in this poem is the assertion of the stolid objecthood of the self: "I am not your sign" because I, as an embodied person existing in this dizzying fullness of sense-able objects, am not contingent, not ancillary to some reality elsewhere. *I am.* That phrasing, with its Exodus echoes, verges on irreverence, but I mean it not as blasphemy but as praise.

JH: There is a well established theological tension between our utter dependence on the divine and our own integrity as individuated beings. The divine has created us to flourish fully as ourselves, though we remain utterly God's without ever becoming merely ancillary to the divine. It seems to me impossible to make all of this come out even. These considerations put me in mind of your study *Made Flesh: Sacrament and Poetics in Post-Reformation England* (2014), where you discuss the complex history of reference and representation with regard to the "phenomenal and epistemological overlap between textuality and sacramental worship." Both poems and sacraments do indeed refer to what is beyond them, though they also manifest presence in their own right (and in their own rite) in the present moment. The poets and poems you explore refuse to fall along clear doctrinal lines. Would you want to comment on where you find yourself concerning these issues of doctrine and tradition? I believe that you identify as a member of the Mormon tradition; because this is an interview for *Presence: A Journal of Catholic Poetry*, I also have to ask about the influence on you, if any, of Catholic tradition.

KJ: I suppose I would self-define as a Christian who participates in communion with the Mormon community, and that stance aligns me to some degree with the evasive poets of the post-Reformation era whose work I have studied. Like those poets, I locate myself between confessions—or perhaps *among* confessions; as someone who has spent a lot of time tunneling around in the tangled theologies of historical Christianity, I find some aspects of many faith traditions appealing. For instance, I find the sacramental theology of Catholicism deeply moving, because it turns upon the live intervention of the divine in the material world; and even though the tradition in which I practice has adopted a low sacramentalism, tipping far onto the Zwinglian end of the ritual spectrum rather than the Roman, the doctrine of transubstantiation aligns suggestively with the Mormon tradition's view of the material world as fundamentally sacred, shot through with palpable divinity, not bleakly fallen but rather immanently glorious. The Catholic tradition's investment in the sacramental potentialities of the material world acknowledges how inextricable are the theological and the aesthetic. I say from time to time that I'm one good oratorio or painting away from converting to Catholicism, and while that's obviously a joke (I mean, there've been plenty of good paintings and oratorios!) it speaks a bit to the register in which I respond to the structures of worship—and clearly it's little wonder that, given these interests on my part, I've ended up pursuing works of poetry (as both a scholar of other people's poems and as someone who tries to write poems) that foreground the aesthetic dimension of worship.

JH: Given the rich array of denominations that exist under the very large canopy of Christian tradition, where do you think we are going, or where should we go? For example, do you look toward some future convergence, a kind of reunification, or are we perhaps better off with a variety of denominations, each with its own genius, style, and intensification? Of course, traditions other than Christian could enter these considerations as well.

KJ: Well, I'd hardly dare to make any predictions, but if the past is any indication, I wouldn't put money on convergence. The history of Christianity in its various expressions is a long drama at the center of which is the work of interpretation. It is a faith tradition whose founding narratives are textual, whose rituals can be traced to passages of scripture, whose earliest thinkers were textual analysts. And that feature of Christianity almost guarantees variety, because the nature of texts is that they are differently interpreted by different readers. Disputation over words' meanings is baked in—think of the debate in the latter part of John 6 about what it means for Jesus to say *I am the bread of life*, and the anxiety about the status of metaphor. Think of Peter and Paul at loggerheads in Acts (and in Paul's epistolary reporting) about how circumcision signifies—is it materially consequential or a figure for some spiritual condition? So divergence is sort of baked in to this interpretation-heavy tradition. And it's likely compounded by each person's idiosyncratic appropriation of religious thought structures and doctrines: I've long thought that there are 7.1 billion religions on the planet (is that how many people there are these days? I think so), each one self-contained and self-defined, albeit nominally affiliated with some more systemic or institutional framework.

JH: Is there one last question, something that I have not yet asked, that you would like to ask yourself and answer?

KJ: I suppose I would dwell a bit longer in a point we've brushed up against and then moved past. I mentioned before how a throughline in my various work has been my perception of "how inextricable are the theological and the aesthetic." It's interesting to me to dwell in the question of what kind of spiritual or theological work, exactly, can poetry do? It's a question I'm keenly invested in thinking about, and much of my scholarly activity has to do with exploring other folks' answers to that question. At the moment, I think that the kinds of productive tension that exist between, say, the spiritual and the material are analogous to the sparks that fly between the form and content of a poem. It's often the case that people read poems paying primary attention to what the poem has to say—its content. That's certainly an important part of the experience of a poem. But a poem often uses its form to advance a surprising para-argument to the one that the content seems to be offering, and that para-argument complicates, elaborates, expands, contradicts, or even subverts the stuff that the sentences of the poem are saying. That very action of thinking about a subject simultaneously in two ways seems to me to offer a rich aesthetic version of what a lot of religious life asks of its adherents: thinking multiply, and sometimes contradictorally, about hard things. This capacity is what draws me both to poetry and to the study of religion, and what makes both pursuits feel so very meaningful.

Kimberly Johnson is the author of three collections of poetry, most recently *Uncommon Prayer* (Persea Books, 2014), and of book-length translations of Virgil and Hesiod. As a scholar of early modern English literature, she has published a monograph, *Made Flesh: Sacrament and Poetics in Post-Reformation England*, and a number of critical essays on Renaissance poetry. Johnson is a recipient of grants and awards from the John Simon Guggenheim Memorial Foundation and the National Endowment for the Arts.

Jerry Harp's books of poems include *Creature* (2003) and *Spirit under Construction* (2017). His scholarly work includes *For Us, What Music? The Life and Poetry of Donald Justice* (2010). He teaches at Lewis & Clark College.

"Hungering for the Emptied God": An Interview with Daniel Tobin on a New Collection Exploring the Person and Work of Simone Weil

by Mark S. Burrows

[In October and November, 2019, Mark S. Burrows interviewed Daniel Tobin regarding his forthcoming book entitled This Broken Symmetry: A Poem. *It is the second of a trilogy of books: the first,* From Nothing *(2016), explored the thought of Jesuit priest and scientist Georges Lemaitre; the third, in process, engages the witness of Teilhard de Chardin, tentatively entitled* At the Grave of Teilhard de Chardin.*]*

MB: How did you discover Simone Weil's writings? What is the trajectory of your involvement in her work?

DT: I discovered Simone Weil's writings initially through Wallace Stevens, surprisingly enough. I'm not sure whether it is widely known how she influenced Stevens' ideas. He makes reference to Weil in *The Necessary Angel* and invokes her concept of decreation as a way of defining the art and poetry of his time. Stevens died in 1955, so he would have discovered Weil in the last decade of his life after her writings started to find wider publication. The other path to my discovery of her work was through Czeslaw Milosz, the great Polish poet, who invokes her in *The Witness of Poetry*. I believe it was in 1982 that Milosz gave the Norton Lectures at Harvard, and those lectures would have formed the blueprint for *The Witness of Poetry*. I attended the Norton lectures during my time as a student at Harvard Divinity School—a thrilling experience since I had read *Bells in Winter* shortly before he won the Nobel Prize in 1980 and found myself completely taken with the poems and the sensibility behind the poems. So Stevens and Milosz would have been the instigators of my fascination with Weil's work and life. I can see myself heading off right out of the lecture, across the Yard, and into the Harvard Bookstore to buy *The Simone Weil Reader*, the big black-covered hardback among the books on sale for discount in the basement. What followed, after I left Harvard for the University of Virginia and my doctorate, would have been Simone Petrement's biography. I wanted to find out more about the life that produced such starkly compelling and challenging ideas about the world, history, faith, God, human suffering, human corruption, the commitment to justice, and the difficult and (dare I say) self-obliterating path to transcendence.

    Now, some thirty-five or more years later, when I crack open my copy of *The Reader*, I see my first underlines, checks, asterisks, where something in the "The Spiritual Autobiography," or "Factory Work," or "The Illiad, Poem of Might," or "The Love of God and Affliction" struck me with the urgency of real discovery as well as recognition. So I would say my trajectory of involvement with her work is characterized as much by a continual return to that first engagement as by my moving ahead through *Waiting for God, Gravity and Grace, The Need for Roots, Lectures on Philosophy* and so on. It is as if my younger self knew something, intuited something relatively early on, that I would be called to discover and re-discover over and over again, and hopefully deepening the encounter.

MB: What led to your decision to write this particular collection? How did the writing take shape?

DT: I wrote *This Broken Symmetry* directly out of my desire to compose a book-length poem on the life of Jesuit priest and scientist Georges Lemaitre, the father of the Big Bang. *From Nothing* came out in 2016, though the inner conversation about the shape of that book really started some six or seven years before its publication. Eventually I decided on a poem in thirty-three sections in tercets, eight stanzas in each section, and the whole book in three parts. That probably tells you that, for good or ill, I have a strong architectural approach to the making of poems. Those tercets are in conversation with the longer poems of Wallace Stevens—each of the three parts of *From Nothing* allude to a poem by Stevens—though obviously the thirty-three sections along with the tercets alludes formally to Dante as well, without assuming a strict *terza rima*.

    As I worked on *From Nothing* it occurred to me that what I wanted beyond the one book-length poem was a still larger design, also in the same form: a total of three book-length poems, each with the same structure, ninety-nine sections in all, with four six–line continuing couplets woven at the beginning and end of each book forming a kind of helix through and across all three. So: three book-length poems forming a single larger whole, ninety-nine sections with the twenty-four line weave forming the final section, not at the end but immanent in the whole design of twenty-four hundred lines. *This Broken Symmetry*, on Simone Weil, forms the center work of the whole. I did not realize at first that the subject of the center work would be Simone Weil. I originally had

Dorothy Day in mind (who surely deserves a poem in her honor!). In the end, Weil asserted herself incontestably, despite being the subject of a number of poems before my own, including Stephanie Strickland's *The Red Virgin*, Kate Daniel's *Four Testaments*, and Anne Carson's *Decreation*, along with a short sequence of poems by Edward Hirsch. There are probably more out there. I had read Edward Hirsch's, and found them beautiful, but I studiously avoided the others for fear of being overly influenced.

In terms of shape and movement, *This Broken Symmetry*, in contrast to *From Nothing* and the expanding universe itself, works contrary to the arrow of time—it starts after Weil's death and ends before her birth. As Weil reflects in *Waiting for God*, "Time as it flows wears down and destroys that which is temporal. Accordingly, there is more eternity in the past than in the present . . . Thus the past presents us with something which is at the same time real and better than ourselves, something which can draw us upwards—a thing the future never does." I wrote each section from the beginning at Weil's end to the end at Weil's beginning, or still on the way as it were in her mother's womb. The design does not mean the book forms a straightforward narrative, but there are motifs running through it, and I've done enough research to give the poem a sub-structure connected to the life but, hopefully, an imaginative life beyond the merely archival. The last book in the trilogy, which I hope to write someday before too long, will be titled *At the Grave of Teilhard de Chardin*.

MB: At the heart of this collection is, as the title suggests, a notion of symmetry, a symmetry we sense, if at all, in the shards and fragments of this world—and of our lives, as Weil knew in the anguish of her life. And yet this is the motive for love in her writings, which you point to in an early poem in this sequence. Why love and not, say, duty or obligation, surely also themes in her writings?

DT: Yes, the title *This Broken Symmetry* is meant to suggest the human experience of the world as somehow fragmented or incomplete, though my first thought was to allude to the physical reality of symmetry breaking, which is the elemental process that brings the universe into being out of the primeval singularity from which it arises. I like to say "arises" rather than "arose" because much of the latest discussion (as I'm familiar with it) conceives of the universe "in creation," as Roy R. Gould of the Harvard-Smithsonian Center for Astrophysics suggests. The point is that the big bang isn't something that happened billions of years ago; rather, it's ongoing—some physicists are coming to the idea that creation wasn't a one-shot event, or an infinite compendium of one-shot events within some "metaverse." In any case, we are in it. I like the theological resonance of a universe in creation, even though from the standpoint of a physicist that reality, if true, implies nothing at all theologically, and probably shouldn't (though Teilhard de Chardin would posit otherwise).

So, as far as the title goes, I wanted it to spin off *From Nothing* and its focus on Lemaitre's work in physics and his theory that became known, derisively at first, as the Big Bang. Simone Weil, like all of us, inhabits this broken symmetry—we are part of it, which is one way to think about our "fallen" natures, and the fallen nature of the world as well conceived of in the broadest sense. Out of some perfect symmetry the universe evolves over vast stretches of time and space to greater complexity, which means it becomes more greatly fretted and involuted as it expands and accelerates in that expansion. One might dare say in human terms we find ourselves more and more at risk, not only from the fundamental conditions of our being but from ourselves. How do you we live in such a world?

I love Simone Weil because she recognizes what is so vitally at stake in how we conceive of reality, and she involves her whole being in the question, which is at once marvelously admirable and fills one with trepidation, precisely because it deepens the risk to the self. And, as we should know, our selves are flawed simply by virtue of being here at all. Hence her longing for the "uncreated." At the same time, one can respond to life in the world as one finds it with a sense of duty and obligation, and if one's sense of duty and obligation is truly moral then, one hopes, one will have added to the sum of worldly justice and betterment. Her attraction to communism surely emerges from this critical moral sense.

On the other hand, her spiritual growth during her short life enters upon the most profound transformation when she comes to feel the presence of love at the core of all that is, as when she was reciting George Herbert's poem "Love III" and Christ in spirit came into her being. Or perhaps it would be more accurate to say she came into the transfiguring apprehension of Christ's being there, as Christ must be, always (though we as human with all our powers of reflection, consciousness, do not feel that presence of the transcendent in the immanent given our adherence to the partial, the broken). She did not die for communism or even the Church—she died for love, transcendent love experienced immanently. One can argue over the extremity of her answer to love's call, or at least admit that extremity—self-starvation—verges on the life denying and may well involve the elusive complexities of psychology and upbringing. Still, I don't think one can deny but that a passionate love for God is at the root.

So, why love? If all that is, is only material, and matter and energy have no aspect and fundament in what we traditionally call the spirit, then there is no need for love—duty and obligation are perfectly suitable to improve incrementally and, if only for a time, the social and cultural conditions of human beings and the environment. It will all eventually pass away anyway. Such a view assumes that one's duty and obligations are directed for the betterment of life's conditions for others. History is rife with those who felt duty and obligation toward some ideology or cause that treated others most contemptuously and brutally, and our contemporary moment is no different. To seek and hopefully find love at the core of all our actions is to see that this broken symmetry isn't fragmented at all, but is bound together by love, and bound toward some more fulfilling symmetry of both being and consciousness, which are obviously mutually enfolded in each other—an All-in-All beyond any static, unmoved One. It means that one keeps faith with love not merely as a template for moral living but as a teleology at the very heart of creation—creation that is ecstatic with God's own ecstasy.

MB: You write of "the emptied God" in one of these poems, an idea that has Pauline roots but reaches as well into Weil's broader philosophical interests. And, in that poem, you point to the power of the imagination to enter, somehow, into that emptiness. Is it fair to see the interplay of absence and waiting, of loss and hunger, so central to Weil's writings, as a dimension of the way you yourself work as a poet? Does this tension express something of the dynamic interplay of the "given" and the "imagined" in your work of rendering Weil's thought and life into poetic form—i.e., something "made" from what we know of her life and work?

DT: I have been drawn to the idea of the emptied God for a long time, since as an undergraduate I took a class on the Pauline epistles and became fascinated with Philippians 2:5 – 11 with its extraordinary, formative hymn of the kenosis or self-emptying incarnation of Christ. I'm aware of the long history of interpretation this early hymn has produced, as well as its ontological and ethical implications, depending on one's Christological approach. I've always read it with a mind toward

God becoming present in the creation through the person of Christ's incarnation, and I suppose one can draw a line from the kenosis of Philippians to the Cosmic Christ of Colossians, as Teilhard does implicitly if not explicitly—God's creation an emptying into becoming from God's own Being: the infinite *I am*. And one can hear, echoing ahead, Eckhart's eternal birth of Christ in the soul out of the Godhead he conceived as God beyond God, in what he called "an eternal boiling." Reading this way leads one to see the being and becoming of things as a kind of surplus, and emptying of God that is simultaneously an overflowing.

Weil's understanding is really the inverse of that vision. God withdraws, and that original primordial creational withdrawal of God is how the universe comes into being and, therefore, into becoming with all of its risk, limitation, and ultimately the human propensity for evil. For Weil, the emptied God highlights God's absence from the creation rather than God's presence within it. I suppose it depends on how one theologically inflects God's emptying—God emptying into the world, or the world emptied of God yet still dependent on God for its being, since there would be no presence without God's original withdrawal, which renders God, from this side of being, *deus absconditus*. Weil's ethical response, to my mind, is very much attuned to Philippians. She takes on the role of the lowly servant, and it would not be going too far to say that she lived a life of emptying herself, perhaps to the point (and beyond) of masochism. Can one make oneself an idol in the desire to empty oneself, even perhaps in imitation of Christ? It's that kind of question that drives my interest in Weil, why I find her so dramatically compelling beyond any theological preoccupations.

So, as far as my own efforts with *This Broken Symmetry* are concerned, I would say yes, the imagination needs to enter the emptiness by listening and waiting. Perhaps the real effort is in readying oneself, always trying to be ready, but more than that to do the steady work of practice. One needs to be a servant to one's subject, needs to be negatively capable rather than positively capable, in Keats's sense of the poet's work. The page before the words begin to appear, however laboriously and, hopefully, graciously, from some capacity more encompassing than the ego, is after all empty.

At the same time, I find it compelling that Weil did not trust the imagination, saw it more in league with human delusion than with human creation—a danger. I would love to overhear Weil in conversation with Coleridge, if such were possible, Coleridge of the primary and secondary imagination—

the imagination of the infinite *I AM* and the human imagination in the image of God's—and Weil with her whole impetus to decreate, to return things to the un-created. I'd invite Teilhard to the table as well, with his essentially Pauline vision of God all-in-all in some evolutionary human future beyond even the death of the species, everything transfigured in and through his Christ Omega; Weil with her vision of the past offering something more real and better than ourselves, Teilhard with his theologically and biologically utopian future.

This last fanciful conclave probably speaks to some deep-seeded spiritual hunger in my work, and one that could easily devolve into dull abstraction. Obviously, one needs to avoid that end. Your last question about the dynamic interplay of the given and the imagined really goes to process. The way in for me requires access to the drama of the life through particular details, scenes, relationships, places. My job as poet is to try to enter them, to let them speak through the poem's formal means at every level and facet of the writing. But I can only enter them if I have begun to lay myself bare before them, to let them enter me.

I don't want to over analyze this, but I am drawn to Weil because of something deeply rooted in me that involves what Seamus Heaney called the definition of a poet's stance toward life, a poet's definition of reality. So, as far as possible, as poet I need to set our stances toward life—mine and Weil's--in dialogue. That can only happen if I am able to render the life credibly and dramatically, and not just by offering her ideas about the life. The boy who appears in the second section, "Roots," really did wait at her door in the Notting Hill rooming house where she lived, not long before she died. He was the landlady's son and was mentally challenged. That is all mere information unless the poem places us there, where the boy curls as if in utero at her door. In the previous section, the first, we are at her burial at Bybrook cemetery, and now we have a child curled in a fetal position, waiting. I have no desire to overstate the resonances, but I can tell you I did not plan any such juxtaposition. The poet has to follow the poem.

That also means in the case of Weil, as in the section "Decreation" (which follows "Roots,"), to let her thought gain dramatic presence: "But to enter the uncreated, Nothing's naked open sea, / Before God abandoned God to these various forms / Of hunger, gravity riveted plumb in every scattered part, // And each I like a standing pole to blot the infinite...." This section ends with the scene in Gethsemane, with God waiting for God under the olive trees. In writing this section I did not arrive in Gethsemane imaginatively by intention but by trying to let the poem lead me, by trying to allow her thinking to inhabit me as much as by trying to represent her thought. Really, the more so letting the habitation take place in me. And before any of that there is listening to how the words move together and in lines and in sentences and in accordance with the poem's formal requirement as imposed or, really, discovered for *From Nothing*. I suppose for all of this, while the desire to be a poet and make a poem is an assertion of self and surely obtains some force of the ego, the poet's work, the maker's work to go back to the etymology of the word, really involves the hope of self-emptying, so the poem can come into being as if of its own accord or from somewhere more significant and abiding than willful desire.

MB: A striking aspect of your collection is the manner in which you create poems "toward" Simone Weil in the voices of others—e.g., Thibon, Picasso, Stein, her brother, father and mother. Here, the "fiction" of poetic invention takes on another richness, a wider complexity. What does it mean for you to enter into such historical persons and "re-create" them within the horizon of Weil's life and witness?

DT: The impetus to imagine a way into these people, some central, some peripheral to Weil's life, came first from the demand of *From Nothing* in which I wanted to view Georges Lemaitre's life through the lens of people like Edwin Hubble, Robert Oppenheimer, and the like. In the case of Weil's mother and father, I wanted to understand, to feel, what it would be like to have a child with this intensity of spiritual genius and worldly commitment to her ideas. Not at all easy I would say. Her mother laments that she is not marriageable and did tell an acquaintance that if they had a daughter to pray she is not a saint. In the case of Thibon, I wanted to try to take on the friend's perspective, to gain a sense of compassion for the extremity of her conviction to the point of turning against her own bodily life—the Manichean streak in her.

There is no evidence I could come across that Stein and Picasso ever encountered Weil, but both lived at least for a time in close proximity to the Luxembourg Gardens in Paris, not far from the Weil apartment on Rue Auguste Comte. What would it be like if they had caught sight of her and knew who she was—really could there be a duo of such significance to the culture and yet more contrary to Weil? The fictional encounter is plausible, and I wanted each to respond to that encounter in a manner commensurate with the tenor of their own lives— both in my view less than exemplary morally and spiritually, if not artistically. Simone de Beauvoir struck me as something of Simone Weil's anti-self, or perhaps Weil is the anti-matter to her materialist twin, whom she encountered at the Sorbonne.

Finally, Andre Weil, one of the great mathematical geniuses of the twentieth century, presents perhaps the biggest problem to his sister because, first, as children they were so close, and, second, because they were divided from each other by the gender roles of the time. "A brother is like a tooth," Simone would say, "a good thing, provided one is not too often forced to know that it exists." Simone Weil, of course, defied those gender roles. I wanted to imagine a way into that complex family dynamic from Andre's point of view. As a whole, these different vantages in *This Broken Symmetry* are meant to enlarge the scope of the poem's engagement with the life. That life, in relief of the infinite in which it shares, cannot be pinpointed. Simone Weil exemplifies in the most urgent and dramatic terms the inexhaustible aspect of every life.

MB: This collection is the second of a trilogy, the first volume devoted to Georges Lemaitre. How will the momentum of this volume carry you into the final volume you have planned, one devoted to the life and work of Teilhard de Chardin? In what sense will that volume be in conversation with this one?

DT: It's been about a decade since I started on what has become the trilogy. *From Nothing* gave structural, thematic and conceptual momentum to *This Broken Symmetry*, and I'm hoping the same will happen for *At the Grave of Teilhard de Chardin*. The overall structural design is a given, but how the sections move from one to the next needs to be discovered along the way. I've been immersing myself in Teilhard's writings, and the work of others, having been drawn to Teilhard since my college days. I had a poem about him in mind for more than twenty years, not knowing how to approach it. There are leitmotifs so to speak connecting *From Nothing* to *This Broken Symmetry*, and I trust the same will be true for the Teilhard poems. *From Nothing* moves along the arrow of time in a linear fashion; *This Broken Symmetry* moves against the arrow of time. I'm not sure yet how these poems will "move," though I suspect in a manner that suggests time as a current within a greater non-temporal reality. But how that works structurally, from section to section, I have no idea as yet. It will need to be discovered in the concentrated effort of composing the piece, appropriately enough, over time. Weil finds more reality in the past; Teilhard in the future, in the *Parousia* of God All-in-All, so that tension needs exploration in dramatic form. For Weil,

God is absent; for Teilhard, Mass is celebrated on the altar of the universe. The other larger issue will be the first-person pronoun—not necessarily Teilhard speaking but perhaps a voice closer to the inner voice of the one seeking the answer. The last enemy to be destroyed is death, according to Teilhard's understanding. That's *Alpha* and *Omega* for the reflective consciousness. The challenge will be for the poem to find a way through.

Daniel Tobin was born in Brooklyn, New York. He is the author of nine books of poems, including *From Nothing*, winner of the Julia Ward Howe Award; *The Stone in the Air*, his suite of versions from the German of Paul Celan; and the newly published *Blood Labors*. He is author of the critical studies *Awake in America, Passage to the Center: Imagination and the Sacred in the Poetry of Seamus Heaney* and *On Serious Earth*. Tobin is also editor of *The Book of Irish American Poetry from the Eighteenth Century to the Present*; *Light in Hand: Selected Early Poems of Lola Ridge*; *Poet's Work, Poet's Play: Essays on the Practice and the Art* (with Pimone Triplett); and *To The Many: Collected Early Poems of Lola Ridge*, which received a Special Commendation from the Poetry Society. His poetry has won the "The Discovery/The Nation Award," The Robert Penn Warren Award, the Robert Frost Fellowship, the Katherine Bakeless Nason Prize, the Stephen J. Meringoff Award, the Massachusetts Book Award, the Pushcart Prize, and fellowships from the National Endowment for the Arts and the John Simon Guggenheim Foundation, among other honors. He teaches at Emerson College in Boston.

Mark S. Burrows is a scholar of historical theology, with an interest in mysticism and poetics; he is also a poet and award-winning translator of German literature. A longtime resident of New England, he currently lives between Bochum, Germany, where he teaches religion and literature at the Protestant University of Applied Sciences, and Camden, Maine. His recent publications include *Meister Eckhart's Book of the Heart. Meditations for the Restless Soul*, with Jon M. Sweeney (2017) and *The Chance of Home: Poems* (2018). He has published several volumes of German poetry in translation, including Rainer Maria Rilke's *Prayers of a Young Poet* (2016) and SAID's *99 psalms*. He was the recipient of a Witter Bynner Prize in Poetry. Current projects include the first full-length translation of the contemporary German-Jewish poet Hilde Domin. www.msburrows.com

Book Reviews

We Became Summer by Amy Barone (NYQ Books, 2018)

    Many of Amy Barone's poems in *We Became Summer* are written in the plain-spoken style popularized during the 1970's and 80's as a reaction against the obscurity of some poetry of the high-modernist era. At its most extreme, a plain-spoken style takes free verse to its freest limit, incorporating few of the conventional tools of poetic craft and using the line break simply to reinforce units of grammar. In poems of this style, lines are broken most often at the ends of phrases, with very few examples of true enjambment, and the poets rely on sonic effects in order to reproduce the rhythms of ordinary speech rather than to compress language into tight lines whose rhythm is often enhanced by alliteration, assonance, and consonance. Barone's poems acknowledge the primary goal of the plain-spoken style, for their language is accessible and their syntax is orthodox, yet they rely on the music of language and the intrigue of metaphor. They are influenced by the plain-spoken style, that is, but they are also influenced by more recent (and perhaps also less recent) strategies that assist the poet's task—to make meaning through language that is beautiful and interesting.

    We Became Summer is arranged into five sections, exploring the poet's interests in music and travel as well as relationships with lovers, parents, other relatives, and friends. "Amelia" is representative of some of those thematic concerns and also of Barone's preference for regular stanzas. Describing the speaker's grandmother, the poem begins, "A lady from Puglia landed / in East Harlem in the early 1900s." The first line is particularly interesting to my ear, with its alliteration and consonance, not only of "lady" and "landed," but also with the "l" in "Puglia." The repeated "d" in "lady" and "landed" enhances the alliteration, as does each "a" following the "l." In addition, the line almost scans, beginning with an iamb, followed by two anapests. Being free verse, the poem itself is not written in a regular meter, but this echo of meter in the first line commands the reader's attention. Here is much of the rest of the poem:

I hear my grandmother held court

from a fluffy sofa
next to a living room staircase.
She insisted her children see no hurdles,

emulate the prosperous WASPs
who settled on Philadelphia's Main Line.
I hear she taught Italian immigrants English.

I hear she served tea from a real silver service
to *paesani* who visited her tiny row home.
I hear she pilfered a close friend's sweater.

My father adored her.
My mother said she was crazy.
I bear her name and want to be
nothing and everything like her.

    For me, the most interesting aspect of this poem's voice is the repetition of "I hear," becoming increasingly frequent as the poem progresses. That bit of slang reveals that this Amelia, this Italian immigrant to a country that preferred its Anglo-Saxon heritage, is a prominent subject of family lore. The lore itself is often interesting, but the "I hear" also makes the speaker interesting. The carefully selected details—"fluffy sofa," "tea from a real silver service"—reveal Amelia's character, as does, most significantly, the climactic detail: "I hear she pilfered a close friend's sweater." The music of that line is also attractive, the repeated short "e" in "friend" and "sweater," the verb "pilfered" so much more interesting than "stole." Having relied on such concrete imagery to describe her grandmother, Barone can get away with the direct statements in the poem's final quatrain. We are perhaps not surprised to learn that an Italian son "adored" his mother, nor that a daughter-in-law would be less entranced by her. The final line, though, confirms the speaker's ambivalence that might have prompted the poem and also confirms a similar ambivalence the reader might feel toward Amelia.
    A few words and phrases in this poem could be cut—"real" and "tiny" for example. The alliteration in "I hear she served tea from a silver service" is more prominent without "real." Earlier, the comparatively flat "see no hurdles" could also be cut as well as "who settled" two lines later. Again, the

tighter rhythm would attract the reader's ear more completely. Even so, the poem is strong in its concrete detail and voice.

A very different poem is "Glad," which consists of a series of specific and surprising commands:

> In the pursuit,
> loosen chains.
>
> Sleep next to a dreamcatcher.
> Live in places smaller than large.
>
> Travel nearer than far.
> Reach for yellow leaves that turn red in October.
>
> Listen to classic soul, not rap.
> Wear silver and turquoise jewelry, if you must.
>
> Speak an alluring language.
> Memorable encounters start with a tongue.

Each of these commands can be interpreted in multiple ways. Some are sensible (shouldn't everyone be freed of their chains?), while others are unexpected (don't we more often urge each other to travel far?). As the poem progresses, the commands become more idiosyncratic (why silver rather than gold, or turquoise rather than jade?), so that readers receive a clearer sense of the speaker. The last couplet, appropriately, is the most surprising. Good things likely do follow if one can "Speak an alluring language," but the subsequent pun is as memorable as the longed-for encounter: "Memorable encounters start with a tongue." The imagery and tone of this poem are particularly effective, and its conclusion is enjoyable—would that more contemporary poems could be this enjoyable.

Prior to *We Became Summer,* Amy Barone had published two chapbooks, and her work has appeared in several national and international periodicals. Her publication record suggests that we will hear more of her. There's nothing better than the anticipation of another book from a poet you enjoy.

Lynn Domina is the author of two collections of poetry, *Corporal Works* and *Framed in Silence,* and the editor of a collection of essays, *Poets on the Psalms.* In addition to her literary studies, she earned an M.Div. at The Earlham School of Religion, where she took courses in the Ministry of Writing.

She serves as Head of the English Department at Northern Michigan University, and she is creative writing editor of *The Other Journal*. She currently lives with her family in Marquette, Michigan, on the beautiful shore of Lake Superior. You can read more here: www.lynndomina.com .

The Virginia State Colony for Epileptics and Feebleminded by Molly McCully Brown (Persea Books, 2017)

In an essay with *The Rumpus*, Molly McCully Brown admits she is "tired of talking about disability." I can see why—it is unfair that the duty and burden of writing about disability so often seems to fall to the differently-abled. There is a roaring silence, a resounding non-representation of people living with disabilities in all facets of our culture. That Brown is "tired of feeling responsible for that silence" makes sense.

> I'm tired of talking about its place in culture and politics. I'm tired of talking about my body and other people's bodies, and of feeling like leaving my house in the morning is a political act. I'm tired of, whatever I write and whatever I'm thinking, feeling disability bang around at the back of my brain and insist on a presence in everything. Get out. Leave me alone. Get out. Get out.

For Brown's continued work in this realm, despite its exhausting nature, I am endlessly grateful.

A confluence of personal lyric, narrative history, and poetic documentary, Molly McCully Brown's *The Virginia State Colony for Epileptics and Feebleminded* is communion with, consolation to, and consecration of a place and people haunted by a disturbing history. The origins of the Colony are introduced in the book's preface:

> The Virginia State Colony for Epileptics and Feebleminded opened in 1910 in Amherst County, Virginia, as the Virginia State Colony for Epileptics, a government-run residential hospital. In 1913, the facility also began serving patients it classified as "feebleminded" and by 1919 the name had been altered

to reflect this fact. In 1924, the Colony became formally enmeshed with the Eugenics movement and began sterilizing, without their consent, patients it deemed "defectives." When, in 1927, the U.S. Supreme Court upheld Virginia sterilization laws in *Buck v. Bell,* eugenic sterilizations became an even more common practice. From the mid-1920s through the mid-1950s, more than 7,000 people were sterilized in Virginia, often without their knowledge. While some patients were sterilized and then released, others spent the better part of their lives at the Colony. Although the last eugenic sterilization is noted in the Colony's annual report for 1956, sterilizations may have continued into the 1970s.

Here, there is violence in the dogwood trees, in shadows cast by the looming colonial revival buildings, in the biting winter wind, in the locks on the heavy oak doors. Set in the mid-1930s, *The Virginia State Colony for Epileptics and Feebleminded* imagines the inner workings of the Colony as well as the lives of the patients and staff, among others. Though the accounts are imaginings, one never has the sense that Brown is attempting to speak for the characters, nor to color over their experiences. Part of what makes this book so masterful an accomplishment is how it returns agency and voice to the characters within, how it empowers and humanizes those from whom the Colony has taken.

    In "The Convulsions Choir," for example, an epileptic speaker considers herself "the worst thing / the reasoned world / has wrought," and imagines linking arms with other epileptic girls, leading them up to the chapel's altar, all of them humming "like hymns," despite the fact that the church was not built for patients, but as refuge for staff. "They did not build / the church / for us," the speaker states twice. *No,* I want to shout through time, *but this book was built for you.*

    The research undertaken to create *The Virginia State Colony* makes clear that the collection was borne of obsession. Molly McCully Brown, who lives with cerebral palsy, grew up near the Colony—a place that, had she been born mere decades before, could very well have been her fate. As considered in the final stanza of the collection's first poem:

> And, by some accident of luck or grace,
> some window less than half a century wide,
> it is my backyard but not what happened
> to my body—

Brown's faith is the stuff in which *The Virginia State Colony* is steeped. Though Catholicism's central rituals are rituals of the body—kneel, now stand, kneel, now genuflect—Brown has described her faith as a framework through which she is capable of understanding her body as meant. Disability is, necessarily, carried at all times: carried as one carries faith. The inextricability of these is present in the sound of caterwauling hymnsong throughout the collection—hymn as both comfort and fright. The crumbling Colony buildings call to mind the Genesitic decree that all eventually returns to the ground from which it was taken, that all returns to dust. This book, in its insistence on communing with the dead, on making space for these narratives, in its realization that moving forward requires looking back, on restoring the fragmented, erased lives of its characters to wholeness, reminds us that a body is never punishment, accident, or mistake.

A collection keenly aware of its own shadow and light, *The Virginia State Colony for Epileptics and Feebleminded* throws open barred doors and pushes aside the stiff, filthy curtains of a ruinous place. It is painful, revelatory, consecrated.

Cydnee Devereaux is a third-year fellow at the Robert Penn Warren Center for Humanities at Vanderbilt University, where she is an MFA candidate. Her work has been supported by the Sewanee Writers' Conference, the Bread Loaf Writers' Conference, and is forthcoming in *Grist Online*.

The Chance of Home by Mark S. Burrows (Paraclete Press, 2018)

As you read through this collection of poems, most of them no longer than a single page, it becomes clearer and clearer that Mark Burrows is a seasoned witness of the extraordinary to be found in what we call the ordinary. In this he reminds us of Thomas Merton in his hard-won meditations, as well as Rilke, whom he has spent years translating. "Each spring," Burrows writes in the opening poem, "I Still Marvel,"

> . . . . I wait for the crocuses to come,
> eager to greet their purple bursts as they rise

>   from the soggy earth and stubborn patches
>   of late-lingering snow, and while I know
>
>   what their veils will show of radiance,
>   this does nothing to blunt my wonder. . .

The language is crisp, accessible, the unrhymed couplets climbing like Jacob's ladder rungs, starting in the wet earth and then ascending upward into another sphere altogether. Pay attention too to the chimes that ring within the lines, as in the repetition of that long *Oh!* sound in "snow" and "know" and "show." Pay attention too to the sibilance of a line like "as if to sing in a gentle soundless way," or the consonantal chiming of the poem's quiet closure, where the poet (and we too) "yearn for, a lure of this long listening."

    What is it the poet hears, or hears beyond or within the sound of words, in these acts of reverential attention? The sway of grass, the clouds morphing above like children without a care, the trees which keep their "vigil in obedience / to gravity and the certainties of place" as we humans race on beneath. And the birds at dawn or midday or evening: the finches and "white-throated sparrows," the "unseen cuckoo" hiding among the trees, the warbler singing "her heart into / this world with an unyielding joy," the thrush feasting on the orange fruit of a mountain ash, the larks and magpies with their "cackle after all a showy sort of praise," the flocks of geese announcing "themselves from afar," then their "swaying line" carving "a wedge through the empty / acres of the sky," following their "long call home."

    Call us home. That's what the splendid, ordinary things of this world seem to do in simply being and doing what they are. They seem to call us home or at least the chance for home. In this Burrows reminds me not only of Augustine and Wordsworth and Rilke, but of Hopkins—a mid-western American version of Hopkins, if you will, with shades of Stevens and Williams and Frost in the mix. The brightness, the light....

    But what of those in pain, like the homeless, the beggars, the sick and orphaned, who wait in the dark night "for light to break the spell of their long / nights and shadowed days"? ("This Somewhere") All at once, like grace breaking in, the poet sees the unspoken, something given to us beyond words themselves, an answer there before him in

>   . . . . a pioneer weed rising at the edge of

> the city lot I walk by each day, a corner strewn
>
> with shards of glass and choked with neglect
> as deep as a stubborn late-November fog.
>
> And there, atop a greening blade, a single
> yellow flower comes to crown this unlikely
>
> majesty, a reminder that not even the grit
> of loss or the grind of grief can ever
>
> finally stay the chance of home.

    Except for a translation of Rilke's "Only the Song," it's the final poem of the book, which gave Burrows his title. Home. That's where the heart is, he tells us. In a deeply-moving afterword, the poet tells us that the title came to him late, after the poems themselves were written, when, reading through the collection, it struck him with the force of an epiphany that this after all was what the poems were about, for it is that sense of home, "our longing for stability" even in the midst of "our awareness of our fragility," which haunts the poet—and us—as we take the journey down and through these lines, the conviction, that, yes, there is after all "a larger whole, rooted...in the heart of things." Something that "comes to us, when it does, from the depth of the unconscious, the moorings where poetry discovers the resilience of its proper voice."

    Burrows is an exceptional poet, really, like Rilke deeply spiritual. His is a voice I believe you can unequivocally trust, a voice, modest enough on the surface, though there's a great deal of learning there, which surely deserves our attention. Read him, and he will feed you, turning the few crumbs of the ordinary—two fishes, five loaves—into a splendid Eucharistic feast.

Paul Mariani, Emeritus Professor of English at Boston College, has published six biographies of poets (William Carlos Williams, Berryman, Lowell, Hart Crane, Hopkins, and Wallace Stevens); seven volumes of poetry, most recently *Epitaphs for the Journey;* and *Thirty Days: on Retreat with the Exercises of St. Ignatius*. His awards include a Guggenheim, an NEA, NEH, and the John Ciardi Award for Lifetime Achievement in Poetry. His life of Hart Crane, *The Broken Tower*, a feature-length film, directed by and starring James Franco, was released in 2012. He served as Poetry Editor of *America Magazine* from 2000—2006. His poetry has appeared there, as well as in such magazines as *Poetry, Image, Presence, First Things,* and The *Hudson Review,* as well as in numerous anthologies. *The Mystery of It All: The Vocation of Poetry in the Twilight of Modernity* is scheduled for publication in 2019.

Night Unto Night by Martha Collins (Milkweed Editions, 2018)

Night Unto Night, Martha Collins' new collection of poems, is a book to savor. The poems are meditations and laments on death, aging, time, love, and the self. They are both playful and philosophical, sometimes intricate and elliptical, other times simpler and syntactically straightforward.

The book invites the reader in, enough white space around the short mostly six or seven line sections to suggest the reader will not be lost in a dense forest, but will be able to see individual trees and find pathways. Then having offered these pathways, the book invites and rewards return visits.

The book is organized into six subdivisions, or poems, as Collins refers to them in the end notes. Each of these poems is dated with a month and year, from March 2010 to November 2015, and each is further subdivided into what Collins calls sections, one for each night of the month. Some dates evoke memories of recent or historic events, among them: the November 2015 Paris Climate Conference, the killing of Osama bin Laden in May 2011, the bombing of Hiroshima and Nagasaki on August 7, Veterans Day on November 11.

There is continuity, repetition, and resonance as well as forward movement from night to night, especially in the two center poems where the last word of one section becomes the first word of the next. Thus the boundaries from night to night become porous, the calendar and the clock not the exclusive measure of the speaker's experience, whether it be of love or grief. Likewise large-scale issues, including war and racism, also breach chronological boundaries of dates, months, and years.

This book tackles poetically challenging material like war and racial justice, not as its primary focus as in *Blue Front* or *Admit One.* Those earlier books made me an enthusiastic Collins' fan for the way her poetic craft made palpable her social justice concerns. Here these concerns are woven into the texture of a full and deeply examined life with a subtle and sure hand.

The title's double reference to night and the fact of its publication in 2018, two years after the death of Collins' husband, might suggest a somber overall tone. Some poems are dark in the usual metaphoric sense of that word. At times, anger and rage break out and are named explicitly or conveyed in specifics that emerge in a powerful volley, such as in August 2012: "Rage / / exploding on streets" and "Rage against polluters, deniers," "Tombstones in the corner / of the dream"; and November 2015: "Trayvon Tamir Dontre Michael / Laquan Eric Rekia John."

Other poems, however, offer the possibility that night is a time of rest and healing. In May 2011, a dream of bird song, for example, is seen as "contra- / puntal lines" that "weave / / a nest for my troubles." Night is also a time of love-making, and exclamations of love help drive the forward momentum of the book. They are brief and fragmentary at first, in May 2011: "oh love / in our bed." Later, they become more imperative: "Stay, Love, beside me in / our bed again," and as the book moves to its conclusion in November 2015, they are most poignant: "missing almost nothing / my love in my arms, in my bed again."

The poems are alive with natural images. Collins seems, for the most part, to be looking upward. Birds and sky provide music and color: "sandpipers, notes, / allegro," "red shadow on pale / moon", "the locust making her flowers / green confetti," and "Water pinks, blues, geese / stretch, ducks stir, green heron / rises". The natural world at times prompts a comparison to something human made, but the human often falls short. Gulls above waters where herring swim, for example, "circled, shrieked, / laboring like, but not— / our drones our extended / hungers for the kill." Later poems move in a quiet way toward moments of peace. Early one morning, "Awake in time   for this red / blaze behind trees" the speaker also awakens to a freeing sense of self: "my little only / life my own to take out / of night into this   given day."

Collins is also attentive to and innovative with form, creating a remarkable range of variations in stanza breaks and line indentions within the short, nightly sections. Here is an example from the first poem:

> Waterfall sculpted
>   itself into water-
>   fall, using cold
> to mold itself solid

>   and still, as if to
>   be forever
>   falling without ever falling.

The opening word "waterfall," hyphenated and enjambed from second to third line, signal a change in form or state, in this case, the change from the liquid to solid state. The long ō sound of "cold" and "mold," convey a chill, and the line break separating them also conveys a sense of falling. The poem ends with an oxymoron, reminiscent of the theme in Keats' "Ode on a Grecian Urn," applied here not to art but to a natural phenomenon, and fitting well into the context of the concern with body, loss, and immortality.

    Here the cascade of lines approximates an S shape, a letter that the poem also alliterates. More importantly, the lines mimic a waterfall, and the last line, even if it is horizontal rather than vertical, suggests the waterfall frozen into the single, unbroken line the words name.

    Time and again I found most sections of the poems likewise reward such careful study of their form. The artistry of the poems in *Night Unto Night* offers a rich and thoughtful experience and a great deal of pleasure.

Margaret Rozga has published four books of poetry. Her most recent book, *Pestiferous Questions: A Life in Poems* (Lit Fest Press, 2017), looks at issues of women's roles, U.S. western expansion, and race as they are woven through the life of politically active and well-connected Jessie Benton Frémont (1824-1902). Research for this book was supported by a creative writer's fellowship at the American Antiquarian Society. Rozga has also been a resident at the Sitka Center for Art and Ecology and at the Ragdale Foundation. Her poems have been published recently in *Presence, Leaping Clear*, and *Sweet Tree Review*.

Street Calligraphy by Jim Daniels (Steel Toe Books, 2017)

    Jim Daniels is a Carnegie Mellon professor and prolific author, with 17 books of poetry, four screenplays, and five collections of short stories to his credit. Daniels' poetry has, for four decades, celebrated industrial Detroit and mythologized both its decay and the poet's corresponding reckless youth. *Street Calligraphy* continues to link these phenomena, reading both against the trials of addiction, the demands of parenthood, and, especially, attempts to balance the two.

The poem "The Rusty Muffler of Nostalgia" reverently details a teenage beach week with "a beer-shotgunning contest," "parking-lot brawls," "drunk-driving lessons," and "hickeys from North Carolina girls." The poem recalls James Wright in its cunning juxtaposition of seemingly basic reverie with the imminent factory life that reverie anticipated. "Rusty Muffler" is also notable for the speaker's matter-of-fact confessions—"[T]he guys razzed me / about Marsha from NC . . . / . . . My girlfriend stopped / rooting for me—left early and alone, / and I was almost glad of it."—which Daniels employs in multiple poems.

In several Detroit pieces, the speaker is mostly a spectator, curating his hardscrabble neighborhood and its demise via unpretentious and devastating storytelling. In "Flightless," the speaker's mother is mugged in her driveway, and white flight ensues while the speaker's family stays. In "Up on Blocks," a neighbor boy dies in Vietnam, and his father unravels thereafter. In "Cutwoman in the Corner House," the speaker's mother, a nurse and "designated secret sharer," patches the wounds of neighbors seeking to conceal their husbands' abuse: "Mrs. Anders tumbled, bruised, over the back fence, / Mrs. Blondell and the glass shard, / Mrs. Laney and the teeth, Mrs. Dodge and the burn— / my mother held ice against sobs."

Notably, however, Daniels is never *just* a spectator, at least not in Detroit, where he refuses to play detached anthropologist. His style artfully reflects Daniels' Detroit itself—ever plainspoken; often abrupt and harsh; eager to exude toughness—although occasional colloquial flourishes feel forced ("I smashed the mother-fucking scale"; "one night some asshole torched it"). Daniels' Detroit poems are especially ripe with plain-but-powerful symbolism. In "The Wave, Tiger Stadium," the speaker recalls The Wave's advent in 1984: "Detroit embraced / its odd magic, how you could both stay in one place / and move . . . / . . . The tang of anarchy / sweet to anyone who worked an assembly line / and knew about standing in place." In "Tennis Practice Wall," the speaker highlights the irony of the wall, never used as intended and caked in profane graffiti, in a neighborhood with problems too pressing for tennis.

Beyond Detroit, Daniels explores parenthood, and, occasionally, his struggle with sobriety while parenting.

"Stagger" and "Last Day in Coldwater" offer graphic and unnerving snapshots of addiction-driven dysfunction. In "Dusk, July, Third Floor," a newly-divorced friend seeks comfort from the speaker, who reminisces, seemingly sans guilt, about sleeping with the friend's ex-wife. These pieces perfectly contextualize "Changing the Name," which is less visually evocative, but transformative for first exposing the speaker's conscience:

> While his wife was at church
> my great-grandfather let his son choke
> on a chicken bone while he mopped out
> his tavern's Saturday night stink
>
> . . . .
> . . . . When I missed my plane in Grand Rapids,
> too stoned to read the watch face, I had to stay
>
> an extra night, lighting and blowing out
> imaginary candles while my two babies
> back home kept my wife up talking in tongues
> about their stoned old man.

Neither great-grandfather nor the speaker can escape his guilt, as Daniels skillfully links the two narratives: "I inherited the watch [great-grandfather] won racing pigeons / a fancy piece too complicated to fix, / yet I hear it ticking."

Several poems document the perils of parenting-while-addicted, such as "Slow Learner," in which the speaker seems indifferent to his 20 years spent in an "artificial fog," but embraces sober parenthood in the closing sequence. Daniels writes, "At age forty / I finally learned how to whistle / blowing love into my daughter's hair." This embrace is punctuated by "Ohio Turnpike Opens New Rest Stop," in which the speaker comforts his daughter who was alarmed by seeing an addict emerge from a rest stop bathroom. "[W]e stand squirming for minutes / until a woman unlocks the door / / and steps out alone, eyes glazed / with locked-door drugs, the sting / of recognition."

Street Calligraphy comes full circle as Daniels' children age into adolescence, which he laments—nostalgic for bedtime stories ("Once Upon a Time") and museum trips ("The Names of Dinosaurs")—despite, and, in part, because of, his love affair with his own wild teenhood. "My son's in 9th grade," Daniels writes in "The Lincoln Death Chair." "The idea of him drinking / sprays buckshot into my chest." However, Daniels' real love affair is with the past itself, and his poetic duty to eulogize bygone moments, is demonstrated in "Talking About the Day":

Each night after reading three books to my two children—
. . . .
I'd turn off the light and sit between their beds
. . . .
and ask them to talk about the day—*we did this,*
we did that, sometimes leading somewhere, sometimes
not, but always ending up at the happy ending of *now.*
. . . .
                                         Grown now, you might've guessed.
The past tense solid, unyielding, against the acidic drip
of recent years. But how it calmed us then, rewinding
the gentle loop, and in the trusting darkness, pressing play.

Jake Oresick's poems have appeared in *St. Peter's B-list: Contemporary Poems Inspired by the Saints* (Ave Maria Press) and the *Pittsburgh Post-Gazette*, as well as literary journals, including *American Literary, Superficial Flesh, Figure Four,* and *Adanna*. He is the author of *The Schenley Experiment: A Social History of Pittsburgh's First Public High School* (Penn State University Press), and his scholarly pieces can be found in *Western Pennsylvania History* magazine, the *Heinz Journal,* and *JURIST*. Oresick was educated at John Carroll University, Carnegie Mellon University, and the University of Pittsburgh. He lives in Pittsburgh where he works as a litigation attorney.

Dear Pilgrims by John F. Deane (Carcanet Press, 2018)

    As fertile a writer as he is, the publication of any book by John F. Deane is always a cause for pause and celebration. In the last ten years alone Deane has published five collections of poetry (A Little Book of Hours, Eye of the Hare, Snow Falling on Chestnut Hill: New and Selected Poems, Semibreve, and, Dear Pilgrims), a memoir (Give Dust a Tongue), and a mosaic text about his beloved childhood home off the west coast of County Mayo, Achill: The Island.
    Dear Pilgrims begins with four poems that honor family and friends. The first poem, "Crocus: A Brief History," is dedicated to a cherished grandson whose life, like a crocus, "will be an oratorio / of hollyhock, lupin, sunflower, / under the

gold-full baton of the light." Two life-in-death poems follow (one, an elegy for Deane's friend Seamus Heaney) before the quartet culminates, as the collection culminates, in a kind of Eucharistic unity. This last poem of the four, "Epithalamium," invokes the nuptial spirit of the classical form, the speaker praying that the beloved couple might have "music, the slow, classical dance" as they make their pilgrim way together, one hopes, to "a better world, of love and mercy, of justice, happiness and peace." The subsequent seven sections of the collection are stitched together with likewise dynamism and illuminate a wide-ranging scope of concern and experience. As always, Deane is a poet who is at once natural, spiritual, and social— a relational, dialogical artist who inhabits a Christian way of being while attracting readers who might otherwise eschew the warm but demanding heart of an advanced sacramental poetics.

 The first three sections—*First Testament, A Small Salvation, A New Testament*—immediately disclose Deane's virtuosity as sacramental artist. These sets of poems, marked by acute observations of place, person, and event, reveal expanding resonances that vibrate inwardly/outwardly, the "intricate and burble-delicate water-music" that plays an essential part in the larger symphony. Explicit biblical allusions in "Rainbow" move us to contemplate the innermost ways that God is known to us in moments "Small, fond, and local" as Mary Karr might say, the ways that, for the speaker in the poem, "Joy made covenant with me / / these decades back, days on the riverbank / when trout responded to stick, twine and pin…" But then to the larger mystery too, Hopkins-like, where, even though there exists the dearest freshness deep-down things, we also must answer in justice for our churlish abuses of the gift—or as Deane has it in "Rainbow, "to purge us of the wars we wage / / on the good earth, who have grown smart / with chemicals and missiles"—we who stand naked and accountable before the "dreary undersides of the clouds."

 While there are so many instances that communicate Deane's integral vision of sacramentality in *Dear Pilgrims*—of the proximate but transcendent "sacred-spirit fuselage" of God's creation—we behold a most stark example in "Dawn to Dusk," from the *A Small Salvation* section:

> here – in the everyday year in which we live
> and labour to effect a small salvation —
> light shifts on towards night,
> night towards light again.

> Heron stands – motionless as a battered
> parasol – among stones in the quiet shallows,
> heron-eye wide and watchful;
> noon-time sunlight will set ablaze
>
> the green flaggers along the marshes;
> angelus is tolling in the distance; now
> is a silence containing in its breathing
> the warmth of sap, of blood flowing.

Deane, ever the master of the apt neologism, encapsulates the eternal now of our lives in God—and the very structures of liturgy and sacramentality—by entering "everyday year" into the lexicon. The revelatory bell of the Angelus rings out alongside the speech of birds (in another poem, "Parlement of Foules," the bird wordplay is most explicit and sustained); and the fragrance of eucalyptus (a dominate scent in the collection) enhances the marsh aromas as birds vacillate between song and silence in the bloodstream of the living God.

The title of the collection is found in "Letter from East Anglia," the last poem of the *A New Testament* section. The poem, dedicated to Rowan Williams, is a love letter to the region. So many poet-pilgrims beloved of Deane are invoked as the speaker moves through the rough terrain of southeast England and the "short, slatternly days" where "skin is ragged" and the North Sea winds "cut to the bones" and "nobody comes calling." Deane juxtaposes the hard climate and ancient, archetypal repetitions of labor (women scraping "fish-scales and blood / from the boards with a killing-knife" against the assurances of Julian of Norwich that every manner of thing (at least) "might be well" because "*Jesus is motherly, comforting in his homelyhood.*"

T.S. Eliot and his *Four Quartets* are likewise present in "Letter from East Anglia" as the speaker engages the "spreading pastures / of the Giddings, pilgrims, moving like flocks of foam / / blown upon the sea." There's also an allusion to Cambridge educated George Herbert (a poet to whom Deane is deeply indebted) as the poem moves toward Walsingham and the center of its Christ-compassed vision:

Listen! The still-young girl in question hears her name
spoken out, with feeling,
in the strangest tongue, hears words announcing nothing on
                                                        this earth
will ever be the same again.

In the "intertestamental sunshine"—even as the speaker has now crossed the Channel and addresses we "dear pilgrims" from the French setting that concludes the poem—time is collapsed. We too can hear "the Virgin's / high shout *Magnificat!*" that responds, however quietly, to the "long, reiterated litanies, humankind's / / polyphony of pleas and pleading" of this fatigued world, pleas for the grace and peace of Christ, the incarnation of love and "the heaven of our hopes."

The exhortation to "Listen!" is perhaps the most central feature of Deane's sacramental poetics. In his 2015 poem "Semibreve," the walls of an empty, far-flung chapel also counsel the speaker to "Listen!"; and by poem's end the speaker is awakened and "tuned for it" because the "tiny chime had happened, vibrated / on my inner listening." Deane reminds us that the prophetic life of poetry is radically dialogical, and that listening—and being in tune—is the other side of poetic speech. Listening pervades the entire collection, not least of which *The World is Charged* section and the poem "Cadenza":

> There was something major key about the scythe
> with father's big-boned body
> slow-waltzing to the rhythm, cadenza, making
> meadow-music, no rain expected;

Like Hopkins (and another Jesuit whom Deane admires, Teilhard de Chardin), Deane finds the embedded music of particular moments—the inscape of them—and understands their cosmic vitality. Just as for Hopkins and his kingfishers "Selves — goes itself; myself it speaks and spells, / Crying Whát I dó is me: for that I came," for Deane the hope is that we awaken to these relational realities so that we ourselves may be turned from untuned to tuned. Deane continues in "Cadenza," observing another kind of bird as she works through her day, tuning her chicks to the rhythm and presence that lives underneath the spectrum of aural harmonies:

> the landrail, in the scurf-grass, had time to crake
> and urge her untuned chicks to safety
> down into the drain, before windows, shakings, hayricks
> rose in choir and lightly hymned in harvest.

Like Hopkins too (and like Herbert, Kavanagh, Levertov, and Merton who go before him), Deane's ecological consciousness does not stand alone; it draws us in to deeper listening and invites us into sacred, transcendent encounter.

Just as he interprets creation expansively, he also employs a variety of poetic forms in order to distill the integrity of particular moments. His section, *According to Lydia*, a series of sonnets spoken by an unknown female disciple of Jesus (of which there were thousands), is a fine example of this. Lydia, who walks the steps of Jesus in Palestine and Israel, serves as an artistic foremother of a Christian poetics of faith. Her experiences with the historical Yeshua become intimate, artful meditations; and Deane's "Papyrus" not only discloses the uniqueness of Yeshua, but announces the birth of Lydia as a poet—for the Word of beauty has touched her implacably and irrevocably:

> The word, I have discovered, is food for my surviving,
> this need to lay down words on strong papyrus, in strait
> and patterned lines, hints of love and yearning…
> . . . . .Words of Yeshua

The collection concludes with a most creative and heartbreaking adaptation of the late 14th century English poem "Pearl." The poem has at its center a girl child who has died young and who consoles the speaker of the poem, her distraught father, and edifies him from beyond the grave with a paschal theology of "Sacred Saturday" conveyed in the April air:

> . . . . As we walked she spoke:
>
> 'It is the great
>   unfolding drama, the beautiful excess of universe,
>   anemone and allium, the wren, toucan, the albatross,
>   eucalyptus, acanthus, the redwood forests,
>   the grain of sand, the water-drop, the billion-oceaned-
>   galaxy…'
>
> and I
>   in bitterness still:

to which Pearl, to assuage the grief of her beloved "Dad," replies:

>   'Be
>
> open,' she said, 'to surprise, to the sacred earth and the
> body and soul of the emergent universe…'

The dream vision of the speaker/father ends soon after in a Eucharistic key as the speaker awakens, a pearl now mysteriously in his hand and

> it was softening, yielding; I raised it to my mouth
> where it melted slowly on my tongue, its purity, its
>   living,
> and I was fed by it, and my thirst was quenched.

Dear Pilgrims lives up to the relationally sustaining and soul nurturing promise of its title and deserves a wide readership. From Lydia to Pearl to the speaker of "The Downs, The Cedars" who enquires after the "suburban Jesus" to see "if he has turned in off the avenue," the collection is a testament to the long lineage and enduring power of sacramental poetics. Even in a world where divine presence is too often eclipsed by the torpor of spiritual indolence and the fog of historical amnesia, Deane demonstrates the unique power of poetry as a faculty of the imagination and as a mode of prayer. The prophetic and poetic uses of language attune us to God and provide for us, in our pilgrim creatureliness, a sure path in any season and any age:

> .... At dawn, at noon, at night
>
> we celebrate what the world has gifted us, the sorrows
> of imperfection, the joys of tenderness; our prayers
>
> to the Lord Creator: he is our peace, we are his poem.

Michael P. Murphy is director of the Hank Center for the Catholic Intellectual Tradition at Loyola University Chicago. Mike is a National Endowment for the Humanities fellow, and his first book, *A Theology of Criticism* (Oxford, 2008), was named a "Distinguished Publication" by the American Academy of Religion. His most recent academic piece is "Breaking Bodies: O'Connor and the Aesthetics of Consecration" in *Revelation & Convergence: Flannery O'Connor and Her Catholic Heritage* (CUA Press, 2017); and he is currently editing a volume of essays for Wipf and Stock: *this need to dance/this need to kneel: Denise Levertov and the Poetics of Faith* (forthcoming in late 2019).

Single Bound: Krypton Nights/Amazon Days by Bryan D. Dietrich (WordFarm, 2018)

Like the superhero whose dedication to truth, justice, and the American way stands at the center of Bryan D. Dietrich's *Single Bound: Krypton Nights/Amazon Days*, some books of poetry are strong enough to survive even the most savage foe. Case in point: Dietrich's *Krypton Nights*, originally published as Richard Howard's choice for the 2001 Paris Review Prize in Poetry and justly praised by that distinguished judge as "a remarkable contribution to American literature." Unfortunately, its publisher—not *The Paris Review* (which merely sponsored the prize) but the notorious Zoo Press—imploded around 2004 when its editor, while continuing to invite submissions and collect reading fees, stopped publishing any actual books or, soon after, answering the panicked communications of sponsors, authors, and creditors. (An overview of the whole mess is available online at *Poets & Writers*, May/June 2006).

While *Krypton Nights* did appear before its publisher went AWOL, the ensuing chaos cost the author editorial support and the more lasting distribution that his debut volume deserved. For a long time, beside the original cover image, Dietrich observed wistfully on his website, "This is my first book. Zoo Press has since gone under…Perhaps some day a new edition will come out through another publisher." Thanks to WordFarm, *Single Bound* is the answer to this plea (one shared by Dietrich's admirers), and goes the first edition one better: along with the Superman-centric *Krypton Nights*, we now have *Amazon Days*, an equally inventive book-length sequence on the larger-than-life mythos of another DC Comics icon: Wonder Woman, daughter of Hippolyta, Zeus, and psychologist/polyamorist William Moulton Marston, eccentric inventor of the real-life lie detector and his most famous character's fictional Lasso of Truth. (Jill Lapore's *The Secret History of Wonder Woman*, published in 2015, offers a fascinating account of Moulton's career and unconventional love life.)

Conceived as roughly parallel book-length sequences—*Krypton Nights* and *Amazon Days* open, respectively, with "I, Kent" and "I, Wonder," each followed by a loosely rhymed, loosely metrical crown of sonnets—Dietrich's twin books may be read separately or together. But their joint appearance underscores how our view of each character reflects the ways that we respond to gender. Dietrich uses this factor to advantage. Reinforcing the heroes' kinship and tying their histories together, Superman resurfaces in the final section of *Amazon Days* in poems that imply a more intimate relationship between the heroes. These are largely narrated by a breathless Superman, overwhelmed by his secret crush (or, perhaps, their clandestine relationship): "Alone with her, I seem to understand / earth, its breath, better, the orgasm of ozone / that rushes out when she describes her own / flight" ("Superman's *Other* Secret"). Here and elsewhere, Dietrich masterfully navigates the difficult waters between our suspension of disbelief (these are, after all, outlandishly costumed comic book characters) and a more serious examination of the archetypes that they embody. To do so within the strictures of various shifting narratives, in poems often framed as dramatic monologue, is especially impressive.

The case of Wonder Woman presents unique challenges. Since at least 1954, when psychologist Frederic Wertham's *The Seduction of the Innocent* asserted that comic books (especially horror and superhero comics) were a key cause of juvenile delinquency, the sexual content of comics has been debated, their idealized—and ideally endowed—male and female protagonists subject to the jaundiced gaze of moralists and censors. At the same time, creator Marston filled Wonder Woman's early adventures with encounters unmistakably shaped by the bondage and submission fantasies he believed are widely held (see Lapore, among others, for further discussion). Dietrich responds in several ways. One is through the dramatic monologue that, taking its title from Wertham's book, features not Wertham but Marston claiming his mantle as "Lord of Lies":

> . . . . Nothing
> could escape my snare.
> Not one woman. Not
> two. Not the one I
> made of my wives,
> gave a lasso to, bound
> with that other
> invention, my intention
> to save us all from men
> like me…

The male gaze that Marston and others bring to women's bodies—to women *as* bodies—raises unavoidable questions regarding a character so often eroticized. Dietrich meets these questions head on in "I, Wonder," a meditative monologue that allows Wonder Woman to crack wise about her own erotic power: "It's all about cleavage, and I don't just mean / what I could do with an arrow and a dozen / ax heads." Elsewhere, Dietrich examines the impulses and myths that resonate through Marston's heroine. "Paradise Island" opens with suitably Miltonic overtones as Queen Hippolyta, Wonder Woman's mother, considers the island's history: "I sing of arms and of a woman who fate made / fugitive, who on her arms *wore* arms, bracelets, bonds / I forged myself from folly." In a contemporary voice, she regrets her daughter's departure with Steve Trevor (the officer nursed back to health after a crash-landing on the island) to join the war against the Axis powers: "This is how it's always been, / some man leaving with the best piece. Even the myth, / the story you tell yourselves of who and where we are, / that too is part of your forgetting." (The Amazons' Themyscira remains beyond the reach of men due to various fictional tropes employed in the comics' near eighty-year history.) In lines like these, Dietrich succeeds on multiple levels: he inhabits a character convincingly, reinvents the DC universe, invokes its basis in Greek myth, and asks serious questions about gender and culture, all the while ensuring that we suspend our disbelief. He is walking a tightrope (or magic lasso?) that Wonder Woman herself might envy.

Along with the gift of *Amazon Days*, the restoration of *Krypton Nights* to print is both welcome and long overdue. In poems whose references reflect the author's immersion in influences as wide-ranging as Homer, Dante, Yeats, and Joseph Campbell, among others, Dietrich expands the poet's standpoint: he is protagonist, myth-gatherer, cultural critic, bard, archivist of popular culture, and seeker of enlightenment. In fulfilling this last role, the title poem, "Krypton Nights," is especially moving, evoking spiritual transcendence despite the burden of fatal knowledge:

> When the last Krypton night simmers over
> the rim of your world, when we meet in the sky
> to find ourselves sharing stars, when what was
> once familiar slinks away, disoriented,
> hungry for the next clarity, remember
>
> shadows cast from nothing in the dark.

The poem appears in "The Jor-El Tapes," a section in the voice of Superman's father as captured by Albuquerque's Very Large Array radio telescope and later transcribed—a delightful conceit. (Throughout the book, cosmic messages and prayer often connect in serious play.) Jor-El is dead by the time his voice has spanned the light years, destroyed by the same apocalypse that brought his son to Earth, only to come of age as the hero who, as Gary Engle observes, flies and wears a cape that "doesn't so much drape his shoulders as stand apart from them and echo their curve, like an angel's wings" (Gary Engle, "What Makes Superman So Darned American?", an essay widely anthologized). Engle points out that the suffix of Superman's Kryptonic name, Kal-El, suggests a Hebrew origin with multiple meanings: for example, "God" in masculine singular form; also, "of God," often the ending of angels' names in the Apocrypha. Having monitored earth from Krypton, Jor-El's persona reflects on the metaphysics of myth, and in poems such as "The Else," "JHVH" (the name for God in Hebrew consonants), and "The Mysteries of Azazel" (one of the fallen angels in the non-canonical Book of Enoch), the poet explores religious traditions for the ways that they prefigure Krypton's semi-divine son—a stranger whose powers promise rescue and protection: "My son will be your Moses. He came from a red sea. / Crossing the dark channel between folds between worlds, / . . . / articulate, astute, uncanny for his age, able / to leap tall buildings in a single bound" ("The Curse of the Pharoahs").

  In their humor, learning, and humanity, both halves of *Single Bound* are challenging, urgent, and, often, deeply moving. Whether or not the success of Patty Jenkins' 2017 hit movie helped nudge *Amazon Days* into print, with *Krypton Nights* thrown into the bargain, both popular culture and literature have long prospered from the inspiration of comics. Think of Michael Chabon's Pulitzer Prize-winning novel *The Amazing Adventures of Kavalier & Clay*, or poems like Lucille Clifton's "note passed to superman," Jo Shapcott's "Superman Sounds Depressed," or Simon Armitage's "Kid," that famously trochaic dramatic monologue from the viewpoint of Batman's Robin. In *Single Bound*, transposing the cosmology of two DC comics characters into another medium allows Dietrich to interrogate the double awareness of readers who know that their beloved characters have no life between panels or beyond the page but who, nevertheless, love to imagine that they do. Fortunately, Bryan D. Dietrich is one of those readers. His imagination has brought us two books that manage to strip away the colorful costumes that entertain us while raising timeless questions—about human aspiration, the need for selfless compassion, and the importance of questioning the place we occupy in Creation.

Ned Balbo's most recent book is *3 Nights of the Perseids* (University of Evansville Press), selected by Erica Dawson for the 2018 Richard Wilbur Award. *The Cylburn Touch-Me-Nots*, selected by Morri Creech for the New Criterion Poetry Prize, will appear in the fall of 2019. His previous books are *The Trials of Edgar Poe and Other Poems* (Story Line Press), awarded the Donald Justice Prize and the Poets' Prize; *Galileo's Banquet*; *Upcycling Paumanok*; and *Lives of the Sleepers* (University of Notre Dame Press), awarded the Ernest Sandeen Prize and a finalist for the Arlin G. Meyer Prize of the Lilly Fellows Program. He recently received an NEA translation grant, and an excerpt from his version of Paul Valéry's *La Jeune Parque* recently appeared in *The Hopkins Review*. See more at https://nedbalbo.com/.

Stichomythia by Tyler Farrell (Salmon Poetry, 2018)

Stichomythia looks small and much like a typical-looking volume for poetry, yet it is a huge book with a huge heart. And not to worry, it comes with the OED definition of /stɪkəʊˈmɪθɪə/ on the title page. Those of you expecting something academic or perhaps just another typical book of poetry, may be surprised at how tough this book is to read and yet how tough it is to put it down.

Even though there are no family pictures, sketches, hand-written notes, or other memorabilia here — reading *Stichomythia,* I felt as if there were tons of photographs, maps of cities and countries, histories of the world, even Lives of the Poets, some Lives of the Saints, parts of The Apocrypha we've all been looking for, and many of the letters we've been meaning to write — this is one man's down-to-earth story, over a hundred pages, almost a hundred poems, and it's all in here.

As you would with a family album or a stack of letters found in a box, I encourage you to jump around, just dump everything out, go back and forth, make your own sequences; you'll find yourself drawing maps, piecing together lives, loves, and histories, and if you stick with it all, enjoying the drama, some music, the colloquial narratives, the dreams, the prayers.

St. John of the Cross says, "In prayer, come empty, do nothing." Martin Luther says, "The fewer the words, the better the prayer." And then, there is the Zen saying: "Complete attention is prayer."

CXD: I feel, Tyler, that I've found more than one litany, certainly requiems, and I can't separate the bars from the cathedrals. Do these definitions of prayer play in a way with your perception of writing, with your gathering of these poems? I'm thinking of the letters, the dreams, the poets you quote and write about. For example, you write to James Joyce and quote him. I remember reading how Joyce, talking to his friend, the painter Frank Budgen, explained he'd written only two sentences that day. Budgen inquired if Joyce was "seeking the mot juste?" Joyce replied, "I have the words already. What I am seeking is the perfect order of the words in the sentence." What is prayer to you as a poet? How would you define prayer?

TF: To me prayer is like devotion, similar to belief in being devoted and filled with adoration. I view poetry as a kind of prayer or my devotion to certain authors as prayer. Every time I write a poem I feel like I might be praying for the person or the subject or the idea. The letters and dreams and poets are all about paying attention and that is a kind of love too. I view the spiritual side of writing to be something that is universal. No matter what is a person's belief, we can always show devotion and love to each other and to the subject. It reminds me of a quote I think about from time to time from a movie called *Frances Ha*. The main character says:

> It's that thing when you're with someone and you love them and they know it and they love you and you know it but it's a party and you're both talking to other people and you're laughing and shining and you look across the room and catch each other's eyes. But not because you're possessive, or it's precisely sexual, but because that is your person in this life and it's funny and sad but only because this life will end and it's this secret world that exists right there.

To me that is a kind of prayer. Knowing something silent and personal and filled with a new understanding. Love and paying attention to something are really the same thing and I think we find all of these ideas in poetry.

I really like that quote you mentioned about James Joyce and Frank Budgen as I feel the same. I'm looking for how poetry can make us feel and how the order and words can take us on a journey and we are always looking for a worthwhile arrangement. And we hope that how we see the world is where we are going and how poetry and words can help us and bring us joy. That is prayer to me.

CXD: When we began this conversation a couple months ago, one of the first things I suggested to Tyler is that we turn the tables on the typical review / interview style and have him ask us some questions about *Stichomythia*. Here are a couple of the author's questions to the reader.

TF: I am always curious as to how people respond to the personal aspect of my writing—the narrative style, the letters, the voice. Perhaps I am talking to the reader as well. Where might these words go in order to give off more emotion or thought?

CXD: First, in reply to the narrative style which, in my reading of *Stichomythia*, your book (as well as the concept/definition of the word) leads right into the question of letters and voice. At first glance, I am concerned about what I might find when I see a title which looks so academic. I should have just jumped in— look, here we are in the opening lines of the first poem, in a Milwaukee bar looking into an iconic Wisconsin beer mirror:

> Large Old Style mirror
> wall of Riverwest, Milwaukee
> tavern. I remain hidden, my flaws, my ideas.

As the poem goes on we are watching and wondering together as "the door opens / suddenly wind overtakes our spirits ..." A perfect opening poem in a voice we can reckon with; yet, more than a voice as we see each other there in the mirror as the wind "sweeps thru the darkened room, away from / the mirror, away from this place." Listen a bit more to the conversation in this poem, "Bar Time Haze, Stray Thoughts," as it sets the stage for the book:

> People themselves never remember
> who they were, are, want to be. The mirror
> never itself either. Mirrors shift, reflect
> distort hide and advertise. Kingdoms
> point to humankind. . . .

The poems continue in this marvelous voice, this inclusive voice, this down-home voice! And we meet James Liddy, mentor and friend, in this first section; and then find a whole slew of *Letters to James*, fifteen of them, making up the entire section two. In these letters, all these poems, Tyler is a story teller who never forgets you are listening; he is a narrator who wants you to join in, come back home with him, write your own letters. Sometimes the title tells it all: "Thoughts in an Empty Bar on Tuesday Afternoon, the First Day of Autumn." I immediately want to be there, too, as I know the poet knows all about a good conversation.

Well, as far as where else these words might go to give off more emotion or thought — I think you've delivered, Tyler Farrell. I mean, you look around, you pay attention, you tell stories, you say your prayers, you write letters, you take us to your favorite taverns, you know how to play and paint — you're a friend and fellow traveler always ready to explore and discover with the reader. You've made us part of the family.

TF: Another question is: Does the reader see the progression of this book? In a lot of ways it is about change and learning and trying to get something out of life that is interesting and full of impact. Does that come across?

CXD: What I saw with *Stichomythia* right away was what I think you'd call *progression,* though not obvious, not forced upon me. Yes, it comes across, the change, I mean. For example, in section four, *Je suis comme ça,* the poems speak for themselves. This quoting of "Waiting for Godot" here (as you've also done to title section three) works, but it seems neither Beckett nor French is needed for the reader "to get it," to join in, to move forward. As we learn in "The History of Finger Painting":

> Art always looks for the trouble with us
> distortion expression pushed reason. There is no reason
> what reason do you need?

A clear theme, it seems, for this section and for the book — pure drama and classical stichomythia at its best.

TF: Thanks. *Stichomythia* is a complete labor of love for me — many sections really look at the idea of having conversations with people — it is the back and forth of the essence of stichomythia and also the ancient Greek notion that is used in drama. There is also a mirror theme — fitting with the reflective aspects of writing and the letters. I use this book to talk with myself and others about themes, thoughts, desires, reflections.

CXD: Yes, mirrors, the opening poem, and Jack Spicer warning us up front: "...one brings the person to the mirror." You say, "I use this book to talk with myself and others about themes, thoughts, desires, reflections." Could you say more about themes? I think all poets (and readers) struggle with that. What exactly is a "theme"? Do you find that the "themes, thoughts, desires, reflections" you talk about are actually synonyms?

TF: Yes, themes are ideas that I like to address in my work. I often come back to authors who have influenced me and friends that I look to for guidance. But I also think there is a lot of love, life, fun, and thoughtfulness in these poems. Poems I write can be about little things — ideas that are not too consequential. I use poems to address the image of the mirror and how life reflects upon us. I also like to emulate writers' works and show how those words can give us guidance. Themes that occur in this book are: thought, relationships, writers, loved ones, our connection to the universe, intuition on how to handle things in life, and practice, and luck for those too. There is inspiration and thoughts. There is a religion and the lore of place. There is love. And Spain and Costa Rica — there are museums and art as a motivator to creating my own art. The movement between poems I think is important. Anyone can read this book and bounce around or read it from cover to cover. There is a journey here, but it doesn't have to follow the order I put it in. That seems to be a theme as well.

CXD: I love the expansive, personal, non-technical approach you have. And what fun — yet, you talk and write about place (cities, bars, churches, classrooms, and meetings) all of which gets me to ask, where is home for you?

TF: First, I want to say how this approach, this conversation we're having, all seems very lively and that is really how I see a lot of my own work. I am from Milwaukee, and I love that city, so I hope there is some of that in there, too. But I have spent a lot of time in other places, too. The smaller poems maybe have more of Ireland in them — but also the personal and reflective, contemplative. I also like the humor in them. Small poems can always have a great impact even with so few lines. And poetry can draw maps too.

CXD: Yes, I think you're right about the smaller poems — in particular those in section three, the *Ephemeral,* as you call them. But Ireland or Milwaukee, long or short, your poems have a way of keeping the conversation going, so we can "bounce around." And in a way, that takes us full circle. I'm hoping that our discussion leads to a better understanding of poetry, prayer, and place.

CX Dillhunt looked at quite a few books before he agreed upon reviewing *Stichomythia*. He liked the title, found the mix of poetic styles intriguing, and has been a big fan of Salmon Poetry books for years. Also, CX felt that he and Tyler Farrell had much in common, explaining in his first note to Tyler: "I've taught letters as a form (which I feel I learned from my mother and her mother); I'm a Wisconsin / Illinois boy (born in Green Bay with roots in Milwaukee, a grad degree from UIUC, son born in Urbana); finally, many of your poets are my poets: O'Hara, Duncan, Crane, Niedecker, Gilbert, Berryman, Baudelaire, Spicer, Roethke, Ovid, Wright, are certainly many of my first loves." CX is editor of *Hummingbird: Magazine of the Short Poem*.

The Lake Michigan Mermaid: A Tale in Poems by Linda Nemec Foster and Anne-Marie Oomen (Wayne State University Press, 2018)

The many layers braided into Linda Nemec Foster and Anne Marie Oomen's slim volume, *The Lake Michigan Mermaid: A Tale in Poems* make this a book one can return to many times over. Each reading invites a new discovery and a different way to delight in how the connections form and inform the narrative tale. A series of 27 poems, the work has been reviewed as a "lyrical story," a "fable," and a "mythical coming of age tale," all of which it is. But it is also much more. Some of that "more-ness" has to do with the imaginative, intelligent and evocative use of voice. In a kind of "call and response" format, four voices bring the tale to life. Meridith Ridl's shimmering illustrations enliven the text and add yet another voice to the narrative.

The story begins with Lykretia or Lyk, a lonely young girl whose world is falling apart. Her name means "joy," but she doesn't feel joyful. She is drawn to the shores of Lake Michigan in search of solace, understanding and healing. There she calls out for "a being who would say *Lyk* like the name / /

was meant to join one joyful thing to some / other joyful thing." She hears the something in the lake respond, *"Phyliadellacia."* She hears an echo of her own voice in the reply and recognizes in it, a name similar to her own.

Two other voices weave their way into the narrative. Lyk's mother is the despairing voice of poverty and isolation that alternates between silence and breaking. Lyk's Grandmother is the ancestral voice of knowledge and wisdom. Her voice contains the past. It holds Lyk's family history, the history of "black haired Potawatomi people," the history of the lake, and the shores that surround it.

How Phyliadellacia's lyrical water voice and Lyk's earthy one communicate is magical, mysterious and mystical. Nemec Foster calls it telepathic. It sounds like "low humming, almost song that runs under the lake, a hint of a lullaby, the heartbeat of the moon, and a mother wrapped in silence." They sense the presence of one another; feel each other in the currents and swells. They hear each other in waves and stone, wind and sea foam, seawater shells and the sandbar. Yearning, loneliness, and the desire to be recognized is the language they share. Ultimately, however, theirs is the poetic language of metaphor, and it is metaphor that turns the pages of this tale. Phyliadellacia, as half-human creature, the lake as water and ice, and the shoreline as middle ground between sea and land all serve as metaphor for the binary nature of creation.

The Lake Michigan Mermaid resists the impulse to separate or categorize. It recognizes the relationship between all creatures, both natural and supernatural as seamless and fluid. Filtered through Meridith Ridl's eyes, this fluidity looks like layers of watery blues and faded greys; ribbons of shells, dune grasses and sequins; overlapping letters, words and arches and waves. Heard through Nemec Foster and Oomen's words it sounds like the "lake's heart of ebb and flow" sea foam in flowing hair and the woven pattern of a blue blanket draped over a chair.

As a binary narrative, it belongs to the world of myth and archetypal tales. Like the very nature of water, the tale is one of ebb and flow, allure and threat, birth and destruction, redemption and forgiveness. The interdependent relationship between wind and water, rock and driftwood, birds and fish, wildflowers and seagrass is its enduring theme. The question this fable-parable-myth asks is "can we recognize our braided and woven existence?"

Lyk's mother didn't. She could not see the silver sequined flashes of water or hear the low thrumming sound residing in the Lake. She was "frozen like the lake's embrace in winter." But Lyk could, and so could her grandmother. The bond they share is a sensitivity to the natural world and the ability to see the supernatural within it. In "The Room Weeps," Lyk's grandmother tells her *"The mermaid's spirit inside our palms— / it asks we pay attention to her."*

  The book remains true to its call and response format with each poem appearing on a separate page, each written in its own discreet voice. But in the final poem, "Contrapuntal: *Two Voices of the Lake*," the lines and the voices unfold in tandem. Like the ebb and flow of lakes, oceans, rivers and ponds, the verses are both separate and inseparable. One is not elevated over the other, and the balance between them is harmoniously elegant.

  No matter how many times we reach for it, *The Lake Michigan Mermaid* continues to open us into a world where water is always speaking and implores us to listen to the many voices flowing through its currents. This important and timely work, lyrically told and lovingly illustrated, has been honored as a 2019 Michigan Notable Book.

Mary Ladany is a Writing Specialist and Adjunct Professor in the Department of English at Caldwell University. She wrote and co-produced a full-length performance piece, *Having Opened the Book*, at a variety of venues in the New York/New Jersey metropolitan area and, most recently, a ten-minute play, *Herstory*, for the New York Theater Workshop's Mind the Gap: Intergenerational Theater. She is currently finishing a hybrid piece, *You Will Find Me in My Poems,* which integrates prose and lyric to form a loosely constructed narrative. Mary is a member of the Caldwell University Tower Poets, a group of working poets, which this year celebrates its twentieth anniversary.

The Best American Poetry 2018. Dana Gioia, guest editor; David Lehman, series editor (Scribner-Simon & Schuster, 2018)

  Compiling an anthology of the year's "best" American poetry is, unavoidably, a challenge. Is it even possible to achieve consensus on which poems are truly the "best" when our aesthetic options are more numerous than ever? Of course, the title of the series is merely good marketing (who would buy *Excellent American Poetry, Some of It the Best in Our Opinion?*). What matters, instead, is how good the contents are, and whether the editor's selection reflects a wide array of styles. In these respects, the current collection is an unqualified success, thanks to Dana Gioia—poet, critic, librettist, Laetare Medal-winner, California's Poet Laureate, and the editor-curator of this year's volume.

Series editor David Lehman contributes a lively foreword that reviews the year's developments, from the death of titans Richard Wilbur and John Ashbery to the rise of the Instagram poets, and poetry's loss (or possible surge) of popularity. Regarding America's public dialogue on poetry, Lehman observes, "The only time articles about poetry appear in the culture pages of our newspapers is when the subject is a counterfeit, the implication being that we'd be prepared to embrace poetry if only it weren't poetry." Later, Lehman concedes, wryly, that one defense of the Instagram poets and their ilk is that "such verse...may serve as 'gateway' to the real stuff."

It's the real stuff that makes up the current book. Gioia's choices range widely across geography and generations, belying his own passing doubt that "any single editor can have sympathies broad enough to evaluate everything fairly." As former chair of the National Endowment for the Arts and author of the influential essay "Can Poetry Matter?", Gioia is a vital figure in the resurgence of narrative and/or metrical work—a role that has sometimes overshadowed his broad taste and tireless efforts in service of *all* poetries, and the arts in general. Keenly attuned to recent developments, Gioia offers an introduction that may be read as a timely update of "Disappearing Ink: Poetry at the End of Print Culture," the title essay of his 2004 collection of literary prose, in which he examined the effect of new technologies on how poetry is viewed, shared, performed, and created.

This time, Gioia reminds us of what's changed in the past fifteen years: "Print now coexists with other equally powerful media for poetry," a fact that accounts for any number of trends—from the renewed emphasis on sound in literary poetry (born of hip-hop and performance poetry's popularity, Gioia asserts), to poetry's increased online presence and as a reference in film or television. Seeking a gathering equal to such scope, Gioia assembles poets from both coasts and every region between: elders secure in (or retired from) academia, middle-agers at the height of their powers, and poets under forty (several under thirty, in fact).

Some are the sons or daughters of immigrants, or immigrants themselves, bringing fresh perspectives to the American experience. As an editor, Gioia's poetic curiosity and enthusiasm for discovery remain undimmed.

There are more fine poems than a brief review can single out, but my own favorites demonstrate the wide range represented. Stephen Kampa's "The Quiet Boy" depicts romantically challenged post-pubescent boys imagining the superpowers they'll never have: in conversational pentameter, they argue, only to pause: "Invisibility? Dumb. Just plain dumb. / Why choose a power you already had?" Equally attuned to teen angst is Hieu Minh Nguyen whose free verse "B.F.F." explores the anguish of remaining a friend while wanting more—wanting, in fact, to *be* the object of desire: "I even took her to the winter formal / watched, in the green glow of the gymnasium / at how I—she danced, chiffon willow / silk mystic." Nkosi Nkululeko (like Kampa, a musician and, like Nguyen, a poet whose contributor's note reveals a love of movies) uses the curt, clear lines of "Skin Deep" to examine national attitudes and private perceptions of race: "I once tried to drown my / skin & be human without it." The work of such a trio, born in the '80s or '90s, bodes well for the future of American verse.

Poets in mid-career make their voices heard as well. A. E. Stallings' use of varying trimeter lends "Pencil," all point and potential erasure, an unsettling precision: Time is "the other implement / That sharpens and grows shorter." Natasha Trethewey's "Shooting Wild," a powerful sonnet, examines a daughter's dawning recognition of the abuse her mother suffers: "Then one morning, the imprint of his hand / / dark on her face, I learned to watch her more…" Aimee Nezhukumatathil's "Invitation" opens playfully—"Come in, come in—the water's fine!"—summoning a world as "oceanic, boundless, limitless" as the "dark sky" or "all / the shades of blue revealed in a glacier"; but in its vivid descriptions of "plankton hurricaning in open / whale mouths" or narwhals that "spin upside down while their singular tooth needles / you like a compass," the poet's unfolding, urgent lines remind us of all we stand to lose.

One of Gioia's most striking selections is Paisley Rekdal's retelling of Philomela's rape in the *Metamorphoses*. Ovid's Philomela is silenced by having her tongue cut out but reveals what happened (and that she is still alive) through a tapestry she weaves. Rekdal's response, "Philomela," is a contemporary narrative: its protagonist visits the barn where a distant cousin displays the large-scale sculptures that capture what cannot be said, including one that, though it resembles "a tree blasted by lightning," depicts a rape that triggers her own painful memory: "the plank face / had been scraped clean; all the fear / and anger burned instead inside / their twisting bodies." Rekdal's poem contains much else as well, its power a testament to her skill in crafting a narrative of impressive scope into subtle, tightly woven free verse lines.

As in Rekdal's poem and others, the defining quality of Gioia's choices may be one too often undervalued. Whatever its stance, style, or structure, each poem is *about* something—a recognizable human experience conveyed in memorable language. Whether celebrating a despot, willingly lost in moral quandaries (see Aaron Poochigian's "Happy Birthday, Herod"), or speaking in praise of flawed splendor (see Nausheen Eusuf's "Pied Beauty"), each poem asks us to enter a world: a person's perspective, striking or strange, based in fact or wholly invented, openly funny or quietly moving. As Gioia quips, American poetry has entered its "anything goes" phase—one where free verse and form "are no longer viewed as mutually exclusive techniques." Thank goodness: one of this collection's singular virtues is that Tracy K. Smith's "An Old Story," the troubling fable of one era's passing into another, can occupy the same poetic cosmos as Alfred Nicol's "Addendum," a darkly witty revision of Christ's instruction to render unto Caesar what is his: "Caesar's arms are open wide; / your whole estate will fit inside."

Happily, authors known to readers of *Presence* are represented, too. James Matthew Wilson's "On a Palm," originally published in these pages, offers a sympathetic, tightly metrical portrait of a psychic already relegated to the past tense by the time the poem begins: "But, when I see my hands gripped round the wheel, / . . . / I think how there is no one who will peel / Them open, lay the fingers gently straight, / And study all those traceries of fate." On the next page, Ryan Wilson weighs in with a fluent sonnet of troubling self-recognition: "That unidentified fleck, approaching and / Receding at once, rapt in the wind's spell— / . . . / That thing that you're becoming, that you are" ("Face It"). A similar unease resides in David Mason's "First Christmas in the Village." On a stormy night after an unexpected birth, the guest of a widow's family finds comfort in their company, in food and fire's sustenance, despite a nagging awareness of violence: "That night all murders were forgotten / in the salt abundance and the storm / and the warm fire in the widow's house . . . ." Another poet familiar from *Presence*, Maryann Corbett, offers a "Prayer Concerning the New, More 'Accurate' Translation of Certain Prayers," a beautifully crafted tetrameter sonnet in gentle protest against unnecessary improvement: "These prayers translated plumb-and-squarely / Pinch and constrict us (though we grant / They broaden our vocabulary.)"

In sum, Gioia's instincts and insights unerringly hit the mark, and this new entry in *The Best American Poetry* series provides a richly rewarding compendium of styles and possibilities. In deftly channeling Auden's "The Fall of Rome," Ernest Hilbert's "Mars Ultor" (another of my favorites in the book) observes, "Brutes push their way to power, / But the muddiest barbarian / Also wants the throne an hour." So, too, do poets, and the seventy-five assembled here have earned their hour of pageantry in this most distinguished gathering.

Ned Balbo's most recent book is *3 Nights of the Perseids* (University of Evansville Press), selected by Erica Dawson for the 2018 Richard Wilbur Award. His previous books are *The Trials of Edgar Poe and Other Poems* (Story Line Press), awarded the Donald Justice Prize and the Poets' Prize; *Galileo's Banquet*; *Upcycling Paumanok*; and *Lives of the Sleepers* (University of Notre Dame Press), awarded the Ernest Sandeen Prize and a finalist for the Arlin G. Meyer Prize of the Lilly Fellows Program. He recently received an NEA translation grant, and an excerpt from his version of Paul Valéry's *La Jeune Parque* recently appeared in *The Hopkins Review*. See more at https://nedbalbo.com/.

Magdalene by Marie Howe (W. W. Norton & Company, 2017)

Closure might be a term to encompass what is important about Marie Howe's latest volume. Not the narrow question of closure as a matter of poetics, of the way poems end, but larger questions: how to close the gap between text considered scripture for a particular group and story considered as a bequest for all humanity; how the sacred and the everyday can find their needed closure in one another; particularly Christian questions of how judgment should find closure in grace, shame in love, knowledge in fruitfulness, self in other.

The book's epigraph sets the sensual and spiritual tone. From the appropriately liminal *The Gospel According to Thomas*, it recounts how the disciples ask Christ: "When will you be visible to us? and when will we see you?" To which Christ responds, "When you undress and are not ashamed." Something seems restored of Eden in the messianic here, a trace of Eve and her goodness recovered. The disciples anticipate what Christian Wiman called rivenness in the title of his 2010 collection, *Every Riven Thing*, and Christ gestures toward the promise of a sensuous, bodily unveiling, to reflect a creation redeemed from shame.

Howe is not a practicing Christian, but the stories of the Bible are the ones she grew up with. Here she writes persona poems from the perspective of Mary Magdalene, the tortured character of the gospels. Tortured, not in the stories themselves—though according to Luke, Magdalene was possessed, at first, by seven demons—but tortured rather, in legacy, contorted, distorted, made to fit this or that often male-centered purpose, not unlike Emily Dickinson, who, Virginia Jackson has argued, has been tortured by literary critics (*Dickinson's Misery*, 2005). In *Magdalene*, Howe endeavors to restore to the heritage of this character a fuller, truer scope of her humanity, bodily and spiritual.

In "Magdalene—The Seven Devils," a touchstone poem in the collection, we make ranging encounters with demons and begin to understand what these mysterious figures of scripture might represent in our modern, everyday lives. There are mild demons, such as the one of being "worried," or the one of being "busy." But in orienting us in the ordinary, Howe does not spare us the potential severity of the demonic. Another demon in the poem inhabits the grotesque, terrifying perception that our bodies are "made of guts and blood with a thin layer / of skin lightly thrown over"; still another, a sense of the intolerability of mere breathing, knowing that all of us share and "expel" the same air. Such demons seem to tempt us towards fear, mistrust, doubt, and separation from others.

As the poem goes on, the series of everyday demons grows more and more various and pervasive, as the poem keeps cycling back, unable to settle on which exactly the seven were, so the tally of devils increases. The poem hesitates sporadically ("No. That was the first one"), a trick Howe may have learned from Wisława Szymborska. At a recent seminar for MFA students at Texas State University, Howe admired Szymborska as the poet of skillful wavering, "the maybe this, the maybe that." What finally ends this modern Magdalene's exposed thinking about demons is closure. The ultimate demon, it turns out, is this one: "that I didn't think you—if I told you—would understand any of this—"

      Howe's poem ends, thus, in the exorcism of the demon that says, "You must not say; they will not understand." As soon as we readers do see, do understand, not only has Magdalene been returned to us, but we have also been returned to Christ, who always heard and had compassion for the demon-possessed. For Howe, it's not the demons that matter, so much as our open seeing of one another, without shame. Another poem, "The Affliction," speaks of the near "unbearable[ness]" of such an encounter with the other: "he saw me see him, / and I saw him see me." This is a "mutual gaze" into which *Magdalene* aspires to draw us, demons and all.

Luke William is pursuing an MFA in Poetry at Texas State University. He completed his Ph.D in English with a Critical Theory emphasis from the University of California, Irvine, in 2014. He received his BA in English from Pepperdine University. Music is a significant part of his life, and most recently he has been at work on a series of albums called *Songs For Children*, some of which are complete and available to listen to and download freely at lukekwilliam.com.

Tropic of Squalor by Mary Karr
(HarperCollins, 2018)

      "Forgive me." These are the first words of Mary Karr's new collection of poems, *Tropic of Squalor*. "I've always loved you" are the last. Between these two sentences—the first the prelude to Confession, the last the conclusion to that sacramental act—lie thirty-seven powerful and provocative poems of observation, meditation, castigation, desolation, and consolation. Karr's Catholicism is on full display in these poems, embodying a worldview evident in her previous collections, especially her post-conversion book *Sinners Welcome*. These are poems in which the speaker looks hard at her flawed self, at the fractured human beings all around her, and at the broken world we all inhabit together. The book would be devastating reading if not for the fact that all of the signs of sin she sees and carefully chronicles are counterbalanced by glimpses of grace, the clear conviction that love governs and redeems the ruins we live in the midst of.

Given the fact that *Tropic of Squalor* takes the form of an extended confession, the book is inevitably dominated by darkness. It begins with a series of apologies—to the animals the speaker neglects and eats, to the madman in the "loony bin" the speaker gladly leaves behind when she gets well, and in one of the most powerful poems in the volume, "The Burning Girl," to a child who sits amid the speaker's sophisticated set ("a herd of hardly troubled rich") on fire with inward agony that manifests itself in starvation and self-mutilation. "I was the facile friend insisting on a hug," she ruefully recalls, "I said / C'mon let's hug it out." All the adults are equally culpable, for who knows what to do in the face of such suffering? "That night we watched / Some fireworks on the dewy lawn for it was / Independence Day. By morning she was gone. / She was the flaming tower we all dared / / To jump from. So she burned."

Many of these poems of confession are also poems of mourning, bearing witness to the private pain of others in addition to her own. In a series of remarkable—and remarkably personal—poems, Karr eulogizes her friend and former lover David Foster Wallace, the celebrated writer who took his own life years after he and Karr had parted ways. In fact, Wallace haunts the first half of this volume, his ghost appearing four times, the image of his hanged body returning to the reader as reliably and terribly as it surely returns to Karr: "What are you doing on this side of the dark? / You chose that side, and those you left / feel your image across their sleeping lids / as a blinding atomic blast" ("Face Down"). The tone in these poems is tremendously various, shifting from resentment, as in the previous poem, to detached irony, as in the devastating conclusion to "Read These," which closes with the grotesque image of the lifeless Wallace, now deprived of all air, "breathlessly lecturing in the hall of silence;" to castigation in "Suicide's Note: An Annual," wherein she asks the dead man to "forgive my conviction / that every suicide's an asshole;" to an expression of playful certainty and belief in eternal life and Wallace's participation in the fact of resurrection: "I just wanted to say ha-ha, despite / your best efforts you are every second / alive in a hard-gnawing way for all who breathed you deeply in, / each set of lungs, those rosy implanted wings, pink balloons. / We sigh you out into air and watch you rise like rain" ("Suicide's Note: An Annual").

These are powerful poems, particularly if one knows the story behind them and is familiar with Wallace's work. One question that arises, however, is how accessible that power is to the reader who lacks this knowledge about Karr's personal background. This potential problem crops up in several other poems in the volume that are highly autobiographical and is most insistent in "The Age of Criticism," a comic yet deadly serious poem that is a modern incarnation of the 18th-century genre of the verse satire, in which Karr recounts a series of escapades shared with poet friends Franz Wright, Tom Lux, and Askald Melnyczuk. The poem makes reference to private moments shared inside their circle, including some terribly sad events and circumstances, among them divorce, suicide, commitment to a mental institution, alcoholism, and anxiety over one's poetic legacy. Karr takes a risk in these poems. At times the latter verges on versified literary gossip (a tendency also evident in the poem's forbears penned by the likes of 18th-century masters Pope and Dryden). Yet, this is a risk inherent in the project of making *mythos* of one's life, an impulse that runs deep in Karr, whose vocation as a memoirist is evident in all of her poetry.

Indeed, *Tropic of Squalor* is devoted to the business of mythmaking and accomplishes this in various ways. While Part I focuses largely on the microcosm of the self, Part II, titled "The Less Holy Bible," offers a much expanded, more capacious vision of the world the self occupies. These twenty poems, each of which is linked by the title to a particular book of the bible, portray the ruined landscapes near and dear to Karr, starting with the East Texas gulf town she grew up in, spoiled by the "chemical stink" and "liquid stench" that comes bubbling up out of the earth and populated by people afflicted by "spongy tumors," "the fistula / in the breast, the bowels, the hanging balls" while the oil barons live a safe distance away ("Genesis: Animal Planet," "Numbers: Poison Profundis," "Leviticus: In Dreams Begin Responsibilities"). She then directs her prophetic gaze to New York City, the place she currently calls home, for the remainder of the volume, wherein Karr's characteristic grittiness is also present. Karr's Manhattan is no playground for happy tourists, nor do the poems tout the blandishments and clichés of the city that supposedly never sleeps. She has a gift for nosing out the ugly and the repulsive, amply evident in the hellish landscape (the stalled traffic, the rat she sees "scramble across her path," the roaches who "flee from my light switch," the filthy subway "befumed by the farts of strangers," and the street carts selling the scorched "flesh / Of many slaughtered lambs").

And yet, the speaker finds beauty in the seemingly forsaken city, a beauty that flashes forth at unexpected moments from its people, the four old ladies who hold their umbrellas over the grunting moving men wheeling a grand piano through a downpour, the cellist at Carnegie Hall who soothes our common mortality by playing her instrument "sending up moans / from the pit we balance on the edge of," the giant Slav in the Garment District who "shoulders a box of Chinese silks—gold butterflies, / Scarlet dragons, white chrysanthemums like fireworks / On emerald cloth." Such visionary moments inspire Karr. In this she takes her cue from the fellow New Yorker and poet to whom she pays homage in "Hey Jude: Prophetic Interlude by the Ghost of Walt Whitman," channeling his prophetic voice: "Out of the ether I have come to speak to you." These people going about their ordinary lives redeem the world, albeit in small, tentative ways, and offer some brief relief to the daily suffering endured by so many on this "island with two million souls" ("Chronicles: Hell's Kitchen"), the latter line and title a clear tribute to another of Karr's mentors, fellow Catholic poet Dante.

Despite these respites, Karr insistently reminds us that this is a world of squalor and sorrow, teetering on the brink of disaster. Her vision is, at times, apocalyptic. If the haunting spirit of Part I of the book is a suicide, the haunting spirit of Part II is the ghost of 9/11. Karr devotes four poems to this defining event of the 21st century (in counterbalance to the four poems about Wallace), featuring an intimate (and creepy) portrait of a suicide bomber ("Malachi: Truckload of Nails"); a powerful tour-de-force narrative that depicts the extraordinary life of one of the victims ("Hebrews: The Mogul"); a poem that chronicles the poet's attempt to bear witness in the aftermath of the horror ("Lamentations: The More Deceived"), and concluding with "Kings: The Obscenity Prayer," a dark parody of The Lord's Prayer suggesting how far we have fallen from grace. Even our attempts at prayer are corrupted.

Karr's vision, however, does not permit the luxury of existential despair. Immediately following the infernal "Our Father," the reader encounters a modern day "Hail, Mary," a poem that in its inception posits faith as the only antidote to evil. In "Marks and Johns: The Blessed Mother Complains to the Lord Her God about the Abundance of Brokenness She Receives," the poet channels the voice of Mary of Nazareth, rather than the voice of the pray-ers, who recounts the sufferings of the supplicants who have come to her altar with their desperate pleas: "I am the rod to their lightning. / Mine is the earhole their stories pierce." When people pray, they are heard, and Mary, along with the rest of the Communion of Saints, suffers with them: "To me, the mother carries the ash contents / of the long-ago incinerated girl." (Perhaps the child in "The Burning Girl," the reader might wonder.) "She begs me for comfort since my own son / was worse tortured," Mary says, reminded of her own trial by fire with each new tormented soul. And yet she bears witness, faithfully absorbs their prayers, and suffers in solidarity, as did her child: 'Each prostrate body I hold my arms out for / is a cross my son is nailed to."

All of Karr's mythmaking, both the microcosmic and macrocosmic, the personal and the prophetic, coalesces in the Judeo-Christian *mythos* that serves as the bedrock of her belief. In one of the final and most arresting images of the book, a messenger arrives at the door of Karr's dark apartment, a young man with hopes that his current life as a lowly laborer will someday be better. His aspiration is to be a carpenter. As he drives off amid the cabs and cars, "dodging a bus that belched smoke," "on battered mountain bike, green wings extended / / behind in wind," an urban angel *en route* to his next destination, the speaker tells us "his name was Jesus." Troubled as it is, the world is not abandoned. Time and time again, in Mary Karr's poems, she finds God in the strangest places. Including, and perhaps especially, in *The Tropic of Squalor*.

Angela Alaimo O'Donnell teaches English at Fordham University and is Associate Director of Fordham's Curran Center for American Catholic Studies. Her sixth collection of poems, *Andalusian Hours: Poems from the Porch of Flannery O'Connor*, is forthcoming (Spring 2020) from Paraclete Press. Previous publications include two chapbooks; five collections of poems, *Moving House* (2009), *Saint Sinatra* (2011), *Waking My Mother* (2013), *Lovers' Almanac* (2015), *Still Pilgrim* (2017), and a memoir, *Mortal Blessings* (2014). Her critical biography, *Flannery O'Connor: Fiction Fired by Faith* (2015), won first prize for excellence in biography from the Association of Catholic Publishers. O'Donnell's work has been nominated for the Pushcart Prize, the Best of the Web Award, and the Arlin G. Meyer Prize in Imaginative Writing. http://angelaalaimoodonnell.com/.

The Night's Magician: Poems about the Moon, edited by Philip C. Kolin and Sue Brannan Walker (Negative Capability Press, 2018)

In *The Sacred and the Profane,* Mircea Eliade argues that we humans navigate the deep processes that rule our lives through the moon—"birth, becoming, death, and resurrection; the waters, plants, woman, fecundity, and immortality; the cosmic darkness, prenatal existence, and life after death," all tied to lunar interpretation. The moon, in other words, drags much more than our tides along with it. And addresses to the moon go back to the earliest poetry we know. Holding *The Night's Magician: Poems about the Moon* in my hands, it feels as if this anthology should have already existed.

That it does exist is thanks to the year 2017, a year of extraordinary performances from our partner-in-gravity: a "snow moon" covered by the earth's shadow in a penumbral eclipse; a partial eclipse encompassing five continents; and the Great Solar Eclipse that darkened much of the United States. It was, after all, a fitting time for this book—a year in which the moon's recurring absences made its presence all the more remarkable.

The poems in this collection are very fine, comprising eighty poets writing the lunar in a diversity of forms and voices with all the tide-restlessness of Eliade's explanatory moon. Some poems in this collection are brief and lyric, some longer and more narrative. Fittingly for poems that sing a recurring yet changing presence in the sky, repetitive forms like the villanelle, pantoum, and sonnet appear. From Ted Kooser's "a lamp held steady" to Chris Forhan's "knucklebone" to Kathleen Hellen's "densely cratered / basin of our darkness," the moon in *Night's Magician* expansively shapeshifts. And the poems offer song, story, chant, and mythology old and newly created—all the magic language our species has loved to spin out while sitting under the moon.

While all the poems in this book have much to offer, several in particular caught my attention. Mary Swander's "Last Day on Inishark Island" tells the story of an Irish island that all but one of its inhabitants deserted in a single day, finally unable to live in a place where "the sun and moon were all." Quietly lyric, beautifully detailed, "Last Day" pulls its energy from that tension between the moon's claim and the demands of modernity, the needs for food, phones, quicker medical care overriding an ancient alignment between the heavens and a particular point on earth.

Swander's is the longest poem in the book. Others balance on a brief lyric tripwire, such as Jianqing Zheng's "Ten Impressions: Moon," brief stanzas that track the autumn moon's progress from new to full. First an innocent "crescent line / of wave foam," the moon grows to become the full moon of Halloween, an antic circle held in "the live oak's gyrating limbs."

"Contemplating the Moon in My Seventy-Seventh Year" by Maria Mazziotti Gillan explores the poet's lifelong relationship with the moon, a planet she saw in the "dark Paterson sky" as a child, composing about it "hundreds of haiku." She watches the moon landing in a married student dormitory at her college, and later reads a news story of the moon "drifting away from the earth." The turn toward considering the moon as emblem of her age feels both surprising and natural, in line with all the things in life that pull away and remain lived but unknowable: "I must accept that the landscape of old age is like the surface / of the moon."

No matter how many poets consider our planetary satellite—no matter how many times even one poet, like Zheng, revisits it—it eludes us. Poets like Ralph Adamo try to put the moon into its material place, "this big rock caught / in the net of our girth"; it refuses to stay. Adamo's rock goes on to clown, speak, communicate with the dead. Gillan's moon may embody her body's changing abilities, but still she ends by praising it, its beauty the thing "that lifts me up."

To paraphrase critic Anne Ferry, a successful anthology does more than collate work piled up by the passing of literary time; it moves literary tradition forward. Good anthologies do this not through dogmatic selection but through suggestion, the subtle narratives that arise when poets, especially poets of an overlapping literary period, exist in dialogue with one another. *The Night's Magician* offers a larger story of literary representation, the urgency and instability of symbolizing, our human need to try to leave our interpretive mark on the world, even as we continually frustrate ourselves and rub those marks away. Read together, these poems offer an array of beautifully crafted verse and an inspiration to other poets to find their own personal and collective moons, to keep the dialogue live.

Susanne Paola Antonetta's *Make Me a Mother* was published by W.W. Norton. A digital book, *Curious Atoms: A History with Physics*, was published by Essay Press in May of 2016. She is also author of *Body Toxic, A Mind Apart,* the novella *Stolen Moments*, and four books of poetry. Awards for her poetry and prose include a *New York Times* Notable Book, an American Book Award, a Library Journal Best Science book of the year, an Oprah Bookshelf pick, a Pushcart prize, and others. Her essays and poems have appeared in *The New York Times, The Washington Post, Orion, The New Republic* and many anthologies. She lives in Bellingham, Washington.

Cures for Hysteria by MaryAnn L. Miller (Finishing Line Press, 2018)

Cultural critic Susan Sontag, in her book *Illness as Metaphor*, contends that historical views of disease commonly include blaming the victim for her own misfortune, citing such causes as "moral failings" or "a lack of passion." The same can be said for some disabilities, including those that have been associated with sexual repression and other psychiatric/psychologic issues. As disease entities become better understood, science-based explanations have replaced many outdated ideas, and others have slowly faded or been debunked. Yet it may be argued that we continue to harbor cruel assumptions about disorders of body and mind still cloaked in mystery. In his 1997 volume *Recovering Bodies: Illness, Disability, and Life Writing*, G. Thomas Couser advocates writing as a way for persons dealing with disability to reclaim the body from marginalization and medical mismanagement. MaryAnn L. Miller employs this approach creatively in her second volume of poetry, *Cures for Hysteria*. Here poetry builds a forceful narrative that documents her lifelong efforts to deal with Hyperkalemic Periodic Paralysis with Myotonia, a rare potassium disorder that causes sudden temporary paralysis. In "Onset, Age Three" Miller introduces us to a terrified child waking up in the night.

> I'm nailed to the bed. I can move only fingers and
>   eyelids.
> I'm going to suffocate.

And in "4 AM Ambush"

> teeth clamp eyelids lag
> heart slams in my ears
> . . . .
> try to move anything
> try to roll, bring a knee up

What follows is the child's desperate effort to cope with a condition she can't control and doesn't understand, one that will bring her ridicule or worse, expose her as different, a potential troublemaker. Again and again she is failed by institutions that should have come to her aid. The poems' exacting language brings us back to that time when we were all at our most vulnerable, recalling efforts to fit in and do what is required at school and at church and on the playground. At St. Michael's, her elementary school, Miller's teachers seem oblivious to her difficulties.

> Everyone is down the fire escape
> practicing safety, but my legs are paralyzed.
>
> Sister stays behind. *What if*
> *there were a real fire?*

In high school, Miller calculates her best options:

> Scan schedule, see where I can fall
> when to go upstairs to the girl's room
> walk the block-long building end to end

When hypervigilance is insufficient to keep her safe, she becomes expert at deflecting attention away from herself and her disability.
    I can personally attest that both parochial and public schools in the post-WWII era of Miller's (and my) childhood were overcrowded. Barely able to keep up with the baby boom, most did not have trained staff available to assess or respond to children's health anomalies. It is harder to excuse the medical profession, and Miller does not. As she enters adolescence her condition is finally given a name. We are as shocked as Miller to hear, "*Exaggerated guilt conversion. Hysteria. / Psychosomatic,*" words from a trusted doctor that exacerbate her and her parents' fears and frustrations.

> *Do you want to end up in a sanitorium?* my mother asks.

    Much later, floundering as a young mother herself, she turns to Christ and throws herself into a bevy of church and charitable activities. It is during this period that her three-year-old son suddenly falls out of his chair in a way that is startlingly familiar. He can't move. In "Help Me Jesus" she writes:

> I am bludgeoned by recognition.
>
> I speak at the World Day of Prayer—how Jesus revealed the cause of my illness through my son.
>
> Father Morris gives the benediction: *May you all take away the truth of what was said today.*
>
> —as if only part of what I said was truth
>
> An oblique message sent and received

Even here she feels herself diminished, not entirely believed.
    But Miller moves beyond personal trials to the broader implications of her experience, enlarging on themes raised by Sontag and Couser, occasionally employing a sly humor. We find poems examining myth, ancient cures, disability as handled by other cultures. Overall, it is fair to say that women have been disproportionately subjected to shame and blame for their disabilities, decreasing the chances of diagnosis and treatment. Miller draws a tender portrait of Giovanna M., spending her long life in a mental hospital because she suffers from recurrent headaches. We see Freud's patient Emma Ekstein subjected to botched nasal surgery in an attempt to cure her of sexual arousal. (It is relevant to remind ourselves that less than a century ago women were sent off to mental institutions for the inconvenient emotional swings of menopause.) But men, too, have suffered and will find themselves represented in Miller's book. In "Diagnosis by Law Enforcement in Philadelphia" we meet a diabetic mistaken for a drunk and beaten by the police, though he wears a bracelet clearly identifying his condition.
    The beauty of forbearance, courage and perseverance permeates these poems, providing a balance to injustices. It is sadly ironic that the end of Miller's fraught journey arrived with the detection of the condition in her son, but with accurate diagnosis came genuine help. The good Dr. Katcher "his compassion edged with excitement ... calls it in / to the station house at Columbia Presbyterian: / 'potassium glide' 'affected gait'." The genetically-linked disorder has a medical name, and there is a drug to bring it under control. The reader shares Miller's belated but heartfelt relief.
    It can be tempting to turn away from probing and difficult poems like these, so deftly rendered in *Cures for Hysteria*. But engagement rewards the reader with

comprehension and hope. I expect to return often to the insights of this compelling, necessary work.

Juditha Dowd is the author of four volumes of poetry, most recently a full-length collection, *Mango in Winter* (Grayson Books, 2013). Her work can be found in *The Florida Review, Poet Lore, Ruminate, Rock & Sling, Cider Press Review, Ekphrastic* and elsewhere. It has been featured on *Poetry Daily* and *Verse Daily*, included in many anthologies, and nominated for the Pushcart Prize. Her mixed-genre, verse narrative *Audubon's Sparrow* is forthcoming from Rose Metal Press. Juditha lives with her husband in Easton, Pennsylvania.

Full Worm Moon by Julie L. Moore (Cascade Books-Wipf & Stock, 2018)

In the newest volume by Julie L. Moore—her longest and most ambitious yet—we find "a veritable storm of story" ("Once,"). Those of us who have followed Moore's work over the years know that she is a poet who writes from her life. We have admired the beauty and wisdom in her autobiographical narratives and observations. Collectively, her poems have invited us to ponder the question, "Do you know any way life comes forth / without pain?" ("Does soil hurt," *Particular Scandals*, 2013). Given what we know of her life and work, her latest book knocks the breath out of us, breaks our hearts, and grips us with a new admiration for Moore as a poet who creates art out of suffering.

The opening poem, "Loose Stone," reveals a shift in the landscape of Moore's life. We see how Moore, whose kids have "cleared out for college," foreshadows a shocking collapse: "This is far from upheaval, / yet everything feels disturbed, / treacherous…." In the second poem, "Full Wolf Moon," we see the beginnings of domestic upheaval: Shining through a window in her home, the moonbeams "illuminat[e] / the collapse within, / / the husband confessing to his wife / he told another woman she was / *beautiful*…." Thus begins Moore's chronicle of the demise of her marriage of twenty-seven years.

Writing about divorce, let alone experiencing it, is no doubt one of the most difficult tasks for Christian authors, as it likely dries up the wellspring of creativity for many—but not for Moore. The abundance of poems in *Full Worm Moon*, organized into three sections, cut a path through this still-taboo topic, inviting readers to walk with her through the trauma and observe how she emerges as a woman, poet, and Christian with just as much intellectual curiosity and capacity for joy as before.

The first section addresses the divorce directly—the tempestuous times leading to the day of "the vows' un- / doing," when a judge made the split official ("Full Long Nights Moon"). In recording personal tragedy and turning the chaos of emotion into art, Moore used a literary constant—a steadying device like the fixed point a dancer's eyes return to with each spin. This is the function of the twelve full moon poems that Moore strategically disperses throughout the book. As the *Old Farmer's Almanac* tells us, many of the poetic names for full moons originate from Native American culture. These names describe distinct aspects of each month and signal a dichotomy of constancy and change. Figuratively speaking, the moon serves as Moore's handhold in a landslide, reminding us of the constancy of Almighty God in the midst of turbulence. In addition to the moon motif, and in the first section especially, Moore uses a consistent third-person speaker. This strategy creates necessary distance not only between the author and the speaker, but also between the author and the traumatic events.

One poem in particular—"Full Thunder Moon," the title poem of the first section—displays these steadying strategies. The poem tells of a woman who seeks refuge in a gazebo outside St. Meinrad Archabbey as a rainstorm begins, the "first drops" of which are "indifferent…to whether her marriage lasted two years or twenty-seven." Unlike the unfeeling storm, the moon brings comfort despite its distance: "…[H]ere beneath / the full thunder moon, she inhales air thick with solace." Soon, "determined" raindrops begin to land "on the bare arms / of a wife who's endured seven surgeries, / whose husband left her, then told her, / *Your health problems have worn me out.*" The cold splash of rain on skin cannot begin to match the sting and treachery of such an accusation, but the comparison is intentional. How could a woman bare to hear, let alone record in a poem, these harsh words? How could she survive the storm of betrayal? As established by the epigraph from Psalm 57:1 (the beloved passage about taking refuge under God's wings), the implication is that like the wife in the poem who finds shelter by the light of a full moon not overtaken by storm clouds—and just as "a bird, say, a sparrow or finch, might glide in / & roost right there, within an inch of her care"—Moore felt the wings of God surrounding her during those difficult days leading to the divorce.

After the first section's series of raw revelations, we encounter a strikingly different tone and a diversity of subjects in sections two and three, aptly titled "Aftershock" and "This is the Landscape Left." The book's stunning title poem brings the hope of spring into Moore's new reality as a divorced woman: "…[T]his moon / announces, in all its fullness, worms / stirring in earth's softening center…." Moore welcomes worms "teeming with prophesy" and calls syrup "born again." And while the theme of solitude emerges, Moore makes a distinction: "It's not loneliness I feel…. What I sense is my singularity" ("Present"). She references her divorce overtly in just a few poems in sections two and three, but of course, we read all the poems in the light of what we have learned: Moore must begin again. On this new path, the "memory of marriage" is "a melodic shadow / / trailing the life / [she] never dreamed of" ("Open Window One Summer Night").

Though her personal circumstances have changed, this poet's signature philosophical moves still richly emerge, as in "Full Flower Moon," when she asks, "Should God suddenly speak, …

> Would it really be so strange
> if the still, small voice broke open
> like a bulb beneath the earth,
>
> then aired something sensible
> as the strong stem lifting high
> its lit lantern, signaling us
>
> to join in, do what we were made to do?

Here, Moore depicts the moon as a medium for the voice of God, urging us to live out our purpose—in Moore's case, to continue in the craft of making masterpiece poems despite everything.

Shanna Powlus Wheeler is the author of *Evensong for Shadows: Poems* (Resource Publications-Wipf & Stock Publishers, 2018) and *Lo & Behold: Poems* (Finishing Line Press, 2009). She teaches and directs the Writing Center at Lycoming College in Williamsport, Pennsylvania. Visit www.shannapowluswheeler.com.

The Five Quintets by Micheal O'Siadhail
(Baylor University Press, 2018)

I teach a course on the epic tradition at Northwest University. We labor with Odysseus as he zigzags across the Aegean Sea, lament Dido's fearsome end, venture with Dante through the incarnate psychology of his *Comedia*, tour the "darkness visible" of Milton's Pandemonium, and find ourselves in Middle Earth by semester's end. The endeavor feels strangely subversive in an age committed to the liturgy of Twitter and the iconography of the meme. For years, I've been on the lookout for contemporary poets as well-read as Eliot's modernists, as ingenious as Emily Dickinson, as comprehensive as the metanarratives that inspire the songs of Antiquity. I have found just such a poet in Micheal O'Siadhail and his *The Five Quintets*.

To say *The Five Quintets* is ambitious is to say *The Aeneid* is summer beach reading. There are moments where the sheer grandeur of the project near-unravels the intricate quintet / canto architecture O'Siadhail has devised, but again and again readers are brought to havens both resonate and rewarding. Like Homer's *Iliad* or Pound's *Cantos*, *The Five Quintets* is a poem readers "go up to over a lifetime" (to cite the late Seamus Heaney). I'm hard pressed to think of another contemporary poem as generous to the past or as stalwart in its effort to give fresh voice to our historic moment. The poem exhibits the "catholic" hospitality all artists should strive toward in a culture of outrage and is astute enough to avoid the essentialist claims that often mar the work of lesser poets. Sonnets, haiku, and Dante's terza rima are O'Siadhail's chief stylistic messengers, and he employs these agents to explore themes of *making*, *dealing*, *steering*, *finding*, and *meaning* in each quintet respectively.

Lest one think O'Siadhail's project too intellectual, *The Five Quintets* abandons highbrow pretension with a tone that is conversational and engaging. O'Siadhail tours a pantheon of poets, intellectuals, musicians, monarchs, and theologians with a keen eye for their shared humanity. The impact of their successes and failures on our contemporary world is observed with wit and precision. The inhabitants of Eliot's wasteland may have shored the fragments of history against their ruin, but O'Siadhail's project is a much needed reformation. *The Five Quintets* is not merely a survey of an intellectual and poetic tradition, what G.K. Chesterton calls the "democracy of the dead," but an active search for a feasible narrative to inform humanity's future. As O'Siadhail comments in his introduction, " ... I believe that poets have a part to play in shaping our public discourse." This search for viability, for a poetry and politic to stave off the creeping nihilism, despondency, and environmental catastrophe of our postmodern age, is a central feature of the poem. Consider this passage from *Steering* (Canto 5):

> Earthlings we belong together now,
> Serving one another's needs and gifts;
> In our trust our future's one shared globe.
> So prestige or standing, what's achieved
> Matters little – there's no starring role.
> Slung between what's past and still to come,
> Bonhoeffer's earned wisdom resonates:
> Let's not play heroic games instead
> Only ask when all is said and done,
> How another generation lives –
> Answering this the thrill of politics.

The sobriety of this appraisal, coupled with its generous spirit, is a recurring virtue of *The Five Quintets*. Just as Auden incanted to his readers in 1939, "We must love one another or die," O'Siadhail quests after the same universal love that compels us to chase after the good, the right, and the beautiful. In his introduction, O'Siadhail writes, "We are no longer in charge of a universe which we are part of and where we, too, belong. We need to re-examine overarching certainties, dreams of excessive individualism, isolation or fixity of borders, ideologies, and –isms. Our world is interwoven for good as we learn to cope with plurality of every kind." O'Siadhail's words provide a fitting summary of *The Five Quintets,* and he proves himself a capable guide as he leads readers through the formidable architecture of history.

The Five Quintets engages with a literary and philosophical tradition I fear many have abandoned like so much "pottage" here in the West and is as observant as Whitman among his spears of summer grass. O'Siadhail enchants his poem with the "cloud of witnesses" who have gone before us, and invites readers to reside in a geography that is both lettered and lyrical. Like all great art, *The Five Quintets* is a demanding work that pays dividends. The ambition and scale of O'Siadhail's poem is both welcome friend and cunning rival to the literary works I tour with my students each year.

Jeremiah Webster is Associate Professor of English at Northwest University. His poems have appeared in *North American Review, Beloit Poetry Journal, Crab Creek Review, The Midwest Quarterly, Dappled Things*, and elsewhere. His poetry collection, *After So Many Fires, and critical introductions for the poetry of T.S. Eliot and W.B. Yeats* are available from Wiseblood Books.

Before the Burning Bush by Brian G. Phipps (University of Saint Katherine Press, 2018)

One of the most formative features of liturgical tradition is to help us know a rite when we see one while also reminding us to whom we owe the glory. In *Before the Burning Bush*, Brian G. Phipps's debut collection of poetry, we accompany a puck-driving Eastern Orthodox poet through the rite of passage that is middle-age—all in terms of ice hockey, family, and prayer.

In the book's first section, *Theosis*, we read "Liturgy," the first poem with hockey as a conceit for spiritual practice:

> .... Exercise like this
> manifests its members as a unity and over
> time builds it up, shapes its posture
> toward the world, rectifying regions even
> deeper than the chemical. The body aches
> without such work...

The second time hockey serves as primary conceit is in a poem called "Prayer and Fasting," which begins by lamenting the late stage into which the speaker begins his ascetic life: "having found / our true vocation in the wake of / disillusionment...." The homily proceeds:

> We must skate even when we don't feel
> like it, even when we've used the last ounce
> of energy the day before, even when we think
> we're kidding ourselves believing in this
> game and our alleged ability to be good
> at it...

Phipps's ability to wring every possible meaning out of an analogy betrays a rhetorical clarity befitting a metaphysical poet of yore. The wisdom is undeniable:

> . . . . But we,
> aware of what we've missed,
> appreciate the wonder of developing
> any skill at all, the joy of being
> able to move like this, attaining
> through the effort of the body
> and the elevation of the spirit
> this graceful state.

    Another Orthodox poet, Scott Cairns, often writes about what he calls "sacramental poetics." At the risk of oversimplification, a poem achieves the level of sacramentality when the language of the poem becomes its own presence while inviting the reader to participate in the act of meaning. Cairns developed this theory as a way to counteract a tendency in contemporary poetry to serve as means of communicating a past event; communicating, to Cairns, is not *communion*, the goal of a sacramental poetics.

    Through the rhythms and materiality of his labors, Phipps teaches us how liturgy and sacrament form us in love, as he reflects upon the limitations of his body, even as he sacrifices it out of love for his family, in "Midlife":

> Two days later, blistered
> and stiff and sore, he'd pay
> for his labor, but now
> he warmed to the work
> of lifting the sledge and bringing it
> down on the concrete slab, breathing
> and limbering and sweating,
> reclaiming at least this portion
> which was lost to a hardened
> layer, to a wall of stone.

    But can explicitly sacramental subject matter compensate for a less-than-sacramental poetics? I don't know. But poems like "Midlife," a meditation on the sad but wise acceptance of the taxing nature of ordinary holiness—of work, prayer, and parenthood—can form in readers a forgiving heart:

> . . . . . . There was this: doing
> things more and more because they needed

> to be done, less and less from desire.
> And this: the first stirrings of anything
> like duty, though not quite
> allegiance and probably much
> too late . . .

Who doesn't buckle under the weight of being too late? Only a word of grace can deter despair. The poems in *Before the Burning Bush* can often settle for communication over communion, but we could do worse than heed the collection's unassuming insistence to attune to the liturgical and sacramental nature of creation, even hockey.

Michael Angel Martín was born and raised in Miami, FL. His poems and book reviews have appeared in *Dappled Things, America, Anglican Theological Review, Apogee,* T*he Living Church,* T*he Offbeat, Modern Literature, Green Mountains Review, Saint Katherine Review, The Mondegreen, Pilgrim, Presence,* and elsewhere.

A Stone to Carry Home by Andrea Potos (Salmon Poetry, 2018)

Creating under Alvaro de Campos, one of his many heteronyms, the Portuguese poet, translator, and critic Fernando Pessoa once wrote, "A place is what it is because of its location. Where we are is who we are." This quote passed over my mind often while reading *A Stone to Carry Home*, the new poetry collection by Andrea Potos. Potos' skilled use of place in these poems tells the reader that there is often a deep lore to place—where we are born, how that place shapes our outlook—strong connections abound to places we find significant, whatever the reason. It is fitting that this book is published by Salmon, a unique and storied Irish publisher, considering that the Irish use the term Dinnseanchas for this kind of adoration of place. Salmon also publishes authors from around the globe, many who engage in deep wanderlust. In this collection, Potos uses her carefully crafted words to recount the origins and significance of place, the traditions of family, and links to the past. Through these poems she often concerns herself with earthy beauty and reflects on events and characters associated with herself, her travels, artists, and especially her family, her mother, and grandfather. There is a softness and beauty to these poems, a reflection through journeys in life and journeys of the mind.

Part One – Widening Spaces begins the tenor of the collection. It touches on the personal and familial, the ways in which we pass memories down through generations. The book is also conceived as a journal to travel and new spaces. Many poems are also formed from a very personal standpoint. The author sees travel and the page as a cathartic space to ponder. Some the most telling poems reflect in an immediate way including: "Midlife, Late," "Morning of My 56th Birthday," "Trying to Talk to my Daughter," "On the Anniversary of My Grandmother's Death," and "In the Café Where I Write." There are also conversations with writers, John Keats and the Brontës, clearly two of Potos' favorite inspirations. There is love and adoration in these poems, a sense of connection that helps the poet reflect on the past and the future, the mythical in words. Here are some lines from "I Ask My Mother to Show Me the Old Greek Church of Her Childhood."

> *It was there,* she said, where
> she, at 14, first saw my father.
> *I told myself, I'm going to marry that boy.*
> I imagine her, waiting at the bottom of that small hill.
> He moved toward her, his white shirt
> shuddering in the breeze off the water, his face
> so clear from afar, olive skin and dark hair
> blazing in air, like a young god,
> the planet spinning
> from her axis onto his.

Here Potos explores connections to the past and reminiscences of where she was born and how she was formed. There is Wisconsin (the author's home state) deeply in this work and the significance of how a spot so close can be remembered and cherished. These poems are signposts leading to a larger, more impactful story, a tale steeped in tradition and past.

Just as Potos takes from her mother and her grandmother for history and connection, she also passes ideas down to her daughter pondering conversations and upbringing, a way to include history and influence, moments in life that claim the strong bonds of family. The author is learning to talk about her history and sending those news items to the next generation in poems like: "Daughter at 16," "Daughter Pearl," "Mother/Daughter," "Visiting Your Child's Chosen College," and "At 18." The sentiment in many of these poems is not so far removed from later Linda Pastan and Anne Sexton poems about the mother and daughter bond. The words contain connections that are seldom done with such insight.

When we reach *Part 2 – The Spell of the Journey* the reader enters the conversation of far off places, and Potos shares the impact they can have on a writer. We see Keats again appearing in poems about art and writing. He becomes a kind of spiritual guide. The reader also experiences the parts of Greece the author calls her ancestral home. The link Potos makes to the land of her grandfather conjures up images of the closeness of her family. Being from far off places in space and time can often show us how we are all very closely related. We see the lineage of family in poems like "My Grandfather's Home" where the author reflects.

> My daughter and I bend, peer under
> a muddy tarp that cloaks
> a rubble of fallen stones,
> as if saved for the day the granddaughter
> and the great-granddaughter could cross
> the Atlantic, drive the dizzying
> mountain roads to kneel
> on the April grass
> and reach their arms inside, pick one stone
> to carry home.

We see the mementos that Potos wants to keep, but also ones to share in her deliberately chosen words.

The collection's final poems are the strongest featuring conversations with Van Gogh or Proust and contemplations in the Musée de l'Orangerie. Art and writers can truly inspire and allow the author to look at the deeper aspects of life, a journey we have with ourselves, a travel log about the voyage of life. In Potos' work we see the connection to our journeys, our family, our significant places—who we are—and the experience all wanderers see through words and deeds, a journey we long to hear and write.

Born in Illinois in 1973, **Tyler Farrell** received his undergraduate degree at Creighton University, Omaha, Nebraska where he studied with Eamonn Wall. In 2002 he received his doctorate from UW-Milwaukee where he studied with James Liddy. He has published three books with Salmon Poetry: *Tethered to the Earth* (2008), *The Land of Give and Take* (2012), and *Stichomythia* (2018); and has contributed a biographical essay on James Liddy for Liddy's *Selected Poems*

(Arlen House, 2011). Farrell is currently a Visiting Assistant Professor at Marquette University where he teaches poetry, drama, writing, and literature. Farrell also leads two study abroad programs; one to Ireland, the other to London. Also, his Morrissey imitations are said to be legendary.

What Will Soon Take Place by Tania Runyan (Paraclete Press, 2018)

Midway through *What Will Soon Take Place,* Tania Runyan re-imagines the angel with a "little scroll" of *Revelation*'s Chapter 10, now casually proffering this "scroll like a golden / Fruit Roll-Up," with the warning: "You're stomach's gonna kill." Undeterred by the threat of intestinal discomfort, the speaker asserts:

> . . . . But I don't care.
> God's got a recipe.
> Once I start unfurling
> and chewing those words,
> I just can't stop. ("The Angel and the Little Scroll")

This image aptly describe both the project Runyan sets herself in her fifth book of poems and my own experience reading this palimpsestic collection in which the symbols and visions of the 1st century *Book of Revelation* co-exist with the objects and narratives of our 21st century lives.

In a "Foreword," Runyan recalls a life-altering introduction to Apocalypticism as a panic-stricken teenager. The evangelical interpretation of the *Book of Revelation* that undergirded her commitment to "receiving Jesus" offered an antidote to fear. Some thirty years later, Runyan had eschewed "pretrib" millennialism to focus on living with Jesus in the present, but confesses she had still never read the whole of *Revelation,* distrustful of a book whose "garish, terrifying imagery had been used to terrify people into Christianity." But now, historicist scripture study ("unfurling / and chewing those words") having taught Runyan to read *Revelation* "in the context of the past rather than the future," she finds true comfort in the mysterious symbols and episodes that promised hope to a struggling early church.

My own confession: as a cradle Catholic, I also had never read straight through *Revelation*; it seemed, indeed, dauntingly indigestible. But having "unfurled" it now with Runyan as a guide, I too "just can't stop" chewing over the words, images, and symbols – both of the scriptures and of Runyan's poems.

These—the words, images, and symbols—are very much the same: whole lines of scripture having found illuminating settings in Runyan's poems. And the structure of the book mirrors the order of *Revelation*—from the angel's appearance to John on Patmos through the final vision of the new heaven and the new earth. As in the scriptures, numbers matter here – Runyan carefully playing with sevens, fours and threes in the collection's structure, stanzas and repetitions. Here, too, are the four horsemen, the lamb and locusts, the woman and the dragon, the whore of Babylon, the 144,000 saved; gemstones and symbolic colors abound. But as Runyon's "Fruit Roll-Up" scroll demonstrates, these familiar figures and patterns are transposed to the key of 21st century American suburban life.

The first poem in the collection, "Patmos," attends to the symbolic value of the things with which we surround ourselves; a "plaster Nessie in the dandelions" bespeaks "some prophecy of beauty." But more darkly, Runyon insists that the detritus of our lives also wields power to direct our destiny. We could dwell in the resurrection symbolized by a concrete angel at the front door,

> But we always enter
>
> through the garage instead: crushed milk bottles,
> mud-scabbed boots, jump ropes coiled
>
> with shovels and bikes. They were never meant to lie
> in our way. Like it or not, they speak.

The poems brim with T-shirts at Old Navy, cell phones, "Velcro Toy Story sandals," selfie filters, Kinkaid prints while the poet laments, "This morning I can't squeeze out / of my smallness." But Runyan also knows the only way out is through: she is attentive to the ways in which our bodily and material lives, while offering temptations to self-absorption and materialism, also reveal our humanity and can lead us to grace. She sees the variegated beauty of "a magnolia bud / stippled with stars;" she feels the "stone / you pressed in my palm" or "salt wind on my neck." The body that "resists exile" on Patmos (John is tormented there by a "burrowing mite" and the fabric of his robe "sticking / in [his] crack") is nevertheless the body which will receive the angel's words "like wounds."

Runyan is teaching us to read our lives for the saving grace in the details just as she seeks an encounter with the Jesus of the Gospels in the confusing labyrinth of *Revelation*'s symbolic patterns. Both impulses coalesce in "The Great Throne," a poem beginning with direct address to the relatable, earthly Jesus who is so hard to recognize in the trappings of an Apocalyptic throne room:

> Rabbi, I'm losing you in all these robes,
> like a kid tunneling through a department store rack,
> pummeled by grown-up fabric.

The Jesus the speaker seeks is not be-robed, but the one with "sand in your hair and leper skin // under your nails." Runyan concludes by admonishing God:

> You don't need thousands of unblinking eyes
>
> staring you down over a great glass sea
> when the fish of Galilee peer at your calloused feet
> skimming the water like sunlight.

But the beauty of her final image: the fish peering up at what to them is surely an unfathomable miracle – serves to precisely undercut her own earthbound view. We are all children lost in the heavy coats, fish peering up through the water: our understanding of what is holy is limited by who we are and what we already know. The mysteries of *Revelation* and the sufferings of this world have something to teach us; Runyon's poems ask us to suspend our own judgments and be open to God's revelations.

There is so much to praise in this collection. Again and again I stopped short in delight at a well-chosen word. Runyan also writes effortless lines whether in free verse or more formally corralled. As a middle-aged woman, mother, wife, I felt a wonderful kinship of experience in so many small details ("Maybe an Idol" offers a hilariously accurate depiction of menopause). But I was also deeply moved by Runyan's repeated evocations of teenaged experiences. No doubt because she first encountered *Revelation* as a distressed teenager, and perhaps because she has mothered or taught them, she remains alert throughout the collection to the suffering of youth. She sympathetically revisits her own teenaged years in "Philadelphia" and "Maybe an Idol." She writes with a wry poignancy about adolescent dreams and desires ("Jasper") and heartbreakingly about teenagers lost to tragedy ("En Route, Tikrit" and "The Rider on a White Horse").

As these last two poems—one about a suicide, the other about "the teenager in a soccer jersey, tossed on a salvage bed like scrap metal" in a massacre in Iraq—illustrate, *What Will Soon Take Place*, although rooted in the mundane world of malls ("The Antichrist at the Mall") and broken jars of mayonnaise ("Our Sins under a Glass Sea"), is threaded with poems that evoke real evil in our world. In that sense this collection, like the *Book of Revelation* itself, is indeed challenging to read. But in the face of this evil, the poet, true to her new understanding of the consolations of *Revelation* and to her own vocation as a writer, like John, with a prophecy to share responds:

> Alpha, Omega: it makes no difference.
> The heavenly city of God has come down.
>
> He makes his dwelling place
> in the muddy corner of your garage,
>
> the oncologist's office,
> the space between paper and pen. ("New Jerusalem")

Mia Schilling Grogan is an Assistant Professor of English at Chestnut Hill College in Philadelphia. She is a medievalist who works on hagiography and women's spiritual writing. She has had poetry published in *America*, *Southern Poetry Review* and *Presence*.

Beyond All Bearing by Susan Delaney Spear (Resource-Wipf & Stock, 2017)

We read books, starting at the beginning. Yet where is the beginning of a life, and what chapter establishes the most meaningful interpretation? In re-reading, we begin with our most pivotal events. This sense of "where to start?" is apt in Susan Delaney Spear's *Beyond All Bearing*, which concludes with the story of Spear's musician son, Peter, dying by his own hand. Spear's preoccupations coalesce to honor her son.

The sequence becomes sadder still, when we understand the circumstances. Those who followed the case thought it was a missing person case, and it turned out to be a suicide. This was especially true for the family. As Spear writes in "Actuary Tables," "It was not the fact that he was dead. / . . . / It was the probability that she / would live another thirty years." Measurement in human and divine time is important—especially in the moment. Once Peter is found, Spear gets to see him: "*Yes. Now.* / / She saw his body / perfectly, / as a mother sees" ("Honeysuckle").

Apologies are currently old-fashioned, but there can be grandeur in a sincere apology: and Spear has a quiet grandeur. "Tender" shows Spear apologizing to her son for going on with her life: "You did not rise and walk. God is slow / and slowly tenders me the strength to go." In the public context, she and her family apologized as well, thanking the mourning community for doing what they could. I remember thinking that this was far beyond what most people would do. It is difficult to communicate grace when everyone is hurting, and yet the Spear family managed to do it.

We begin with our most pivotal moments.

Given this focus, other poems in the volume receive new resonance, especially poems about trauma. For instance, "Old Ralph," a gay bashing poem, is about two interpretations of a piano teacher, Ralph: one, the joy of his students who play the piano with him; the other, the prejudice of those who would make a statement such as "That guy's a fag." When a group harasses Ralph, "ransacking cupboards, plates breaking on the floor," Ralph has a stroke. While he can no longer play music, he hears "a soprano singing: / *Sheep may safely graze and pasture / where a shepherd guards them well*" ("Old Ralph"). There may have been no intention to cause a stroke, but it is the result nonetheless. We may anticipate one outcome in the moment, but be startled—even shocked—by the long-term. Every person is situated in a community and a life, and Spear, repeatedly, shows the unexpected reverberations in her collection.

Other poems of loss are noteworthy, some sweet and touching, some funny. For example, in "Pricey Recipe," the maker of stroganoff lovingly assembles the expensive ingredients for the meal, from cognac, to cremini mushrooms. The poem is an Italian sonnet, which also takes some preparation and which Spear handles with finesse, just like the meal in the poem, even though the recipient has lost interest: "his lips had wandered off." While there are many gifts in the poem, the most satisfying may be the concluding couplet, with the rhyme "wandered off" and "stroganoff." Here Spear reminds me of a poet like Anne Sexton, who loved the complications of rhymeand seeing how far she could take them.

It is no surprise that Spear, who teaches at Colorado Christian University, is drawn to Biblical stories, and, from them, she gleans valuable lessons. Stand-outs for me are "Outliers" and "Consider These Lilies." "Outliers" has a more contemporary feel, in terms of its title, and illustrates women being strong as they shape the genealogy of Jesus, whether they realize the full ramifications of their actions or not. "Consider These Lilies" is more traditional, with a poignant theme of growth:

> Now they thrive, bright offspring of agony.
> Their perennial blooms climb verdant ladders
> like ivory-robed apostles, open-mouthed,
> or brassy trumpets sounding weighty matters.

In terms of the Bible, Spear makes us realize that the lessons there are living stories, from which we can gather hope. While Spear is an optimistic person, the reader senses it is from faith she receives the source of her strength.

Spear is an admirable craftsperson. While she handles many forms well—particularly the short-lined sestina and the sonnet—Spear's strengths in other areas can make us take her skills for granted. That would be a mistake. That her poems sound so natural is to Spear's credit and should be praised. One of her particular strengths is the concluding couplet variation in the Italian sonnet. She is also good at runs of long rhymes, as in "Salt Water." Short lines are difficult in themselves, and rhyming short lines more difficult still. Extend the length of the rhyme: and it is a pressurized wonder.

The end leads us to the beginning. The poem "An Invocation in Ordinary Time" opens the book for the reader, saying

> Come, Holy
> Ghost, hum
>
> in common places
> Prove to me
>
> your extraord-
> inary graces

That is exactly what happens in the book. And so we begin—and end—here.

Kim Bridgford is the director of Poetry by the Sea and the editor of *Mezzo Cammin*. The author of ten books, she is the recipient of grants from the NEA, the Connecticut Commission on the Arts, and the Ucross Foundation. With Russell Goings, she rang the closing bell of the New York Stock Exchange, in honor of his book *The Children of Children Keep Coming*, for which she wrote the introduction. Bridgford has been called "America's First Lady of Form."

The Consequence of Moonlight by Sofia Starnes (Paraclete Press, 2018)

Sofia Starnes, recent Poet Laureate of Virginia (2012-2014), poetry editor of *Anglican Theological Review*, author of four previous, highly regarded poetry collections, has stunned again with her latest book, *The Consequence of Moonlight*. If that seems hyperbolic for a poetry review, then get ready, because the poems in this collection warrant all manner of extravagant praise.

Starnes has wizardry skill with language. Many poems I stopped reading midstream and thought—*how did she do this? It is so beautiful*. I even found myself reading some poems, without understanding what the words meant and, instead of being annoyed or impatient, I didn't care. The sounds were enjoyment enough: the largely iambic rhythms, the constant, unexpected interplay of rhyme and off-rhyme, the interesting word choices and juxtapositions, all the little language jolts along the way. It is possible to get lost in this collection, to keep reading for sound, and to let, meanwhile, the sense seep into your consciousness.

These poems are forthright in taking on life's stickiest questions of meaning, yet they avoid being dogmatic or cloying or cowardly or self-involved. In fact, Starnes makes herself largely absent from the collection, often using the plural pronoun *we* or addressing the reader directly as *you*, including the first poem, "Invitation," "it's all about *intent*— / as with the eye, no more surveyor / / but a lover in the momentary light." As a guide, Starnes functions almost like Dante's Beatrice, troubled by what she sees, but her own eyes securely fixed on the eternal, about which she has no doubt. The final section of the four-part "Meditation on a Lenten Corpus" concludes:

> .... part need, part instinct—no, *all* instinct, true
> as genuflect love. Lose and God gives.
> So ready, ready to resurrect.

In her final "Note to Readers," Starnes unequivocally states her hope that this book "be a poetic invitation to an awareness of this underlying Presence, as well as a call to be present as a loving witness to valuable and vulnerable things." In several poems, she limns Elena as an archetype with whom to identify as we discover our true identities. Starnes also directs our attention to the Moon, a frequent touchstone throughout the book and the crux of the title; the Moon, which she writes, "underscores a quality we rarely mention in our daily lives, but which the poems attempt to express as well: the quality of sainthood. Saints always meet the dark with light."

The Elena poems are complex and deserve careful readings. We arrive at the first one, "Elena Leaves Home," after initiation to the possibilities in the previous two poems: "Our story waits its turn, as stories do" ("Tenebrae") and "Walk up the sidewalk, wake it with your name" ("By Name, We Called You"). While there are no Elena poems in the second section, the poem "Archetypes" there serves as a guide to how to read her:

> You've heard me say "Elena" for a girl,
> and "Carlos" for a faraway young boy;
> they run home, so the rule says,
> when it rains ....
>
> I'm sure that Carlos clamors his in haste—
> he, of the archetypal kind,
> who'll lift a sword without excessive qualm,
> but who remains a child before the dark.
>
> When shall I draw them out, free from the woods,
> he and Elena, and others, fresh from myth?

We say goodbye to her in the final, "Elena's Reprieve": "So, here she is, on this redemptive / / bench, her name upon it. / *You must return*, it says;"

Moon and moonlight show up in numerous, unexpected contexts, always shape-shifting. From folksy wisdom in "Old Wives' Tales"—"Full moon: we never plant against her gravity,

/ nor hammer nails"—to observation: "A hound bays at the moon," in "Beasts in Prayer," where moonlight works as a springboard to divine presence: "Oh, bless the beasts / / whose moorings hold no doubt, no mask— / whose moon (like God?) spills on their grass, / unasked." The most detailed development of this metaphor occurs in the title poem, "The Consequence of Moonlight." No way these saints invited to the garden, a consequence of moonlight, can be captured in words. "And so, from word we turn to wordless." Finally, with or without words, "these saints will lift our consequence, / our sigh— / their moonlight bodies storying up our sky."

In language, characteristically delicate and lyrical, Starnes also celebrates human stories, human connections, all the "valuable and vulnerable things," she calls us to witness:

> Ah, stories you'll need
> to greet a boy, to live a life, to love a child,
> to spell the moon, to heed
>
> the sempiternal word
> your ache already knows above.
> ("Lessons from Galicia")

So many favorites, "The Search for Good," "Unknowing," "God's Renter," "The Ways of Touch," I could go on. Is there a more poignant way to allude to love's fragile hold than this line from "The Corporal's Wedding": "He loves her, loves the birdcage presence / / of her ribs"? Or these lines from "Why Honeymoons Are Brief": "No matter if they pull the shades, latch inwardly / the locks; the world must sneak its aches, its carbon in." And maybe one of my now and future favorite love poems, "A Mode of Permanence," celebrates love's brittle stand in the face of mortality.

Starnes has produced a significant body of work. While her poems are frequently demanding, they are well worth the effort. Deeply grounded in this world, they reach beyond it with clarity and vision. They bear up well with repeated readings; in fact, they improve. Because Starnes keeps always centermost "Oh, the beauty a bevy forgets, / / pure, particular life" ("White Crow").

Maryanne Hannan has published poetry in *Gargoyle, the minnesota review, Oxford Poetry* (UK), *Rabbit* (AU), *Rattle, Ruminate* and *Windhover*. Several poems have been reprinted in anthologies, including *The Great American Wise Ass Poetry Anthology, St. Peter's B-list: Contemporary Poems Inspired by* the Saints, *The World Is Charged: Poetic Engagements with Gerard Manley Hopkins.* Her book reviews have appeared in *Anglican Theological Review, Innisfree Poetry Journal, Web del Sol Review of Books, Sentence,* and elsewhere. Her website is www.mhannan.com.

Gloved Against Blood by Cindy Veach (CavanKerry Press, 2017)

In Cindy Veach's debut collection, *Gloved Against Blood*, she reaches back in order to move forward and tell a story that has much contemporary resonance in terms of class, gender, and immigration. In an age where the treatment of women, immigrants, and the working class all seem to be worsening, Veach treats these lives with the dignity and emotional insight they deserve.

In these spare yet lush poems, Veach evokes both Susan Eisenberg's personal poems about becoming one of the first female electricians and Diane Gilliam Fisher's *Kettlebottom*, a book of historical poems about the West Virginia coal mining wars. Veach balances the personal and historical to create an intimate, expansive portrait of women in the textile mills of Lowell, Massachusetts.

The author, an award-winning quilter herself, interweaves personal family history with the larger history of the textile mills to create an emotional landscape that reveals the costs both at work and at home. She draws on generations of family experiences and stories while also drawing on research on the mills and how the women were treated. The stories of her Nanny and Mémé, (great-grandmother and grandmother), her mother, and her self, are placed alongside poems inspired by *The Lowell Offering: Writings by Mill Women 1840–1945*, a found poem from *Factory Rules from the Handbook to Lowell (1848)* and Ex-Slave Narratives conducted by the Works Progress Administration (WPA) in the 1930s.

Veach is not just a documentarian of history; she is also a skillful, nuanced poet. She employs a variety of techniques to strengthen the emotional power of the poems. For example, in "Lowell Cloth Narratives, " she interweaves the italicized lines from individual ex-slave narratives with repeated unitalicized lines that evoke the difficult conditions of the work that they all experienced, as seen below in examples from the first two narratives:

State: Arkansas Interviewee: Bear, Dina (in italics)

I was born in slavery time—a world away
we wove we wove away. *I was born in the field
under a tree.* Thirteen hours a day we toiled
cotton into cloth....

State: Arkansas Interviewee: Tatum, Fannie (in italics)

I wasn't allowed to sat at the table—a world away
we wove we wove away. *I et on the edge
of the porch with the dogs with my fingers*—
thirteen hours a day we toiled cotton
into cloth....

The technique brilliantly emphasizes the unique voices of the ex-slaves against the common experiences of the work.
    Juxtaposition is also a common technique throughout the collection. The contrast of work and home lives with sharp, vivid imagery establishes the authority in these poems for documenting the harsh realities of these lives. In addition, she explores the internal versus external contrast that is inherent in monotonous repetitive labor, the tension between functioning like a machine while the mind wanders, as in "Drawn": "And what of the visions / / you threaded your shuttle / with?"
    Veach skillfully uses repetition and anaphora throughout the book as a unifying and rhythmic device to evoke the repetitious quality of the work while also conjuring the generational constancy of the mill in this community. In two separate poems, she uses "How" as part of repeated phrasing. The impossible luxury of thinking about "how" the characters ended up in such circumstances is driven home, as in these lines from the aptly titled "Theft":

How I came down from Quebec to work in the mills—
How I never imagined it would be such hell. How industry.
How factory bell. How many miles of cloth I conjured
from the bloody cotton. . . .

    For its part, the home life of these characters is also difficult. Some of the family poems deal with the grandmother's loss of faith after her husband left her for another woman. In "The Other Woman," Veach explores the difficulties of an abandoned woman in this era:

> .... For she believed
> believed. Read her *Maryknolls*, went
> to daily mass, confessed to the gauzy man
> shadow who at the end mimed his blessing
> making of his hand a steeple that knifed the air
> she breathed as he pronounced her penance—
> which could erase every black mark
> but one...

Veach employs the letter poem form to great effect in the "Dear Francis Cabot Lowell"—*founder of the first textile mill that transformed raw cotton into cloth under one roof increasing productivity and the demand for cotton*. Here, her outrage tears open history to directly confront the inhumanity created by Lowell:

> They bleed I weave. I weave they bleed. Why can't
> you see—blood threads your looms all down the row?

Veach's book is an important addition to the poetry of work. Work—a subject that has often been neglected or distorted in our literature when the reality is that work shapes our lives in every way. The toll work takes—hard, physical work—on our emotional lives, from generation to generation. Many work poets try to preserve the people's history against those who would erase it or obscure it with numbers and the slanted lens of the privileged. How many of us have worked jobs that required gloves for protection. When the mills and factories come down, who can conjure their stories from those vacant lots of rubble? Or, perhaps even worse, where the history is obiterated by repurposing, as in the "Great Red Wall":

> And this—the red brick of mills,
> the home of warp and weft
> that lured them from their failing farms
> to toil cotton into cloth thirteen hours a day.
> And this—red brick on brick on brick
> is all that's left of sweat and linty lungs.
> Can you see them years later—in these offices,
> these cubicles, these cute boutiques
> with clothes made in Bangladesh
> or sitting in the hip cafés that sell espresso
> fifteen ways? . . .

In "Field Trip: Boot Cotton Mills," Veach seems conscious of the responsibility placed on her as someone who has both the sewing skills and the writing skills, and as someone who has her memory intact (dementia, another inheritance—"What happens now/as you disappear/as she did/brain cell by brain cell—/is that our story?"):

> It's possible
> > I was born imprinted
>
> beginning with *loom*
> > from the old word *gelōme*
>
> stitched beside my fate line
> > so I may salvage our history:

Often, it is left to the poets to bring history to life—the physical and emotional struggles to survive against oppression. Bringing the past to life is no easy task, but Veach breathes life into it with the rhythmic music and rich imagery of her poems.
Like poetry itself, Veach finds much meaning compressed into small things, as in "Thimbleful":

and this quilt reminds me
of the silver and gold filigreed thimble
that belonged to my great-grandmother, grandmother, mother--
the way it protects me from the quick stick
of sharps and betweens
at the same time it is a vessel, repository, crèche
for the spiraled remnants of their making.

The thimble, the perfect symbol for this book, a world packed into it—one small hard thing—both vessel and repository.

Jim Daniels' recent poetry books include *Rowing Inland* and *Street Calligraphy* (2017) and *The Middle Ages* (2018). He is the author of five collections of fiction, four produced screenplays, and has edited six anthologies, including the forthcoming *R E S P E C T: The Poetry of Detroit Music*, forthcoming in 2019 from Michigan State University Press, along with his next collection of short fiction, *The Perp Walk*.

The Stranger World by Ryan Wilson (Measure Press, 2017)

Walker Percy, late in life, declared to the average reader: "of all the billions and billions of strange objects in the Cosmos — novas, quasars, pulsars, black holes — you are beyond doubt the strangest."

That paradox — the normality of strangeness — could stand as the ordering principle of Ryan Wilson's first collection, *The Stranger World*.

Winner of the Donald Justice Prize, the book appeared in 2017 to accolades from Robert Pinsky, David Yezzi, and many others. It includes thirty-five poems, seven of them translations from Villon, Baudelaire, and Horace.

Wilson's characters are ordinary people living in American suburbs. Their "stranger world" is recognizably our world. Its culture is ours, with Lynyrd Skynyrd on the jukebox, the Kardashians on TV, and Mr. Coffee on the kitchen counter. But the protagonists experience dislocation and personal dissolution, alone even at parties and in crowded piazzas. They are aliens at home, and yet they find oddly familiar faces and places in foreign lands. Death, of course, looms as the abiding threat to any order they might establish: a shadow on the ultrasound reveals that "Unbeing now will flourish soon."

Melancholy marks the book's early poems, and night is never far off: "dusk fades to dark" ... "winged dark that haunts the clean light's glare . . ."You can hear, if you're quiet, the dark night on march." And yet the poems never fall to mawkishness. Wilson's subtle, wry humor is everywhere the esthetic safety net.

His masterpiece is the long poem "Authority," a horror story in blank verse; like much of the best horror, it's also satire.

"Authority" is the Book of Job rewritten for secularist America. The narrator is an exemplary, genteel suburban liberal, who makes all the socially correct choices and yet suffers a series of trials, beginning with appliance failure and ending with some serious gore. He's bewildered.

> . . . . I voted Democrat
> And do my nine-to-five like everyone else,
> Which is precisely why it doesn't make sense.
> Why me?

A long-lapsed Catholic, he clings to some vestigial sense of cosmic justice. With his wife, he submits his trials to wonky economic and ecological analysis, but he finds no satisfactory answers. Accusatory Post-It notes begin to appear in their house. The police are useless, though kind.

An inexplicable fault line has opened up in his life, and yet he finds he can do no more than passively suffer its effects. He has done nothing to deserve the plagues he endures. But he has no heaven to rage against. In the end, he devotes his remaining days to writing a monumental "history of religious doubt." "Authority" is as funny and strangely familiar as anything in Kafka.

Wilson is resolutely formalist, a virtuoso metrist. He is at ease with dimeter ("Yo La Tengo") and hexameter ("Lullabye for a Suburban Summer Evening") and, of course, everything in between. The collection includes, in addition to blank verse, sonnets, a villanelle, and a ballade. The book's single instance of terza rima, "For a Dog," is the greatest dog poem ever written — true to life and utterly unsentimental — and it has no close rival. This is a small sample:

> .... Dumb—you were dumb,
> Like all dogs, snuffling up to snakes, afraid
> Of mice. When we said "come," you wouldn't come;
>
> You capered when commanded to play dead,
> And when we wanted most to be alone
> You'd offer up that imbecilic head
>
> Until we crowned your pity with a bone.
> Our lives took on the shape you spun from need ...

The melancholy of the early poems would be unbearable over the course of the book. It breaks for the note-perfect translations, and it returns to resolve in the book's final pages. The data is no different there, but the understanding is spiritually profound.

> The sagging fence will never stand up straight.
> Whatever's not ripe now will never be.
> That pain tormenting you will not abate,
> And in the windows of vacated banks
> You'll see yourself, passing by aimlessly.
> You cannot change your life. Give up; give thanks.
>   ("In the Harvest Season")

With those last two words, the poem moves from mere resignation to something far greater: trust that God has permitted every loss and cross for a greater good.

The poet's hope rings almost liturgical in the volume's closer, aptly titled "The View on Waking."

> There is a kind of crypt, between
> This window and the window-screen,
> In which fine silken webs, unseen,
>
> Like wires in levitating tricks,
> Accumulate, somehow, and fix
> Bits of the outer world: small sticks
>
> And past years' leaves and wisps of straw
> All hang, suspended in mid-fall,
> Ensorcelled by some happy flaw ...

It's unseemly, I suppose, for a critic to cite an Amazon product review in the pages of a prestigious journal. But I am reviewing a book that I bought with my own credit card, from Amazon, after reading the reviews that were already there — especially one that recommended *The Stranger World* as a gift "for your brother-in-law who loves T.S. Eliot and ... for your grandmother who loves Garrison Keillor."

There's something to that. Ryan Wilson writes with clarity and authority. His poems are simple in the way living things are simple. I find in them a quality of beauty that's abundant in the more mature work of Frost and Wilbur. I'm not exaggerating. I await the next collection.

Mike Aquilina is author of many books, including *Terms and Conditions: Assorted Poems, 1985-2014* (Serif Press, 2014). His poems have appeared in *First Things, Dappled Things, Plains Poetry Journal, St. Austin Review,* and elsewhere. His song lyrics have been sung by Grammy Award winners Paul Simon and Dion. He has hosted a dozen television series and two documentary films. He is a contributing editor for *Angelus News* and executive vice-president of the St. Paul Center for Biblical Theology. He has been married since 1985.

Life's Work

"Faith's Ardor in [an] Air-Conditioned Tomb": Dana Gioia's Sights of the Unseen in a Secular Age
by Joshua Hren

In its earliest usage (c. 1300) the adjective *secular* meant not godlessness but "living in the world but not belonging to a religious order." However, from the 1850s *secular* has been used "in reference to humanism and the exclusion of belief in God from matters of ethics and morality." That is to say, secularization is bound up with the religious against which it defines itself; the religious, with the secular. In *Partial Faiths,* John McClure strives to define a body of literature, which he gives the ugly if useful name "postsecular." Such a literature merits this appellation because it contains stories that "trace the turn of secular-minded characters back toward the religious; because its ontological signature is a religiously inflected disruption of secular constructions of the real; and because its ideological signature is the rearticulation of a dramatically 'weakened' religiosity with secular, progressive values and projects" (3). Dana Gioia's poetics of faith in a secular age has given us a number of poems that embody the first two of these characteristics, even as it departs from the third. Instead of dramatizing a weakened religiosity that fits cozily into the humanist project, Gioia give us "secular-minded" persons who are "drawn back toward the sacred by promptings [they do] not invite but cannot ignore" (9–10).

Robert McPhillips wryly captures the businessman poet's paradoxical beginnings, noting that Gioia "launched his literary career from the unlikely campus of the General Foods Corporation in suburban Westchester County, New York" (34). David Mason furthers McPhillips' portrait when he observes that, "[Many] consider Gioia the ultimate insider—a man with his fingers in many cultural pies, a man of privilege, educated in the Ivy League, prosperous, prolific, and political. Dana Gioia, the corporate poet, who had attained a vice presidency at General Foods when he resigned his position there to write full-time" (133). The list could go on: Gioia the Bush appointee as chairman of the National Endowment for the Arts, the Poet Laureate of California, etc. And yet Gioia's deep preoccupation with metaphysical questions and sacramental realities, as well as his emergence as the foremost public presence galvanizing the Catholic literary revival that has emerged over the course of these last ten years, situates him—in spite of his superficial station as "insider"—as a perpetual outsider. It is no wonder, then, that in many of his poems the sacral haunts and interrupts lives spent inhabiting the mundane, materialistic, and abstracted spaces of a secular age, unveiling the unseen and reorienting the soul.

As Charles Taylor relates, disenchantment "designat[es] one of the main features of the phenomenon we know as secularization" (287). The German word for "disenchantment" is "entzauberung," which contains the word "zauber," or *magic*: it literally translates as *de-magicification*." Taylor traces two main features of the enchanted world that "disenchantment did away with" (287). The first is that the world "was once filled with spirits [God, angels, Satan, demons, spirits of the wood]" that were "almost indistinguishable from the loci they inhabit" and "moral forces [that] impinged on human beings" (the boundary between humans and these were "porous") (290, 287).

Although secularization has advanced a rosy understanding of disenchantment, any reduction of reality to materiality and mundanity ignores the magic that persists in a purportedly demystified world. Consider the mysteries of commerce that Marx unveils in his treatment of commodities: "A commodity appears at first sight an extremely obvious, trivial thing. But its analysis brings out that it is a very strange thing, abounding in metaphysical subtleties and theological niceties" (163). For Marx, when a person transforms a tree into a table, in spite of the fact that it has changed, it remains a common, everyday thing: wood. However, as soon as this table is changed into a commodity, it becomes "transcendent," assumes a "mystical character." In a passage that proves that *Das Kapital* is not without humor, he writes: "But, so soon as it steps forth as a commodity, it is changed into something transcendent. It not only stands with its feet on the ground, but, in relation to all other commodities, it stands on its head, and evolves out of its wooden brain grotesque ideas, far more wonderful than 'table- turning' ever was" (164). Marx names this transformation "commodity fetishism," borrowing from anthropology the word "fetish," which denotes the belief that divinities and gods inhere in material things. Although he may depart from the labor theory by which Marx explicates this fetish, nonetheless Gioia captures the "enchantment" of commodity fetishism in his poem "Shopping," wherein the narrator proclaims "Blessed are the acquisitive, / For theirs is the kingdom of commerce," after he has "enter[ed] the temple of [his] people but [does] not pray," this even as he "[envies] the acolytes" of abundance "their passionate faith."

In her essay "Dana Gioia: A Contemporary Metaphysics," Janet McCann contends that, "cognizant of the difficulty [of a deeper] quest [in modernity]—in a flat surface, where everything is only itself, [Gioia's work] asks: where can we find the power that went with the old mythologies when they were believed in?" (204). In "Shopping" at least one answer to McCann's question is "the mall." Instead of satirizing or ironizing the mall in a mode that enunciates its secular vapidity, Gioia dramatizes a mystical and religious register that gives a compelling account of why devotees of secularity find such satisfaction in a purportedly materialistic place. The mall, with its "hymns of no cash down and the installment plan, / Of custom fit, remote control, and priced to move," with its pseudo-incense of "coffee, musk, and cinnamon" offered in celebration of "Mercury, protector of cell phones and fax machines, / Venus, patroness of bath and bedroom chains, / Tantalus, guardian of the food court," "beguile[s]" us (Gioia 47). Why? Because the arts of commerce have seemingly surpassed nature itself; piles of crepe de chine, silk, and satin heap "like cumuli in the morning sky" (46). Because all of this seems to have been brought not by mechanistic semi-trucks and overnight airplane deliveries, but by "caravans and argosies"—emblems of the exotic east (46). And yet, if at first this mall-pilgrim experiences a *mysterium termendum* before the "crowded countertops and eager cashiers," he ends by "spending only . . . time, discounting all [he] see[s]," for "There is no angel among the vending stalls and signage" and this absence of the sacramental stokes a visceral search for the "errant soul and innermost companion" (47).

That this pilgrim would fail in such a place was evident from the poem's beginning, for, wandering the "arcades of abundance," he is "empty of desire" (46). That is to say, although he envies the faithful their passionate faith in the fetishes that fill the mall, although he "spends his time" trying to acquire it, he receives no answer to his demand that someone "Tell [him] in what department [his] desire shall be found" (47). What he desires, and what, he confesses, he would buy if he could, is "happiness," and here we encounter that enduring problem, noted by Aristotle in the *Nicomachean Ethics* and which St. Augustine addresses with characteristic jocularity in *City of God:* "That all men desire happiness is a certitude for anyone who can think. But so long as human intelligence remains incapable of deciding which men are happy [and, he elaborates elsewhere, why], endless controversies arise in which philosophers waste their toil" (186).[1] The narrator of "Shopping" pronounces the equally wasted toil of the "footsore customers" standing and waiting in their "sullen lines" (47). That this pilgrim departs from his peers is no guarantee that his new direction will be guided by a more profound beatitude. However, because he experienced the mall as an enchanted realm rather than a merely materialistic, secular space, this spiritually-charged vision permits a turn toward the soul, whom he looks for "among the pressing crowds" (47). If his experience of this commercial temple could be explained as mere configurations of chemicals, with dopamine falling while one waits in line and peaking from the time he sees that satin and silk until he makes a purchase, his disappointment would need to be resolved materially, through some sort of mundane divertissement. But, seeing the spiritual and mystical dimensions of the mall, knowing that the goddess of love herself protects and assists the lingerie stores, he also has eyes for his mysterious soul, whom he addresses in ardent apostrophe: "Where are you, my fugitive" (47)? His epiphany, coming after he has exhausted time spent "stalk[ing] the leased arcades," elicits a series of questions, whose rhetorical expression and effect carries echoes of the beginning of St. Augustine's *Confessions*:

> How shall I call upon my God, my God and Lord? Surely when I call on him, I am calling on him to come into me. But what place is there in me where my God can enter into me? 'God made heaven and earth' (Gen. 1:1). Where may he come to me? Lord my God, is there any room in me which does not contain you? Can heaven and earth, which you have made and in which you have made me, contain you? Without you, whatever exists would not exist. Then can what exists contain you? I also have being. So why do I request you to come into me when, unless you were within me, I would have no being at all. I am not now possessed by Hades; yet even there are you (Ps. 138:8) (4-5).

---

[1] In an *Image: Art, Faith, Mystery* interview, Gioia says that St. Augustine's *The City of God* "probably shaped my adult life more than any other book except the Gospels."

After asking where his soul is, he questions, in confessional form, "Why else have I stalked the leased arcades / Searching the kiosks and the cash machines" (47)? And then the Augustinian inquiry crescendos:

> Where are you, my errant soul and innermost companion?
> Are you outside amid the potted palm trees,
> Bumming a cigarette or joking with the guards,
> Or are you wandering the parking lot
> Lost among the rows of Subarus and Audis?
>
> Or is that you I catch a sudden glimpse of
> Smiling behind the greasy window of the bus
> As it disappears into the evening rush? (47-48).

The poem ends here, without answers. Still, the barrage of inquiries provokes the reader to also seek after the nature of the soul. Further, the questions contain clues as to the nature of the narrator's crisis. One thing cannot, on a literal level, be simultaneously errant and innermost, and so we are cued into the symbolic key of these final inquiries. His soul cannot literally be outside amidst the potted palm trees, but the key word here is "outside." The soul either refused to enter the mall, or the man left the soul there—again, not literally, but metaphorically. Left outside, the soul might be joking with the guards, a gesture suggestive of joy. But perhaps the outside of the mall is also foreign territory for the soul, and it is misplaced, drifting without a clear destination through the sea of cars. Or, finally, is the soul "smiling"—again here suggestive of that joy that the narrator had sought without knowing it—behind a window so different than those that line the leased arcades? Perhaps, and here the chill of the ending emerges, the soul simply departed. The pilgrim sought too long in the mall, did not accept or act upon the soul's jealous insistence upon a joy that can only come with beatitude, so that epiphany the man may have had, but this epiphany does not preclude the possibility of irreversible tragedy, of a case wherein the soul has been veritably excluded and at last excised from his existence.

    We move from the mall to the museum as we leave "Shopping" and consider "The Angel with the Broken Wing." Both of these spaces can be read as temples. As Giorgio Agamben argues, "the Museum occupies the space and function once reserved for the Temple as the place of sacrifice. The faithful in the Temple—the pilgrims who would travel across the earth from temple to temple, from sanctuary to sanctuary—

correspond today the tourists who restlessly travel in a world that has been abstracted into a Museum . . . " (84–85). It would be absurd to declare Agamben's contention absolutely true, but he rightly reads the phenomenon of a secular space replacing a sacred one, a pattern evident in "Shopping" and repeated in "The Angel with the Broken Wing." In the latter, the beautiful is replaced by the aesthetic, which is to say that when sacred art has been "abstracted into a Museum," it is cut off from its relation to the sacred order: art's metaphysical meaning is "mercifully" mummified and put to sleep.

    McCann is right to note that in Gioia's poems, "The bedrock of Catholicism is glimpsed sometimes within, sometimes just beyond their margins. Their sacramental vision and their insistence on the accountability of art are rooted in their religious faith" (204-205). This is perhaps clearest in "The Angel with the Broken Wing," where the poem's protagonist and narrator is an angel statue who has been exiled to solitary confinement ("one large statue in this quiet room") in a museum (Gioia 16). The angel alleges that this fate grows out of the fact that "the staff finds [him] too fierce," which leads them to "shut / Faith's ardor in [an] air-conditioned tomb" (16). Here the poem registers the terrible irony: the angel's purported advancement from "a country church" to a museum complete with air-conditioning and quiet is actually a death. This death comes in large part because the rarefied docents, and presumably the "chatter[ing]" museumgoers, relegate their praise to the angel's "elegant design." Such a reductive reading of the angel elicits his sardonic, melancholic conclusion that if he is a "masterpiece of sorts," it is only in the sense that he is "the perfect emblem of futility" (16).

    Describing the convergence of atheism and aestheticism, Philip Rieff: "having abandoned their belief in God, poetry—art generally—can take its place as the style of redemption" (17). One of the consequences of this replacement is that art comes to be judged only according to the categories of aesthetics. For Thomas Aquinas, the beautiful cannot be compartmentalized: where there is beauty there is also goodness and truth. Further, we cannot draw from an object all its beauty. This implies that when we behold a beautiful object we are captivated by it in part because some of its beauty fastens us to itself in that, so to speak, it does not quite arrive. "To experience the beautiful is not only to be satisfied," John Milbank writes, "but also to be frustrated satisfyingly; a desire to see more of what arrives . . . is always involved" (2). For Milbank, this desire to see *more* is actually a desire to see the unseen; to truly see the beautiful is to see the invisible in the visible. He notes that Hans Urs Von Balthasar aptly articulated "Glory," as it occurs in the Bible, as the experience of a, "hidden, divine force irradiating the finite surface" (2). Wherever this possibility of knowing both the true through the beautiful and the invisible through the visible remains, aestheticism has not conquered. There was, in the Medieval period, no branch of philosophy called "aesthetics." Kant, the supreme theorist of modernity's aesthetic maintains that the beautiful is ineffable, but he locates this ineffability, "on the side of subjective feeling alone" (Milbank 4). He refuses the possibility of glory, or the *presence* of the invisible in the visible. Superficially, the museum docents do the same, limiting their critiques to the "elegant design," but we cannot forget that, though they may not admit this to be the case, they have confined the angel to solitude in part because they "find [him] too fierce" (16). That is to say, they *cannot* mute the way in which the invisible irradiates the visible: their aesthetic categories *cannot* clip the wings of the transcendentals: the beautiful angel bespeaks truth to them, a truth that feels fierce to those who have inherited and who proselytize a horizontal world.

    For Rieff, a world ordered around the horizontal leaves us with an understanding and experience of culture that is all-too-human: in such a social order, the truths do not intersect with and so do not inflect our culture. However, "Our own motions in sacred order are locatable once each of us has restored to himself the notion of sacred order. The basic restorative is to understand the purity and inviolate nature of the vertical in authority . . . That we do not now find safety . . . reflects our loss of the radically contemporaneous memory of sacred order and our present time and place in it" (13). According to the angel, though, the docents have not been able to forget this memory of the sacred order: taxonomize him according to the categories of a museum's secularized aesthetics they may, but encountering him they cannot help but know terror when they glimpse their existences as transcending that which can be empirically mapped. As Rieff continues to explain, "Cultures give readings of sacred order and ourselves somewhere in it. Culture and sacred order are inseparable, the former the registration of the latter as a systemic expression of the practical relation between humans and the shadow aspect of reality as it is lived. No culture has ever preserved itself where it is not a registration of sacred order. The [secularist] notion of a culture that persists independent of all sacred orders is unprecedented in human history" (15).

The poem, Gioia notes, "is spoken by a *santo*, a devotional wooden statue carved by a Mexican folk artist" (71). As the angel narrates the story of his life, we see the docents' recognition of that which transcends his design shared by the Mexican revolutionaries who entered his "country church" of origin and broke his (left) wing ("Even a saint can savor irony") (16). Sent to vandalize the chapel, the troops could do no more than "hit [him] once," "For even the godless feel something in a church, / A twinge of hope, fear? Who knows what it is? / A trembling unaccounted by their laws, / An ancient memory they can't dismiss" (16). Their violence to the statue reinvigorates its—and faith's—ardor, to introduce a sacredness whose beauty is tied to numinous laws that announce truths that reveal the revolutionary's commandments to be radically incomplete and even inimical to the persistent divine.

At the poem's end, the angel with the broken wing recognizes "so many things [he] must tell God!" and yet finds himself "like a dead thing nailed to a perch, / A crippled saint against a painted sky" (17). In Gioia's poems, then, sacramental realities are revealed through their failings: the prospective failure of the mallgoer to retrieve his soul in time; the failure of the revolutionaries or the docents to duly order their cultures around the angel's revelations; the pitiable, beautiful angel's failure to tell "so many things" to God, even though he knows he "must." He cannot, for it was not he alone who can tongue things to God. When he inhabited that "country church" for which he was carved, he "stood beside a gilded altar where / The hopeless offered God their misery" (16). He became "the hunger that they fed"; that is to say, the faithful's "prayers for the lost, the dying, and the dead," were pulled forth upon seeing him. Without him their prayers would not achieve the verticality to which the poem gives literal articulation in the line, "Their candles stretched my shadow up the wall," and beyond the visible ceiling (16). Once again, though, it is this poem's tragic ending, wherein the heights of the cosmos are reduced to the museum's "painted sky," that reveals the awful superiority of the sacred order. Secularity, ushered in by violent revolutionaries or elegant docents, makes us claustrophobic, crippling our souls, and even ("I stand like a dead thing") crippling us. But the poem's tragic end solicits our pity for those necessary angels of beauty who are ready to resurrect faith's ardor even from within the "air-conditioned tomb."

Works Cited

Agamben, Giorgio. "In Praise of Profanation." Trans. Kevin Attell. *Profanations*. Ed. Jeff Fort. New York: Zone Books, 2007. 73-92.

Aristotle. *The Nicomachean Ethics*. Trans. David Ross. New York: Oxford University Press, 2009.

Augustine, *Confessions*. Trans. Henry Chadwick. New York: Oxford University Press, 1991.

Augustine. *The City of God*. Trans. Gerald Walsh. New York: Image Books, 1958.

Gioia, Dana. *99 Poems : New & Selected*. Minneapolis, MN: Graywolf Press, 2016. Print.

Koss, Erica. "A Conversation with Dana Gioia," *Image: Art, Faith, Mystery*, https://imagejournal.org/article/conversation-dana-gioia/.

Marx, Karl. *Capital: A Critique of Political Economy*. Vol. 1. Trans. Ben Fowkes. New York: Vintage, 1977.

Mason, David, "The Inner Exile of Dana Gioia." *Sewanee Review* 123.1 (2015): 133-146.

McCann, Janet. "Dana Gioia: A Contemporary Metaphysics." *Renascence: Essays on Values in Literature* 61.3 (2009): 193-206.

McClure, John A. *Partial Faiths: Postsecular Fiction in the Age of Pynchon and Morrison*. Athens: University of Georgia Press, 2007.

McPhillips, Robert, *The New Formalists*. Cincinnati, OH: Textos Books, 2005.

Milbank, John. *Theological Perspectives on God and Beauty*. Harrisburg, PA: Trinity Press International, 2003.

Rieff, Philip, and Kenneth S. Piver. *My Life among the Deathworks : Illustrations of the Aesthetics of Authority*. Introduction by James Davison Hunter. Charlottesville: University of Virginia Press, 2006.

Taylor, Charles. *A Secular Age*. Cambridge, MA: Belknap Press-Harvard University Press, 2007.

Joshua Hren, Ph.D. is Assistant Director of the Honors College at Belmont Abbey. For many years he served as editor of *Dappled Things: A Quarterly of Ideas, Art, and Faith,* and is presently editor-in-chief of Wiseblood Books. Joshua has published numerous poems, short stories, and scholarly articles. His first collection of short stories, *This Our Exile,* was published through Angelico Press in January 2018.

Extraordinary Spirit: The Poems of Anya Krugovoy Silver
by Susan L. Miller

When, in August of 2018, Anya Krugovoy Silver died, the world lost a poet of great generosity and intensity. Anya was granted a Guggenheim in April, and it seemed that after a career of prolific and urgent writing, accomplished while working, mothering, and bearing up under metastatic breast cancer, she would be granted the leisure to focus primarily on her poetry. Instead, on Monday, August 6, she died. She had been preparing most of the past decade for death, thinking and writing about it, but even so, her death felt sudden and unexpected.

One of the astounding effects of Anya's life's work is that it was so equally balanced between a joyful appreciation of the beauty of the world and a steely understanding of the brutal and horrific. Each book she wrote tried her themes in new ways, but as a body of work, the four books stand as a record of her consistent concerns: beauty and mortality. Her work engages with history as well as with the domestic. Because Anya held a PhD in English, her poems also allude to many works of literature, demonstrating the strength of her reading. In the poems, she is unashamed to be feminine, feminist, religious, rebellious, ecstatic, woeful, a child, a woman. Her vulnerability and her strength do not admit weakness. Instead, like the authors of the Psalms, she rages, complains, questions, and argues with God. In an early poem, "Good Friday," an angel appears to her in a dream and says, "*Obey the law.*" She argues until he amends his order: "*Obey the spirit of the law.*" She is fierce in her pursuit of the spiritual world, and effusive in her praise of the beauty she lived to witness.

Her first book, *The Ninety-Third Name of God* (2010), contains poems she wrote over a long span of time, between thirty-four and forty. During this span, she was diagnosed with inflammatory breast cancer while she was pregnant with her only child. The first section of the book is brief, including poems about her childhood, her youth, and her marriage. In "The Poem in My Childhood," many of her poetic concerns are laid out. The first line says "The poem was the wood and the way out of the wood, the dog I summoned with my tears, my father's proof for the efficacy of prayer." This line is rooted in folktales and the Bible: the wood is a forest, trouble, the crucifixion, the miracle of the lost one being found and rescued. "In church, the poem, male and female, stood half with my father and half with my mother," she writes, evoking family, religion, and power in one image. A grandmother appears, then dies: "I was afraid at my grandmother's funeral to lean down and kiss her face. / The poem growing inside me shriveled. It had grown fat on my grandmother's butter and icons." Silver recalls a story from her childhood, in which her teacher repeatedly scolded her for gazing out the window: "At school...the poem hid in my pocket. / The teacher accused me of daydreams and stealing pencils." The poem ends with a benediction: "[The poem] draped a stole over my head and heard my confession." With its various images of Silver's family life, her parents Swiss and Ukrainian, and her religious upbringing, she positions her own work in the lineage of both American confessional and European poetry. The poem becomes a sacrament, an identity, a sense of power, and a tradition.

The second section of the book contains poems about cancer. Many of them are focused on other cancer patients. "Everything is Perfect" is especially moving, memorializing "the one who knew / she was dying, who turned/ to the man wiping clean her face / / and said, *Everything is perfect.*" The majority of the poems focus on her own cancer, from the beginning of her treatment ("Biopsy") to her evolving status as a metastatic cancer patient ("Letter to Myself, In Remission, From Myself, Terminal") to her acceptance of her lot in life. In "Nothing," she contrasts her body as it was to its current state, "convulsed and reconfigured:"

> And yet, when I lower myself into the bath
> and receive from my husband's hands the naked body
> of our infant son, the curve of his back nestling
> against my belly, his head against my scar,
> I remember the crescent of skull I saw emerging
> between my legs, its damp promise of life.
> Sitting in the tub, my toes turning water off, then on,
> what would I trade for the life I have now?
>
> The word is *nothing*.

This poem contains two of the elements which would characterize her work and life henceforward: the sober fact of her own mortality, and her joy in the life she had borne and chosen.

The final section bears an epigraph from the Talmud, admonishing that "whoever partakes of this world without offering a benediction has committed an act of sacrilege." The final poems explicitly offer that benediction. Especially appropriate to this theme is the poem "A Handful of Berakhot," ("blessings" in Hebrew). She crafts blessings for many daily activities, including "buckling my son's shoes," "slipping my prosthetic breast into my bra," "viewing a fetus on a sonogram," "a brain scan," "going to the post office," and "hearing of a friend's remission." Each blessing feels like an extension of a traditional Jewish prayer—"Blessed art thou, O Lord, Our God, Ruler of the Universe," they begin, nodding to her husband's religious background. In addition, this section praises and glorifies the family, focusing on her son's birth and her husband's love. "French Toast" is a love poem for a lengthy marriage, an extended metaphor in which the oldest, stalest bread is perfect for making French toast. The final poem in this volume imagines the most transcendent possibilities. In "The Ninety-Third Name of God" she names God "O Light," and she ends the book:

> . . . . If I could immerse
> myself in the ninety-third name of God, I would fear
> no longer tumor or death. I would drink light,
> I would rinse my hair in light, I would rub my shoulders
> with its grains and seeds, I would anoint myself in lunar
> oil, I would make love with every wide-open, glowing
> humming luminous cell of my body pulsing and aflame.

This ecstatic voice reminds us of the most impassioned religious narratives: St. Thérèse of Lisieux or St. Teresa of Avila. The sensual and the spiritual join together, making the body an integral part of the subject's religious feeling. This defiance of her body's illness is the act of a masterful imagination—the kind of imagination which faith, in its purer moments, can engender.

Anya published her next three books rapidly: *I Watched You Disappear* came out in 2014, *From Nothing* in 2016, *Second Bloom* in 2017. (My copy of *Second Bloom*, in fact, is dated 8/10/2017, exactly one year before her obituary in the *New York Times*.) Considering the slowness of publication cycles, the gap between writing her first book and writing these other three is even shorter than it appears. If her first book covered a span of 6 to 8 years of her life, her final books were written increasingly quickly. Her final manuscripts must have been written in one-year increments. (In addition to her full volumes of poetry, Anya also published a chapbook, *Saints of Autumn,* in 2006, and a critical work, *Victorian Literature and the Anorexic Body,* in 2002.) Anya confessed to me that she wrote urgently because of her illness, but the astounding thing about this prolific output is the strength of these poems.

I Watched You Disappear differs significantly from the first book, though many of its concerns remain the same. It begins with "Dedication," addressed to friends with cancer "Because I know that healthy people fear us."

> To you, I dedicate these words.
> Let them stand before God
> like a sheet of flame, smoking
> your precious, flickering names.

The book delves more deeply into feelings of alienation, grief, and suffering, and frames the poems not just as personal narratives, but as stories retold from fairy tales, paintings, and other poems. A whole section of the book imagines tales from Grimm as lenses through which to understand illness, disability, and loss. The poems transform folktales into cancer narratives. In "Owl Maiden," "Her hair fell out first, replaced by quills... Her beloved stands rooted, / watching her flap her hollow bones." In "Maiden in the Glass Mountain," "Still she sits, pretending to be part of the life around her. ... She knows she'll never find a way out, now. / The villagers want her to smile. So she smiles." This metaphor of living with a knowledge that one is dying, the alienation from everyone else's normal business, illuminates how she feels as "she, too, watches the world move past." Several of them are violent—"The Flowered Skull" imagines burning "her captor up to grease and ash"—and others pitiful, as in "Silver Hands," where the protagonist "offered her wrists to the knife. / Two stumps, cauterized by weeping." The final Grimm-inspired poem, "The Hazel Tree," uses a softer tone: the mother in the poem has died, turning herself into a tree, "each nut a word she'd grown to tell her son / now that her speaking human voice was gone: / that she'd chanted stories in his blood, / sown language in his eyes so he could dream."

Other poems, though, confront illness with a new, direct intensity, even rage: "I Watched You Disappear" begins "That fucking doctor killed you. *Killed* you." In "Aren't we all so brave?" she questions, "Why didn't she scream as the smiling doctor / showed her slides of her lung, collapsed like a ball / sieved by a dog's gnawing incisors?" Even the poems about other art examine extremes of suffering and disintegration: a long sequence, "Valentine Gode-Darel (1873-1915)" looks at five paintings Ferdinand Hodler painted of his dying mistress. The images are not pretty, and Silver lingers on their details. "Her body is a solitary animal / on its way to the dirt," reads one part of the sequence. Another watches as "A green stripe / crawls up her neck." "Her nose is larger now. / Her eyes and mouth are wide open, she is almost a corpse," says another. The cool appraisal of her voice in these poems is not entirely dispassionate, though—the poem's sequence goes backwards in time, from the death portrait to a portrait of Valentine as a young, pregnant woman, the object of desire. In this way, Silver shows her wish to turn time around, so that our final image of the woman is not of her end, but of her youth and desirability (though this was only two years before the muse's death from ovarian cancer). However, Silver harbors no illusions about the direction of life.

For a woman so aware of the ravages of illness, Silver insists on beauty, intimacy, and passion. An early poem in the book, "Russian Bells," reads, "That's the prayer I want. / To open my mouth / and ring with my Mother's / voice." "Three Salvations," a poem which begins with the death of Silver's great-uncle, "shot with his wife as passing armies smoked / the village empty, spoiling the yellow fields," also crows, in a different section, "Let husbands feel the round arms of their wives, / and wives laugh in voices rich as custard." In its third section, "Real nuts, we ate on Advent evenings, / sitting around the burning wreath, cracking / hazelnuts and almonds, peeling tangerines." "Sorting Peaches," a poem dedicated to her sister, reads, "And what a gift to palm that globe, / that little world fashioned of sun, / flesh, honeyed veins, napped cheeks." These are poems of ecstasy, family intimacy, love, sensuality. They don't deny their shadow counterparts, and sometimes include them:

Paper Mill, Macon

When the sulfuric stench of the paper mill
wakes me at night, I rise from bed
to find my vial of vanilla cologne
and spritz it twice on the pillow case.
Now, face-down on scented cotton,
I escape the fetid downwind creep
and fall asleep to the false
sweetness of rising yellow cake.
And sometimes, too, I spray perfume
on my son's sheets, or hold my wrist
to his nose, so that after I've died,
the smell of vanilla will return me to him--
overcoming, briefly, the foul smell of loss.

The next book, *From Nothing*, carries on the same work. The poems attend to stories of death even as Silver stubbornly refuses to falter. The title poem is the first: it takes a John Donne quotation as epigraph, "I am re-begot, / Of absence, darkness, death, things which are not." Donne, of course, was a master of the double meaning: "things which are not" here may mean that death is not reborn, but it can also mean that there is no death. Christ's sacrifice for us ensures that our life is eternal, and Silver's poem too makes an argument that we go on. She says "each death I witness makes me more my own," a line which can be read in two ways as well: the deaths of her friends make her more fully herself, and each death brings her into more intimate connection to her own death. Her images—"each excess line of mine erased, / each muscle shredded, each bone sheared"—strip away the body, and finally, as she envisions her body's disintegration, she surprises the reader. "Then I'll be re-begot—the air will shimmer / and my molecules will vault, emerging free. / From darkening days, the light will surge and flee." This pair of images contains the tension of contemplation of her death. While the molecules' flight engenders freedom, the light both surges and flees—leaving us with the image of light growing and darkening almost at the same moment. As a conversation with Donne, Silver's poem plays with the same ambiguities; St. Lucy's Day, of course, celebrates the virgin saint whose eyes were removed and who is always depicted with a crown of lights. From the pain and blindness of her experience, she became a light-bearer—another resonance with the final lines of this poem.

Anya chose a female saint deliberately to preside over these poems about women—breast cancer survivors, wives, mothers, lovers. Two striking poems in this volume argue for fashion as a site of resistance against grief and despair, one which ultimately fails, but can temporarily sustain the subject. "Just Red" begins "while my mother sleeps," and tells us that both Silver's father is "ailing in a nursing home" while her friend is "dying in the hospital." The speaker of the poem is looking in Walgreen's for "lipstick. / As pure a red as I can find—no coral / undertones, no rust or fawn. Just red." Of course these colors are notes in commercial lipsticks, but coral, rust, fawn are also nouns. The coral is from Shakespeare: "Full fathom five thy father lies; / Of his bones are coral made." Rust is the inevitable result of disintegration and oxidation. The fawn symbolizes vulnerability and youth. Silver rejects all these in favor of red: the color of living blood is underscored by the image of scrawling "each color on my wrist, / till the blue veins beneath my skin / disappear behind smeared bars." Back home with the new lipstick, the speaker says, "I limn my lips back out of my wan face. / There they are again: smacky and wanting." The image of the color making her lips reappear seems to imply that her closeness to the deaths of others has robbed her of her own vivacity. The act of painting returns her to the land of the living. Later in the book, though, the poem "Red Never Lasts" takes the image of red nail polish and its thrills—"*Russian Roulette, First Dance, Aperitif, Cherry Pop*"— and admits that

> the chips begin, first at the very tips and edges,
> where you hardly notice, then whole shards.
> Eventually, the fuss is too much to maintain.
> Time to settle into the neutral tones.
> *Baby's Breath, Curtain Call, Bone.*

The names of the colors are intentional. The reds are dangerous, sensual, sexual. The others evoke death, as Baby's Breath is a filler for florists' bouquets, the curtain call is a metaphor for leave-taking, and bone is not even a metaphor.

A few of the poems in this book are the most brutal of her career. "Maid Maleen" and "In the Sanatorium" both deal with murder and suffering, refraining from offering platitudes about it. "Maid Maleen" comes again from a Grimm fairy tale, but it is more severe than the other poems inspired by Grimm. In the story, "she and her servant knife their way through the stone tower" to discover "the country's burned and smashed, the banners rent. / No one alive in the castle or village, the farms just soot." Silver reports, ironically, that "the tale will be made right again. / A prince will fall in love with Maid Maleen, she will prosper / in her gold necklace and never want for food or home." She argues against this kind of myth-making: "Never safety again. Once the smoke's in one's lungs, / it remains forever. The charred trees. The murdered bodies." The effects of trauma in the poem are not abstract reflections, as the reader sees in the next poem, "In the Sanatorium." As Silver's father, "after the war," suffers from tuberculosis, his roommate, "a young Soviet veteran / needed to confess to another Russian." The narrative terrifies: "Under orders, he had taken enemies of the state, shoved them between two stopped trains, / and burned them to death. Then swept away remains." Among them, reports the speaker, was "my father's father." Though the veteran is unaware of this fact and asks "Could he ever be forgiven for such a sin?" the father is "unable to respond"— possibly due to the weakness of his lungs, possibly due to his horror. The father nevertheless remains "Riven, six more decades, between two ghosts… Both beyond any word he might have spoken." This descent into the darkest human stories shows Silver's capacity for looking human suffering in the face, refusing to qualify or deny true evil. Such poems take their place in a lineage of profound war poetry, much of it European, which deals with the horrors of the twentieth century.

As a counterpoint, the surprise of the book is its frank sexuality, both in portraits of marital happiness and in images of the female body of the subject. Though her love poems for her husband are tender, intimate, and restrained, others are forward. In "St. Paul's Letter to the Ephesians, Lent," Silver argues with Paul's damnation of "fornicators." "As if all the earth were bleak midwinter," she scoffs. "Meanwhile, Paul, plum trees are bruising / the church parking lot, cherry trees readying / their exuberant and joyful climax of pink," she admonishes. The poem is frankly sexy: "the palest pink, nipple-pink, pink of my dry / (I lick them) lips, of my amoral animal body." The way she describes the female body is an act of open rebellion. She ends, "I love that keen, painful twisting of desire, / the tight bud of it straining against its husk." The red lips of "Just Red" are a call to live; the pinks of this poem evoke orgasms. Reading her words, the reader experiences her intelligence, her defiance, and her honesty as well as her sexiness, and Silver asserts sexuality as another form of worship. The final poem of the collection, "Three Roses," describes the two breasts of the speaker, a breast cancer survivor, as a red rose (where her mastectomy scar lives) and a white one, adding a third, golden rose in her sternum. The red rose is a mystical lens: "My eyes watch through the rose's flaming center, / crimson, as if through a hundred desiring eyes, / till the world prisms: quartz pink, blush, vermilion." The juxtaposition of the Sacred Heart and the gaze of a type of third eye makes the scarred area active, a presence rather than an absence. The white rose is described in various images: "milk-soaked lace, a newborn ewe's plush," "eager to be touched, soft as talcum to the finger." Though it is sensual, the images of milk and talcum lead us to images of mothering and nursing. The third, "rarest rose of all," "spreads petals in the chambers of my heart, / gold touching every dark cell of my body with love." Her final lines evoke Keats, another poet who died too young: "Lay your hands on my chest—here, I give it to you. / Feel your palm on my skin heat and spark." Keats' own "This living hand, now warm and capable" ends with the image of his hand extended: "see here it is—I hold it toward you," but his intention in that poem is to *challenge* the reader to connect to him in life, as he has invoked his own death to bring survivor's guilt to his beloved. Rather than challenging, Silver offers herself as a gift. The rose as a symbol of Mary's love, and divine love, communicates through her body and her words—an enactment of the penultimate poem's exhortation to "Listen to the Holy Ghost. / She blows through you, / she blows her poems right through."

The final book she published in her living days, *Second Bloom*, is the longest of the four. The poems range in subject and tone. They include earlier subjects: the suffering of friends, her love for her husband and son, elegies for her father, hospital poems. They also make her religious practice most explicit: though previous books discuss worship and prayer, rites and rituals, especially her Ash Wednesday poems, this book has an entire section devoted to poems that follow the liturgical calendar. Though all of her previous books of poetry were published by LSU, Anya chose the Poiema poetry series for this final volume, partly because she felt committed to these religious poems. They have a tone of persistence and insistence, even as they grieve. Despite a certain rawness here, Anya remained committed to beauty.

Many of these poems emerged as her metastasis progressed, and she clearly faces up to her cancer here. In "How to Talk to a Sick Woman" her tone is sharp; Anya had lost patience with the ways many well people talked about illness. (This poem feels very much like the Anya I knew: though she was incredibly gracious, she didn't censor herself in our conversations, and I had heard about the occasions that inspired this poem.) "Do not make me your nightmare," she begins, and lists off the ways one shouldn't address cancer patients. "Refrain from invoking me among / the *A, B, C's of your fear*," she states flatly. "My bad luck is not your good luck. / (And by the way, fuck you.)" She runs down those who make her an object of pity: "I find it dreary. / Nor am I the Madonna of cancer, / your bow-arched Amazon." The Amazon image resonates especially well: in the age of Jeff Bezos, people forget that Amazon warriors cut off their breasts so their aim could be sharper. But breast cancer survivors don't choose to lose a breast, nor is it a cancer survivor's job to be anyone's superhero. Anya didn't want to be a symbol, just a human being. Her irony proceeds:

> I don't deserve praise.
> My days are as ordinary as yours.
> And when I die, what will you do?
> You'll have lost your light-strung Santos.

The cutting tone of these lines—"what will you do?"—should give anyone pause and prevent turning those among us into objects of pity or piety. "I don't dread death more than you do. / Only I get to say I'm tragic" she closes, claiming ownership of her narrative.

Even in illness, she retained hope, as the religious poems show, but her faith was not blind. In "Third Advent," she plays on the pink candle, representative of joy, that is placed on the third Sunday. The poem marks time: "This winter, I turn forty-eight. Another year has grown to fullness." Then we realize the reason for her personal celebration: "Cancer has not yet killed me. / I have drunk again from the unicorn's / horn; it has healed me, for now," she says. "God kicks against the rocking womb, waiting," the poem ends. But in other poems in this sequence, her faith in mercy is shaken. "Fourth Advent" begins as a lament:

> I lie beside a friend in bed,
> weeping, because she doesn't want *a better place*.
> How bleak the next life to her grieving sons,
> who need their mother here, on earth—
> her silly wigs, her marathons, her fingers
> deftly pinching dumplings for the feast.

Even for the faithful, death is hard to take, and the details she offers here particularize her friend as a mother, an athlete, a person with a sense of humor. (Anya shared that sense of humor, wearing a cotton-candy pink wig in her Facebook profile picture after being told she'd need to enter chemo again, and proudly reporting that her son cracked up when her prosthetic breast ended up at her waist.) Some of the moral weight of these poems lies in their refusal of metaphor: their directness about what will be lost suffices. Our human lives are precious to those we love, always, enough that she ends the poem with complaint: "Merciful one, begotten of woman, understand / how difficult it is to trust that you are kind." The plangent irony of "begotten of woman" helps us to remember how this particular injustice affects women disproportionately. In Christian practice, we recognize suffering as redemptive, drawing us closer to Christ, but witnessing the suffering of others still feels specifically painful and engenders frustration and anger when those we love cannot complete their promise on earth.

The final two poems of the book, "A Briar" and "August," are a matched set, sharing the symbol of the briar and the rose. In the first, the briar

> bore into her sternum,
> then wound through her lungs,
> its little thorns pricking
> the sleeves of her breath.

This metaphor for her cancer is clear: it "caused her to cough, / or slashed her chest muscles / till her body spasmed in pain." Though it reads like a fairy tale illness, the body inside it is real. In the final lines of the poem, surprisingly, the briar bursts into "blossoms as big as saucers, / claret roses of petal on petal, / for which, grateful, she wept." Roses, the reader will recall, ended *From Nothing*, and so the final reflection of "August," in which the rose itself "doesn't turn" its "many-hooded gaze" "away / from what approaches" transforms those original roses yet again into a way that the poet can address her life. "To bloom is so foolish / that it must be wisdom," she writes, providing a rationale for her aesthetic. Her insistence on the beauty of the world, even in her lowest moments, shows her tremendous spirit. She refused to only admit the painful parts of life and willed herself to experience the joy that roots itself in beauty.

If *Second Bloom* had been Anya's last book, she still would have produced an extraordinary body of work. However, since her death, her husband Andrew tells me that he has a final manuscript, which she was completing the week she died, and over 500 unpublished poems. This essay is only the first part of an evaluation of her work, and I hope that the future will allow for the second installment, as I become more aware of the work I have not yet seen.

Susan L. Miller is the author of *Communion of Saints* (Paraclete Press, 2017). She has published poems in journals, such as *Iowa Review*, *Meridian*, *Los Angeles Review*, *Image*, *Sewanee Theological Review*, and *Commonweal* as well as in the anthologies *Collective Brightness: LGBTIQ Poets on Faith, Religion, and Spirituality* and *St. Peter's B-list: Contemporary Poems Inspired by the Saints*. Miller has twice been the recipient of the Dorothy Sargent Rosenberg prize and also received a nomination for the Pushcart Prize. She teaches creative writing at Rutgers University and lives in Brooklyn, New York.

The Charlotte Poems of Richard Wilbur and the Shape of a Marriage
by Kathleen Marks

    Married 65 years to Charlotte Ward (Charlee), Richard Wilbur would on the occasion of a birthday or anniversary write a poem for or about his wife. Ten such recognized poems— "June Light," "Piazza di Spagna, Early Morning," "A Simile for Her Smile," "Galveston, 1961," "A Late Aubade," "C Minor," "The Catch," "For C.," "The Reader," "The House"— reveal the shape of Wilbur's happy marriage as a foundational source of order, lending the balance that marks Wilbur's whole body of poetry, the perfection of which seemed inaccessible to some critics. Yet when he died in 2017 at the age of 96, Wilbur's "inaccessible perfection" had led him to be generally considered one of the finest American poets in the formalist tradition of his mentor, Robert Frost—having served as Poet Laureate of the United States in 1987. A sometime muse, Charlotte—whose "grandfather had in 1894 been the first editor to publish Frost's poems" (Gioia par.8)—was a good reader of Wilbur's poetry as he celebrates in a later poem about her, "The Reader" (*Collected Poems*, 2004). She was also a good ward, as her name suggests, of her husband's direction: Wilbur once said, "I know that I would be capable of great disorder and emotional confusion if I were out of my wife's orbit; she really has greatly steadied me" (Brooker 517). Written between 1947 and shortly after her death in 2007, the Charlotte poems give us a look into Richard Wilbur's "universe [...] wherein chaos tends to move towards meaningful shape" (Lenz par. 6). These poems trace the orbital path of his marriage, a love incarnate, as fundamental to his life's work.

    Charlotte's love is likened in its completeness to a pear, long seen as an image of the female shape, in the first poem about her and their new marriage, "June Light" (*The Beautiful Changes*, 1947). With many of these poems, the poet addresses his wife in the second person: in the light of Juno's month, he recollects, "your love looked as simple and entire / As that picked pear you tossed me, and your face / As legible as pearskin's fleck and trace." If "The Apology" (*Things of this World*, 1956) is yet an additional poem about Charlotte, where the speaker addresses his love as "apple-heart," she may be seen as at the core of things for him. Certainly, this June woman's handing over an Edenic fruit to her husband recalls that primary union of Eve and Adam; indeed, as the tossed pear falls into his hands, signifying perhaps a love that will endure ups and downs, "it seemed as blessed with truth and new delight / As must have been the first great gift of all." In the "naïve," youthful light, the poet turns in these final lines of his sonnet, to affirm the felicity of *the* fall, and thereby all falls, as redeemed. The reader may see a thematic consistency with Wilbur's oft-anthologized poem, "Love Calls us to the Things of This World" (*Things of This World*, 1956), where love—to the poet who was a life-long member of the Episcopal Church—is a redemptive descent into, yet elevation of, this world.

In the second, shorter poem written for Charlee, "Piazza di Spagna, Early Morning" (*Things of This World*, 1956), marriage means that Wilbur can see as though directly something she described to him: "I can't forget" he writes, "How she stood at the top of that long marble stair / Amazed, and then with a sleepy pirouette / Went dancing down to the fountain-quieted square." Charlee had spent a late night out with a male friend when Richard was too sick to tag along, and she returned with a happy tale of her adventures of drinking from Roman fountains (Bagg 160). Something maybe about the "impersonal loneliness" on his wife's face, puts to his imagination that Charlee is "not then a girl / But as it were a reverie of that place," and as a sort of frolic or daydream, she comes down the Spanish steps toward the fountain "As when a leaf, petal, or thin chip / Is drawn to the falls of a pool and, / circling a moment above it, / Rides on over the lip- / Perfectly beautiful, perfectly ignorant of it." A recent biography, *Let us Watch Richard Wilbur*, notes that this poem is "Fellini-esque" in its "cinematic focus" and, in this moment of literal drinking in the city, the movement is toward the Bernini "fountain shaped like a sinking ship" (160). Here we get a sense of Charlee as drawn by forces other than her husband, and yet as one who, despite a quality of loneliness, circles back, "perfectly beautiful" in her "ignorance" of the potential danger of these forces.

Perhaps there is a touch of jealousy in this poem or a sense that he could lose her. There seems to be a threat to the form of his marriage, a fear of devolving into chaos, a bit of the "terror" that Wilbur tells us is there in his poetry, a "feeling that the order of things is in peril or in doubt, that there are holes in things through which one might drop" (Mariani par. 24). Yet his young but strong marriage is as a stay against confusion and anxiety, and Charlee figures as a center that holds and does not drop or sink. Her orbit, imaged as "circling a moment above" never goes too far in or over; like the "fixed foot" of John Donne's famous compass, she justifies her husband's journey, and yet persists in her own place, ever rooted in love and ever revolving closely around love's source.

Just as location and directionality are present in many of the Charlotte poems, so too is water, in fountains or as bodies. "Simile for her Smile," (*Things of This World*, 1956), arises from the cliché of a smile stopping, or "Balking the hasty traffic." This poem marks an exchange of his simile for her smile, which seems not to come for him *per se*, but does come regularly in response to her reading his poetry, perhaps especially to his poems for or about Charlotte. The very anticipation of her response lends to the boat's passing its poetic quality as smile, as though it is creative of his simile, inspiring both poem and critical reception, of which hers counts the most. In the coming of the boat-as-smile, it's "smooth approach" yet interrupts the filmy surface of this water where "oil-smoke rarifies," producing the "slip / Slip of the silken river past the sides." The smile is for Wilbur a revelation, a slipping off of the sheen of the "silken river"—something like the "liquefaction" of Herrick's "silks" or the "silken tent" of Frost— to momentarily expose the body—that mysterious and fluid place of materials where the secret poetic churning, the "cascading of the paddle wheel" operates. Charlotte seems something of a figure of speech for him and for his poetry and, without her, he would be without a muse.

Charlotte's body is glimpsed as something more in the sea imagery marking "Galveston, 1961," composed at the time but not published until 2009 in *The New Yorker*. In this love poem, with words that remind of Hopkins and reference myth, the speaker addresses a nymph no more, but a "goddess," who came out of the ocean Venus-like, one supposes, "And still half seem to be, / Though close and clear you lie, / Whom droplets of the sea / Emboss and magnify." As though the sea is where transformation into something rich and strange can occur, he begins: "You who in crazy-lensed / Clear water fled your shape, / By choppy shallows flensed / And shaken like a cape." The sea becomes a glass to see the ways in which the beautiful changes and in which the graceful energy of Charlee can, even on a family beach day, become spliced with ancient forces and sources of life.

How the mundane and the universal interact is crucial to the balance of Wilbur's vision, as we are beginning to see, but his stable marriage allows him a certain relaxation not afforded many lovers. "A Late Aubade" (*Walking to Sleep*, 1969) is a longer *carpe diem* poem without the same kind of time urgency. It might better be termed a *festina lente* ("hurry up slowly") poem wherein the poet praises leisure. After listing all the things Charlee could be off in different directions doing (reading at the library, or shopping, or "lunching") instead of spending the morning in bed with him, the speaker asks, "Isn't this better?" Women want to save time, he suggests, and so he importunes, "Think of all the time you are not / Wasting." He responds to her real or imagined question: "It's almost noon, you say? / "If so, Time flies, and I need not rehearse / The rosebuds-theme of centuries of verse." This is, however, the opposite of "gather ye rosebuds." This is no one-morning stand, and the day is less seized than embraced.

Because time goes by when one makes the love that animates all activities, the poet has neglected his aubade, or musical announcement of dawn, until almost midday. But, "if you *must* go, / Wait for a while," he says. A "while" might allow forces that press against themselves to achieve the balance between the masculine and the feminine, the profane and the sacred, the night and the day. But, he goes on, "then slip downstairs / And bring us up some chilled white wine, / And some blue cheese, and crackers, and some fine Ruddy-skinned pears." Here, I think, is a coded message from the man who was a cryptographer in the war: the white, blue, and red of American lovers in France? Charlee does not strike as a woman to be sent to the kitchen, and she is surely a woman who, as the poet writes of her in "The Catch" (*New and Collected*, 1987), can deliver a "fierce frown and hard-pursed lips," even if only about herself.

Yet the image evoked here in "Aubade" reiterates the security of the return that was seen in "Piazza di Spagna, Early Morning." Charlotte is not a Porphyria to be captured by her lover; she would understand the offer of more love hinted at in Wilbur's mention of "Ruddy-skinned pears"—to a woman who, according to him, "had rather lie in bed and kiss / Than anything"—as a promise to write her into one of his poems, as another gift exchange of simile for smile, where she would be sung by the artist to whom she is, perhaps somewhat despite herself, very attracted. They are nourished not only by food as fuel, but as art. Wine, cheese, crackers, and pears are things made and retrieved quickly, but they are to be savored together as though part of a still life, a waiting life, with the potential lively break of a cracker. For the man of faith, this marriage is a coming together, a Eucharistic giving of thanks for the commutual possibilities of opposites, a feast of the senses and things of this world that is more than a foretaste of what is to come.

Wilbur refers to Charlotte as "C" in the titles of two of the poems. "C Minor" (*Mind Reader*, 1976) is a nod to the influence of Beethoven's favorite key as a great organizer of experience and its kinship with Charlotte. His "For C.," first published by *The New Yorker* in the Valentine's Day issue of 1997, is less evocative of Cupid than his mother Venus—as the brightest body with a traceable path in the visible heavens. It stands as one of Wilbur's great poems as it provides some rub against the perfection of even the ideal marriage. While each of the first three stanzas reflects on a pair of lovers who break up, and the final two stanzas are about his marriage that has endured, there are signs that the angst of lost love has not gone unnoticed and has maybe been momentarily desired. In Wilbur's life, there was an incident over which two sides have argued: one insisting there was an affair during the war years and the other saying there is no evidence except a photograph. Wilbur sent word of the existence of a photo with a "sexy-looking French Frail," as Charlotte called her in a letter of response to her husband that shows a Penelopean cleverness to rival his poetry. She continued, "You must remember that I have great respect for your essential *taste* [. . .] and great faith in [. . .] our common love so that whatever you did couldn't possibly touch the good that ties us irrevocably together" (Cynthia Haven blog). If a pull on their marriage, it seems only to have lent the properly elliptical shape to Charlotte's steadying orbit, the marriage having reached its 55th anniversary at the time of this poem's writing.

But the poet lends such a "grand scale" to the parting lovers' goodbyes that some readers might wonder, if only for the span of the first three stanzas, whether Wilbur might find attractive the freedom of a lack of commitment. Be it the "clash of elevator gates," as the woman in the first stanza leaves "bound forever west;" or the "Bright Perseids" that "flash and crumble" for the second "high romance;" or the "three thousand miles of knitting seas" it takes to "unmake / The amorous rough and tumble" of the third couple's "wake," there is excitement and drama here.

The "fine tristesse" in the lovers' regrets, both bitter and sweet, are denied Wilbur. In turning to Charlotte, "my love," it takes a couple of final stanzas to avoid defining their marriage merely against the broken-hearted. These married lovers "cannot share / the frequent vistas" of the "large despair" that is fodder for many a poem, and where everything, including love, is "swept to nothingness:" a nothingness that has the appeal of passion but may not after all be a relief to a love poet. For, like Dylan Thomas' laboring not apart from lovers' griefs, "but for the common wages / of their most secret heart," the Wilburs' marriage "has the quality of something made," or crafted, that gives shape and form to the loves of the above stanzas. Because "Still," says the poet, "there's a certain scope in that long love / Which constant spirits are the keepers of." The "Still" is a pivot away from the lure of the highly romantic downward into the love that critics may call "tame and staid," speaking of Wilbur's marriage or his poetry.

The poet's "certain scope," however, allows him to pronounce almost in a doubling down that his love derives from stillness, not from tameness—from the "pause" in "Simile for her Smile," from the "wait" of "A Late Aubade," from Charlee's willingness to return and share from the well of love's source that has been repeated in the many poetic gifts for C. Here in "For C." their love is, therefore, so far from being "staid" along the lines of the criticism leveled at him, that it is in fact "a wild sostenuto of the heart." This couple's love is the central sustaining pedal that prolongs only those notes in a musical passage that are pressed down. Wilbur's marriage, placed at the bottom of the poem, is pressured and activated to sustain itself as the base, or pillar, or pattern for all lovers. But, there is more: theirs is "A passion joined to courtesy and art" that seems akin to the Dantean pleasure that arises from the union of reason and art and that reaches its highest poetic expression in the light of heaven. Here, it is not only the passion of sexual love, but the passion of suffering, which this load-bearing love in the poem's foundational stanzas endures, that dignifies the "long love" of their marriage.

Wilbur tells us that the line in the Mass he responds to most is "Lift up your hearts!" (Mariani par. 24). Being joined to courtesy and art, the passion is shared and thus less burdensome; it lifts itself, and us, up in the poem's last two lines that are as a conceit—an extended metaphor of love as something made and not made, "Like a good fiddle, like the rose's scent, / Like a rose window or the firmament." Wilbur has said of these lines, "It's rather a lot to have a love poem soar into the firmament," but he gets away with it because, as he says further, it is "balanced by something as modest and earthly as a good fiddle" (Poetry Readings). This balance of scales achieved in the poem is earned, and the "firmament," while indicating the heavens above, is also firmly rooted, by definition and by its position as the poem's final, all-encompassing word—giving solid, steadfast support and rounded, architectural shape to the whole poem and to their marriage as sacrament.

As we move from the sexually suggestive, pear-shaped "good fiddle" to the likewise suggestive "rose's scent" and upward to the almost fragrant "rose window" that yet beholds church, the things of this world are never left behind, but partake of the firmament. Love itself is not "swept to nothingness," but is preserved in the stillness of marriage, distilled even further in lyric. In fact, this series of images seems to make present the goddess whose birth was implied in "Galveston, 1961." Venus, as a primordial love, manifests herself in *her* rose—in the flower's scent and in her planet's orbital path patterned in the cinquefoil of beautifully fashioned rose windows. The shapely being who came out of the sea fully formed, stains white roses red with the blood of her cut foot as she runs, but—unlike the overarching sense of fortunate timing that tracks this married couple—arrives too late to save her lover. And Shakespeare's "Venus and Adonis" is seen in both the content and heroic sestet form of "For C."

The firmament, then, is as much of this world as it is of the next; it is as though the poet sees the point in time where the made and the unmade are joined. The world of lyric has its own primal sense of time in which there is, says Louise Cowan, "a yearning for the moment of creation, when the form of things existed in the divine mind, imprinting matter with the supernally joyous stamp of form" (13). This Wilbur marriage stretches the boundaries of its own existence, and its shape purportedly existed in Charlotte's mind since her childhood. Her friends say Charlotte knew that her "ideal husband had to be a prominent man from Amherst [. . .] and a poet whose first name was Richard" (Bagg 7). By titling his poem "For C.," as in "foresee," a word found elsewhere in his poetry, Wilbur seems to be honoring his wife's foresight as well as seeing that the scope of his lyrics springs from a deep and abiding love of the world in which Charlotte is both herself and yet a Venusian muse—in this world but not of it, lonely and yet a constant presence—measuring the trajectory of the poet's own vision.

The final Charlotte poem, published after her death, returns to the domestic. In "The House," from his last volume of poetry (*Anterooms*, 2010), the poet struggles to remember his late wife's description of a house—known to her only in her dreams—as though they are truly separated: "What did she tell me of that house of hers? / White gatepost, terrace; fanlight of the door; / a widow's walk above the bouldered shore." Since he outlived her, this widower ponders her whereabouts, knowing that without her he knows not quite where to find her: "Only a foolish man would hope to find / That haven." Sad though it is, Wilbur is also saying that he wishes to continue on the orbital path she helped set for him.

He remembers that "sometimes, on waking, she would close her eyes / For a last look at that white house she knew."

The "impersonal loneliness" that belongs to her as well as the generous sharing of herself through stories about the source of love flowing from the fountains in "Piazza di Spagna" was and always will be Charlotte, and now she remains as absent and present as ever. Sensing this presence, he still tells her about his dreams: "Night after night, my love, I put to sea." Wilbur can echo the confident "my love" from "For C." because Charlee has provided him with a vision of the architecture of her dream house. Her destination has been seen, its foundations laid. Her foresightful inclusion of a "widow's walk," as though she knew she would be the first to go, provides her a prospect. From it she can have an unimpeded vision of her husband at sea where he has often found his Venusian Charlee. Thus, as "fixed foot," does she see his journey through to its rounded fullness. Wilbur is a love poet for "the long run" (Rose par. 4), one whose "long love" will be better appreciated, perhaps now and in the future.

Works Cited

Bagg, Robert and Mary Bagg. *Let Us Watch Richard Wilbur: A Biographical Study*. Amherst: University of Massachusetts Press, 2017.

Brooker, Jewel Spears. "A Conversation with Richard Wilbur." *Christianity and Literature*. 42.4 (1993): 517-539.

Cowan, Louise. "Introduction: The Lyric Nostalgia." *The Prospect of Lyric*. Ed. Bainard Cowan. Dallas: Dallas Institute Publications, 2012.

Gioia, Dana. "Richard Wilbur: A Critical Survey of His Career." http://danagioia.com/essays/reviews-and-authors-notes/richard-wilbur-a-critical-survey-of-his-career/. Accessed 19 Feb. 2019.

Haven, Cynthia. "'Touching the Good': on Richard Wilbur: and Charlee Wilbur gets the last word." *The Book Haven: Cynthia Haven's Blog for the Written Word*. Stanford University. http://bookhaven.stanford.edu/2017/11/touching-the-good-on-richard-wilbur/. Accessed 21 Dec. 2018.

Lenz, Millicent. "Laying Claim to the World: The 'Glorious Energy' of Richard Wilbur's Poetry for Children." *Alice's Academy*. Ed. Elizabeth L. Pandolfo Briggs. https://www lib.latrobe.edu.au/ojs/index.php/tlg/article/view/237/234 . Accessed 21 Dec. 2018.

Mariani, Paul. "A 1995 interview with Richard Wilbur from *Image: A Journal of the Arts and Religion*." *Modern American Poetry*. http://www.english.illinois.edu/

maps/poets/s_z/wilbur/imageinterview.htm. Accessed 8 Feb. 2019.

Poetry Readings: 'For C'. Richard Wilbur-Poet (52/83)." *Youtube*, Web Stories - Life Stories of Remarkable People, uploaded 10 Oct. 2017. https://www.youtube.com/ watch?v=-g-b9oyAzm0&t=5s.

Rose, Phyllis. "Citizen Poet." *Poetry Foundation*. https://www.poetryfoundation.org/poetrymagazine/articles/68325/citizen-poet. Accessed 8 Feb. 2018.

Kathleen Marks is Associate Professor, and Interim Chair, of English and Speech in the College of Professional Studies at St. John's University, NYC. She received her Ph.D. at the University of Dallas in 2000 and has written several articles on classical and modern works of literature, such as Homer's *Odyssey*, Vergil's *Aeneid*, and Toni Morrison's *The Bluest Eye*. Author of the book, *Toni Morrison's* Beloved *and the Apotropaic Imagination* (University of Missouri Press, 2002)—about the intersection between African-American literature and ancient Greek religion—Kathleen lives in Queens, New York City, with her professor husband and high-school-aged daughter.

Poets' Biographies

Joseph Bathanti is former Poet Laureate of North Carolina (2012-14) and recipient of the 2016 North Carolina Award for Literature. He is the author of seventeen books, including the novel,*The Life of the World to Come*, from University of South Carolina Press in 2014, and *The 13th Sunday after Pentecost*, from LSU Press in 2016. Bathanti is McFarlane Family Distinguished Professor of Interdisciplinary Education & Writer-in-Residence of Appalachian State University's Watauga Residential College.

Jill Peláez Baumgaertner is the author of five collections of poetry; a textbook/anthology, *Poetry*; and *Flannery O'Connor: A Proper Scaring*, in addition to over forty essays. She also edited the poetry anthology, *Imago Dei*. She has been a Fulbright scholar and is the winner of several poetry awards. She is Professor of English Emerita and former Dean of Humanities and Theological Studies at Wheaton College, where she also served as Acting Provost. She currently serves as poetry editor of *The Christian Century*.

Alan Berecka now works at Del Mar College in Corpus Christi where he has refrained from chasing any library patrons for over 20 years. He has published four collections of poems, the latest of which is *The Hamlet of Stittville*. His poetry has appeared in *The Christian Century, Ruminate, The Windhover, The Penwood Review* and the anthology *St. Peter's B-list*. In 2017, he was named the first poet laureate of Corpus Christi. aberecka@yahoo.com.

Tim Bete, OCDS, is poetry editor at *IntegratedCatholicLife.org* and former director of the University of Dayton's national writers' workshop. He is author of *In the Beginning...There Were No Diapers*, a book of essays on the mysteries of parenting, as well as the poetry book, *The Raw Stillness of Heaven*. More of his work can be found at www.GrayRising.com

Kathleen Bradley is a retired art teacher residing in an artist's community in San Francisco, California.

Pat Brisson writes books for children and poetry for adults. Her picture book, *The Summer My Father Was Ten,* won the Christopher Award in 1998. Her poem, "The Cleverness of Seeds," recently won an honorable mention in the Thomas Merton Poetry of the Sacred contest. She has two poems forthcoming in *Third and Fourth Wave Feminism: The Future of Unruly Women in the Catholic Church.* She lives with her husband in Phillipsburg, New Jersey.

Debra Bruce's most recent book is *Survivors' Picnic*, and her poems have been published widely in journals including *The Cincinnati Review, Innisfree Poetry Journal, Mezzo Cammin*, and *Poetry*. She is Professor Emeritus at Northeastern Illinois University in Chicago and sings in the choir at St. Nicholas parish in Evanston, Illinois. Visit debrabrucepoet.com

Mary Buchinger is the author of three books of poetry, most recently e i n f ü h l u n g/*in feeling* (2018) and *Aerialist* (2015). Her poetry is permanently installed in the city of Cambridge where she lives and has served as a Cambridge Poetry Ambassador. She was a Peace Corps volunteer, is President of the New England Poetry Club (founded by Robert Frost, Amy Lowell, Conrad Aiken) and teaches at MCPHS University in Boston.

Roxana L. Cazan is an Assistant Professor of English and Women's Studies at Saint Francis University, Pennsylvania, where she teaches world and postcolonial literature and creative writing. Most recently, her poems appeared in *Construction Magazine, Cold Creek Review, The Healing Muse, Adanna Literary Journal, Watershed Review, Allegro Poetry, the Peeking Cat Anthology,* and others. She is the author of a poetry book, *The Accident of Birth* (Main Street Rag, 2017)

Yuan Changming started to learn the English alphabet in Shanghai at age 19 and published monographs on translation before leaving China. Currently, Yuan lives a semi-retired life in Vancouver, where he edits *Poetry Pacific* with Allen Qing Yuan. Credits include ten Pushcart nominations, *Best of the Best Canadian Poetry (2008-2017)* and *BestNewPoemsOnline* among others.

Erica Charis-Molling's writing has been published in *Glass, Dark Matter, Anchor, Vinyl, Entropy,* and *Mezzo Cammin*. She was the Eco-Justice Anthology Support Intern at Split This Rock for *Ghost Fishing*, released in April 2018. She's an alum of the Bread Loaf Writers' Conference and nearing graduation in her M.F.A. in Creative Writing at Antioch University. She lives in Boston, where she works as a creative writing instructor and librarian.

Richard Cole has published two books of poetry: *The Glass Children* (The University of Georgia Press) and *Success Stories* (Limestone Books). His latest book is a memoir, *Catholic by Choice* (Loyola Press). His work has appeared in *The New Yorker, Poetry, Ruminate, Dappled Things and Image Journal.* Cole works as a freelance business writer in Austin, Texas. More at www.richard-cole.net.

Maryann Corbett's most recent book is *Street View*, her fourth. She is a past winner of the Willis Barnstone Translation Prize and the Richard Wilbur Award, and one of her poems is included in *The Best American Poetry 2018*. Retired now after many years of work for the Minnesota Legislature, she lives in Saint Paul, Minnesota.

A former contributor to *Presence,* **Barbara Crooker**'s most recent book is *The Book of Kells*, with her ninth book, *Some Glad Morning* forthcoming in the Pitt Poetry Series in fall 2019. Her work has appeared in many journals, including *The Christian Century, America,* and *Sojourners.* She was the recipient of the Thomas Merton Poetry of the Sacred Award and is a poetry editor for *Italian American.* Crooker lives and works in rural northeastern Pennsylvania.

Joanna Currey is a second-year MFA candidate in poetry at Vanderbilt University in Nashville, Tennessee. She earned a BA in English and Poetry Writing from the University of Virginia and writes mostly about plants, bodies, and religion. Joanna serves as the art editor and poetry co-editor for *Nashville Review*, and she hopes one day to record a pop/rock album, read every book she owns, and become a pretty good gardener.

Jim Daniels' recent poetry books include *Rowing Inland* and *Street Calligraphy* (2017) and *The Middle Ages* (2018). He is the author of five collections of fiction, four produced screenplays, and has edited six anthologies, including the forthcoming *R E S P E C T: The Poetry of Detroit Music*, forthcoming in 2019 from Michigan State University Press, along with his next collection of short fiction, *The Perp Walk.*

P. S. Dean is a Mississippi native, and he received an MFA in poetry from the University of Mississippi in 2013. Currently, he lives in New Orleans and is working on his first book.

Jessica G. de Koninck is the author of one full-length collection, *Cutting Room*, and one chapbook, *Repairs*. Her work has appeared in *Diode, Mom Egg Review, Poetry Magazine* and twice been featured on *Verse Daily*. A long-time resident of Montclair, New Jersey, and a retired attorney, she serves on the editorial board of *Jewish Currents* magazine.

Lynn Domina is the author of eight books, including her most recent collection of poetry, *Framed in Silence*. Her work also appears or is forthcoming in *The Saranac Review, The Anglican Theological Review, Tiferet,* and several other anthologies and periodicals. She serves as Head of the English Department at Northern Michigan University and as creative writing editor at *The Other Journal*. She lives with her family in Marquette, Michigan.

Sharif S. Elmusa co-edited with Gregory Orfalea *Grape Leaves: A Century of Arab-American Poetry* and is author of a book of poems, *Flawed Landscape*. His poems and essays appeared in numerous print and online magazines, including most recently, *The Massachusetts Review, Mizna, The Indian Quarterly* (India), *Jadaliyya.com, Voxpopulisphere.com*. Elmusa taught at the American University in Cairo, Egypt, for many years, and also at Georgetown, Qatar, and Yale. He is Palestinian by birth and American by citizenship.

Katie Farris is the author of *BOYSGIRLS* (Marick Press) and co-editor of *Gossip and Metaphysics: Russian Modernist Writers* (Tupelo Press). Her work has won awards from *The Massachusetts Review* and *Fairy Tale Review*, among others.

Andrew Frisardi's poems appear recently or are forthcoming in *Able Muse, Alabama Literary Review, First Things*, Measure, *The Modern Age, New Verse News, The Orchards*, and *Think*; and in a collection, *Death of a Dissembler* (White Violet Press). His most recent book is an annotated translation: *Dante's Convivio: A Dual-Language Critical Edition* (Cambridge UP). He has received a Guggenheim Fellowship, a Hawthornden Fellowship, and the Raizis / de Palchi Translation Award from the Academy of American Poets.

Stephen Gibson's *Self-Portrait in a Door-Length Mirror* won the 2017 Miller Williams Prize, selected by Billy Collins, University of Arkansas Press. Earlier collections include *The Garden of Earthly Delights Book of Ghazals* (Texas Review Press), *Rorschach Art Too* (2014 Donald Justice Prize, Story Line Press), *Paradise* (Miller Williams finalist, University of Arkansas Press), *Frescoes* (Idaho Book Prize, Lost Horse Press), *Masaccio's Expulsion* (MARGIE/Intuit House Book Prize), and *Rorschach Art* (Red Hen).

Dominic Gideon is a seminarian for the Diocese of Cleveland in his first year of theological studies at St. Mary Seminary in Cleveland, Ohio. Prior to that, he spent four years at Borromeo Seminary and obtained a B.A. in English and philosophy from John Carroll University. Gideon is a Cleveland native with a Rust-belt influence to his work and a Catholic worldview steeped into his imagery.

Maria Mazziotti Gillan, American Book Award recipient for *All That Lies Between Us* (Guernica Editions) and author of twenty-three books, founded the Poetry Center in Paterson, New Jersey, is editor of the *Paterson Literary Review* and is Professor Emerita of English and creative writing at Binghamton University-SUNY. Recent publications include *What Blooms in Winter* (NYQ 2016) and the poetry and photography collaboration with Mark Hillringhouse, *Paterson Light and Shadow* (Serving House Books, 2017).

Ed Granger lives in Lancaster County, Pennsylvania. His poems have appeared in *Little Patuxent Review, Potomac Review, Naugatuck River Review, River Heron Review, Loch Raven Review,* and other journals.

Maryanne Hannan has published poetry in *Gargoyle, the minnesota review, Oxford Poetry* (UK), *Rabbit* (AU), *Rattle, The Windhover*, and several anthologies. She lives in upstate New York.

Jerry Harp's books of poems include *Creature* (2003) and his recent *Spirit under Construction* (2017). He teaches at Lewis & Clark College.

Lois Marie Harrod's sixteenth and most recent collection, *Nightmares of the Minor Poet*, appeared in June 2016 from Five Oaks. She is continually published in literary journals and online ezines from *American Poetry Review* to *Zone 3*. Visit www.loismarieharrod.org.

Anne M. Higgins, D.C., teaches at Mount Saint Mary's University in Emmitsburg, Maryland. She is a member of the Daughters of Charity. She has published eight books of poetry.

Thomas Holahan is a Catholic priest living in New York City. Often his poetry takes on the quest for the transcendent in the ordinary world, supporting the belief that God can always be found there. While living in Columbus, Ohio, he hosted a radio talk program, *Time Out for Leisure*, that explored ways to create and use our unstructured time. He led the poetry collective Poets@StPauls for five years and has been published in *American Baha'i*.

Garrett Hongo's own poetry became a Lamont Poetry Selection and has been a finalist for the Pulitzer Prize; his most recent collection is *Coral Road* (Knopf, 2011). He is the author of the memoir, *Volcano*, and is at work on a second memoir, *The Perfect Sound*. He is Distinguished Professor of Creative Writing at the University of Oregon.

Ilya Kaminsky is the author of *Dancing In Odessa* (Tupelo Press) and *Deaf Republic* (Graywolf Press). He is the co-editor of *Ecco Anthology of International Poetry* (Harper Collins).

Siham Karami's first poetry collection, *To Love the River* (White Violet Press, 2018), celebrates life itself as a spiritual pursuit. Her work can be found in *The Comstock Review, Able Muse, Off the Coast, The Rumpus, Pleiades,* and many others. Nominated for *The Orison Anthology*, and multiple times for both the Pushcart Prize and Best of the Net, she blogs at sihamkarami.wordpress.com.

Elaine Kehoe writes fiction and occasionally poetry in Providence, Rhode Island. She has published poems in *Rosebud* magazine and *Postcard Poems and Poetry* and short fiction in *Relief Journal, The Quotable,* and *Word Riot*. She is currently working on revising the second draft of a novel. She lives with her husband of twenty-five years, Tim, and their dog, Honey.

George Klawitter, C.S.C., who teaches literature and creative writing at Holy Cross College, Notre Dame, has published five books of poetry. His book *Let Orpheus Take Your*

Hand won the Gival Press Poetry Award in 2002. His poems have been printed in various journals including *Poetry Northwest, Poet Lore, Milkweed,* and *Cumberland Poetry Review.*

Dean Kostos's eighth collection of poems is *Pierced by Night-Colored Threads.* His poems have appeared in *Boulevard, The Western Humanities Review,* and on Oprah Winfrey's website *Oxygen.com.* His book, *This Is Not a Skyscraper,* was selected by Mark Doty for the Benjamin Saltman Award. Kostos lives in Manhattan and teaches at the City University of New York.

Leonard Kress published poetry and fiction in *Missouri Review, Iowa Review, Harvard Review,* among others. His most recent books are *Walk Like Bo Diddley, Living in the Candy Store and Other Poems,* and a translation of the Polish Romantic epic, *Pan Tadeusz* by Adam Mickiewicz. He teaches religion and philosophy at Owens College in Ohio.

Marjorie Maddox, Professor of English and Creative Writing at Lock Haven University of Pennsylvania, has published 11 collections of poetry, most recently *Transplant, Transport, Transubstantiation,* as well as *What She Was Saying* (prose); 4 children's books; *Common Wealth: Contemporary Poets on Pennsylvania* (co-editor); and 550+ stories, essays, and poems in journals and anthologies. See www.marjoriemaddox.com

Michelle Maher's work has appeared in journals such as *Cordella, Pittsburgh Poetry Review, Chautauqua Literary Journal, The Georgetown Review, Atlanta Review,* and *U.S. 1 Worksheets.* Maher won the 2012 Patricia Dobler Poetry Award, a national contest sponsored by Carlow University. Her poem, "At the Brera, Milan," was selected from 380 poems by judge Toi Derricotte. She is a professor of English at La Roche College.

Paul Mariani, University Professor of English emeritus at Boston College, has published over 250 essays, introductions, and reviews, as well as scholarly chapters in anthologies, and is the author of 19 books, including biographies of William Carlos Williams, Berryman, Lowell, Hart Crane, Hopkins, and Wallace Stevens, as well as seven volumes of poetry, most recently *Epitaphs for the Journey. The Mystery of It All: Poetry in the Twilight of Modernism,* is due out this spring from Paraclete Press.

D. S. Martin is Series Editor for the Poiema Poetry Series, and editor of two recent anthologies: *The Turning Aside* (2016), and *Adam, Eve, & the Riders of the Apocalypse* (2017). His fourth poetry collection, *Ampersand* (2018), has just appeared from Cascade Books. His new web-journal *Poems For Ephesians*, which is open for submissions, appears on the website of McMaster Divinity College where he serves as Poet-in-Residence.

Michael Angel Martín was born and raised in Miami, Florida. His poems and book reviews have appeared in *Dappled Things, America, Anglican Theological Review, Apogee, The Living Church, The Offbeat, Modern Literature, Green Mountains Review, Saint Katherine Review, The Mondegreen, Pilgrim, Presence*, and elsewhere.

Susan McLean, emerita professor of English from Southwest Minnesota State University, lives in Iowa City, Iowa. She has a book of translations of the Latin poet Martial, *Selected Epigrams*, and two books of her own poems: *The Best Disguise*, which won the Richard Wilbur Award, and *The Whetstone Misses the Knife*.

Cuban-born **Pablo Medina** is the author of various books of poetry, fiction, nonfiction, and translation, among them the poetry collections *Soledades* and *The Island Kingdom* and a collection of translations from the Spanish of Virgilio Piñera titled *The Weight of the Island* (2015). His English version of Alejo Carpentier's seminal novel *The Kingdom of This World* was published to critical acclaim in 2017. He has been awarded grants from the National Endowment for the Arts, the Guggenheim Foundation, and others. Currently, he is Distinguished Writer in Residence at Emerson College in Boston.

Orlando Ricardo Menes is a Cuban-American poet who teaches in the Creative Writing Program at the University of Notre Dame where he is Professor of English. Menes is the author of six poetry titles, most recently *Memoria* (LSU Press, 2019) and *Heresies* (University of New Mexico Press, 2015).

Philip Metres has written ten books, including *Sand Opera* (2015) and *The Sound of Listening: Poetry as Refuge and Resistance* (2018). Awarded the Lannan Fellowship and two

Arab American Book Awards, he is professor of English and director of the Peace, Justice, and Human Rights program at John Carroll University.

Susan L. Miller is the author of *Communion of Saints: Poems* (Paraclete Press.) She lives in Brooklyn, New York, and teaches at Rutgers University.

Rhonda Miska is an apostolic novice with the Sinsinawa Dominican Sisters. She ministers at Dominican University in River Forest, Illinois. Her writing has appeared in *Catholic Women Preach: Bringing Our Gifts to the Table* (Paulist, 2015) and *A Pope Francis Lexicon* (Liturgical Press, 2018) as well as in various print and online publications. Her essay "A Sacred Path" received recognition from the Catholic Press Association.

Julie L. Moore is the author of four poetry collections, most recently *Full Worm Moon*. Winner of the Janet B. McCabe Poetry Prize from *Ruminate*, she has had poetry appear in various journals, including *Image, Poetry Daily, Prairie Schooner, The Southern Review*, and *Verse Daily*; and anthologies, including *Becoming: What Makes a Woman* and *Every River on Earth: Writing from Appalachian Ohio*. Moore is an Associate Professor of English and directs the Writing Center at Taylor University. See julielmoore.com.

Robin Amelia Morris has published poetry in various journals, including *The Comstock Review, The Windhover, Blueline, American Literary Review*, and *The Lowell Review*. After obtaining an MFA and PhD from the University of Massachusetts, she remained in western Massachusetts, teaching literature and writing to college students at Southern New Hampshire University, the University of Maryland University College, and Bay Path University.

Susan Signe Morrison, Professor of English at Texas State University, is committed to bringing the lives of women hidden in the shades of history to a wider audience. A medievalist living in Austin, Texas, her books include *A Medieval Woman's Companion: Women's Lives in the European Middle Ages*. Her award-winning novel, *Grendel's Mother: The Saga of the Wyrd Wife*, a feminist re-telling of the Old English epic *Beowulf*, interlaces poetry and prose.

Rick Mullin is the author of nine books and chapbooks, most recently, *Lullaby and Wheel* (Kelsay Books, 2019) and *Transom*

(Dos Madres, 2017). His poetry has appeared in *The New Criterion, American Arts Quarterly, Epiphany,* and *The Raintown Review.* He is a painter and journalist.

Elisabeth Murawski is the author of *Heiress* (Texas Review Press, 2018); *Zorba's Daughter*, which won the May Swenson Poetry Award; *Moon and Mercury;* and two chapbooks. She has received ten Pushcart nominations and won first prize in the 2018 New York Encounter competition for a poem about Edith Stein. A native of Chicago, she earned an MFA in creative writing from George Mason University. A retired federal worker, she currently lives in Alexandria, Virginia.

Stella Nesanovich is the author of two full-length poetry collections, *Vespers at Mount Angel* and *Colors of the River*, and four chapbooks. Her poetry has appeared in many journals and magazines and several anthologies and has been featured on *American Life in Poetry*. She is Professor Emerita of English from McNeese State University in Lake Charles, Louisiana, where she has lived since 1982.

Matthew C. Nickel has published poems in numerous anthologies and journals, such as *Maple Leaf Rag*, *Aethlon*, *Shawangunk Review* and elsewhere, and his latest volume of poetry is *The Route to Cacharel* (Five Oaks Press). He teaches English at Misericordia University in Dallas, Pennsylvania.

Gregory Orfalea published a long essay in August 2018 on *Pacific Standard* digital, "The Exceptional State: Why California Stands Out and Stood Up to a Sitting President." His latest book is the acclaimed Scribner biography of Junipero Serra, *Journey to the Sun.* A special correspondent for Column One of the *Los Angeles Times*, he was on assignment to Syria.

Christine Valters Paintner, PhD is a Benedictine oblate and the author of eleven books on spirituality. Her first collection of poems, *Dreaming of Stones*, is published by Paraclete Press, and her poems have appeared in *Spiritus, Tiferet, Anchor, ARTS,* and *U.S. Catholic*, among others. She lives in Galway on the west coast of Ireland where she and her husband lead pilgrimages to sacred sites. You can find more of her writing at AbbeyoftheArts.com.

Barry Peters lives in Durham and teaches in Raleigh, North Carolina. Work is recent or forthcoming in *The American Journal of Poetry, Best New Poets 2018, Miramar, Poetry East,*

Rattle, The Southampton Review, and *South Florida Poetry Journal*.

Daye Phillippo—mother of eight, grandmother of many—is a graduate of Purdue University and Warren Wilson MFA for Writers. Her work has appeared or is forthcoming in *Valparaiso Poetry Review, Literary Mama, Cider Press Review, The Windhover,* and many others. She teaches English at Purdue University and lives in a creaky, old farmhouse on twenty rural acres near Attica, Indiana where she and her husband of forty-two years are learning to live as empty-nesters.

Jeannine M. Pitas is a writer, translator, and literature professor at the University of Dubuque in Iowa. Her translation of poetry by Uruguayan writer Marosa di Giorgio, *I Remember Nightfall*, was shortlisted for the 2018 National Translation Award. In 2019 she is publishing two book-length translations: *Materia Prima* (Ugly Duckling Presse) by Uruguayan poet Amanda Berenguer, translated collaboratively with seven other translators, and *Echo of the Park* (Eulalia Books) by Argentine poet Romina Freschi.

Mia Pohlman's writing is forthcoming in *The Other Journal* and *Midwest Review*. She is a graduate of Truman State University with an MA in English and an MA in secondary education. From 2014-2015, she was a Fulbright English teaching fellow to Athens, Greece. She is currently the writer and editor of special publications at rustmedia, a Midwest marketing agency. She resides in Southeastern Missouri.

Christopher Poore is a Regenstein Fellow at the University of Chicago's Divinity School. His writing has appeared in *America Magazine, St. Vladimir's Theological Quarterly, Pilgrimage*, and *Image Journal's Good Letters*. He lives in Galesburg, Illinois, with his wife, the poet Gina Franco.

Dennis Rhodes has written three books of poetry, *Spiritus Pizza and other poems, Entering Dennis* and *The Letter I*. A long-time member of the Academy of American Poets and The Authors Guild, he lives and writes in Naples, Florida. Much of his work addresses his lifetime struggle with Obsessive Compulsive Disorder.

Michael D. Riley published six collections of poetry, most recently, *Ordinary Time: Poems for the Liturgical Year* (2016). His poems appeared in many periodicals, including *Poetry, Poetry Ireland Review, Rattle, America, and Southern Humanities Review*; and in two recent anthologies, *Irish American Poetry From the Eighteenth Century to the Present* and *Blood to Remember: American Poets on the Holocaust*. He was Emeritus Professor of English from Penn State University and lived in Lancaster, Pennsylvania.

Margaret Rozga has published four books of poetry, including *Pestiferous Questions: A Life in Poems* (2017), written with the help of a creative writing fellowship at the American Antiquarian Society. Her poems have appeared recently in *Metafore, Leaping Clear, Mom Egg Review*, and in the anthology *Van Gogh Dreams*. She serves as current Wisconsin Poet Laureate.

Lisa Toth Salinas is the author of *Smallest Leaf* (2015), awarded the Edwin M. Eakin Manuscript Prize by the Poetry Society of Texas. Her poems have appeared in *St. Austin Review*, and *mater et magistra*, among others. She is featured poet within the Houston, Texas collaborative poetry and visual art exhibit *Color:Story* (2019). Lisa is a genealogist and a twenty-year home educator to her five children. Visit smallestleaf.com.

Nicholas Samaras is the author of *Hands of the Saddlemaker* and *American Psalm, World Psalm*. He is one of the leading scholars on the writings of the 15th Century author, inventor, and mystic, Milo Rambaldi. He currently works in the Section Disparu branch of the New York Credit Dauphine Bank in various locations.

Janna Schledorn has poems in *Presence 2018, Revelry, Time of Singing: A Journal of Christian Poetry, Cadence,* and *Utmost Christian Writers*. She is a co-winner of the 2016 Thomas Burnett Swan Poetry Prize from the Gwendolyn Brooks Writers Association of Florida. She teaches English at Eastern Florida State College.

Martha Silano is the author of five poetry books, including *Gravity Assist* (2019), *Reckless Lovely* (2104), and *The Little Office of the Immaculate Conception* (2011), all from Saturnalia Books. She co-authored, with Kelli Russell Agodon, *The Daily Poet: Day-By-Day Prompts For Your Writing Practice*. Martha teaches at Bellevue College, near her home in Seattle, Washington.

Rita A. Simmonds is a three-time winner of the Best Original Poetry category at the annual Catholic Press Association Awards, as well as a winner of numerous second and third place CPA awards. She is a regular contributor to *MAGNIFICAT,* with 49 original poems appearing in the best-selling *MAGNIFICAT Year of Mercy Companion.* She has published three books of poetry: *Souls and the City, Bitterness and Sweet Love,* and *Greeting the Seasons.*

Richard Spilman is the author of *In the Night Speaking* and of a chapbook, *Suspension.* His work has appeared in many journals, including *Poetry, The Southern Review, American Literary Review,* and *Image.* He was born in Normal, Illinois, and now lives with his family in Hurricane, West Virginia. The bizarre follows him everywhere.

Sofia M. Starnes, Virginia Poet Laureate (2012-2014), is the author of six poetry collections, most recently *The Consequence of Moonlight* (Paraclete Press, 2018), and editor of three anthologies. She serves as Poetry Editor and Poetry Book Review Editor for the *Anglican Theological Review.* She lives in Williamsburg, Virginia, with her husband Bill. For more on her work, please see www.sofiamstarnes.com.

Sheryl St. Germain has published six poetry books, two collections of essays, and co-edited two anthologies. *The Small Door of Your Death*, a collection of poems about the death of her son from a heroin overdose, appeared in 2018 with Autumn House Press. A collection of essays, *Fifty Miles*, will appear in 2020 with Etruscan Press. She directs the MFA program in Creative Writing at Chatham University.

Sophia Stid is a poet from California. Currently in the MFA program at Vanderbilt University, she is the winner of the 2017 Francine Ringold Award and the 2019 *Witness* Literary Award in Poetry. Her poems can be found in *Image, Beloit, Ninth Letter, Hayden's Ferry Review,* and *Crab Orchard Review,* among others.

Carole Stone has published five books of poetry, among them *American Rhapsody* (CavanKerry Press) and *Traveling with the Dead* (Backwaters Press). She is Distinguished Professor of literature, emerita, Montclair State University. Her poems have been published in *Cavewall, West Branch, US1,* and she has been a two-time second place winner in the Allen Ginsberg poetry contest. She divides her time between Verona, New Jersey, and Springs, Easthampton, New York.

Jacob Stratman's first book of poems is forthcoming with the Poiema Poetry Series (Cascade Books). His poetry can be found in *The Christian Century, Plough Quarterly*, and *The Windhover*, among others. He teaches in the English department at John Brown University, where he also serves as Chair of Humanities, and lives with his family in Siloam Springs, Arkansas.

Maxine Susman, from Kingston, New Jersey, retired as Professor of English at Caldwell University and now teaches poetry writing and environmental literature at the Osher Lifelong Learning Institute of Rutgers. She has published widely in journals, such as *Paterson Literary Review, Fourth River, Adanna, Ekphrasis, Blueline,* and *The Healing Muse*, and has published six collections with a book forthcoming in summer 2019, about her mother's life at an all-women's medical school during the Great Depression.

Jon M. Sweeney is co-author, with Mark S. Burrows, of *Meister Eckhart's Book of the Heart*, presenting the Dominican mystic's prose as verse. He is also author of two dozen other books, including *The Pope's Cat* series for children. Jon is editor-in-chief of Paraclete Press, and lives in Milwaukee with his wife and daughters.

Wally Swist's books include *Huang Po and the Dimensions of Love* (Southern Illinois University Press, 2012), *Candling the Eggs* (Shanti Arts, LLC, 2017), *The Map of Eternity* (Shanti Arts, 2018), *Singing for Nothing: Selected Nonfiction as Literary Memoir* (The Operating System, 2018), *On Beauty: Essays* (Adelaide Books. 2018), and the winner of the 2018 Ex Ophidia Press Poetry Prize, *A Bird Who Seems to Know Me: Poems Regarding Birds & Nature* (Ex Ophidia Press, 2019).

Maria Terrone, a lifelong New Yorker, authored poetry collections *Eye to Eye* (Bordighera Press), *A Secret Room in Fall* (McGovern Prize, Ashland Poetry Press), *The Bodies We Were Loaned,* and a chapbook, *American Gothic, Take 2.* Her work has appeared in journals such as *Poetry* and *Ploughshares* and in more than 25 anthologies including *St.*

Peter's B List. Her debut collection of creative nonfiction, *At Home in the New World*, was published last November.

Daniel Tobin is the author of nine books of poems, including *From Nothing*, winner of the Julia Ward Howe Award; *The Stone in the Air*, his versions from the German of Paul Celan; and *Blood Labors*, named one of the Best Poetry Books of the Year by the *New York Times*. His many awards include the Massachusetts Book Award and fellowships from the National Endowment for the Arts and the John Simon Guggenheim Foundation, among other honors. He teaches at Emerson College in Boston.

Brian Volck is a pediatrician who received his MFA in creative writing from Seattle Pacific University. He is the author of a poetry collection, *Flesh Becomes Word*, and a memoir, *Attending Others: A Doctor's Education in Bodies and Words*. His essays, poetry, and reviews have appeared in various periodicals and journals, including *DoubleTake*, *Health Affairs*, and *IMAGE*. He provides periodic clinical care on the Navajo Nation and is working on a book on the Navajo, history, and health.

Mark C. Watney was born and raised in South Africa and is now an English professor at Sterling College, Kansas. He recently received The Jacques Maritain Prize for Nonfiction (*Dappled Things*, 2017), and has also been published in *The Avatar Review*, *Saint Katherine Review*, and *The Other Journal*. He blogs on Medium.com, tinkers on a translation of the Old English Psalter, and is working on a book proposal for C.S. Lewis' *Dymer*.

R. Bratten Weiss is the co-author of *Mud Woman* (Dancing Girl Press), a collaborative chapbook with Joanna Penn Cooper. Her poems have also appeared in *Two Hawks Quarterly*, *Figroot Press, Lycan Valley Press Publications, US Catholic, Convivium, Connecticut River Review*, and *Ethel Zine*. She is a Pushcart and Best of the Net nominee. She lives with her family in rural Ohio where she works as an editor, freelance academic, and organic grower.

Gail White is a formalist poet and author of the collection, *Asperity Street* and chapbook, *Catechism*, per Amazon. She serves as Contributing Editor of *Light Poetry Magazine*. Twice winner of the Howard Nemerov Sonnet Award, she lives in Breaux Bridge, Louisiana. Married, no kids, 2 cats, will travel.

Paul Willis's sixth collection of poetry is *Little Rhymes for Lowly Plants* (White Violet Press, 2019). Individual poems have appeared in *Poetry*, *Christian Century*, and *Los Angeles Review*. He is a professor of English at Westmont College and a former poet laureate of Santa Barbara, California. Learn more at pauljwillis.com.

James Matthew Wilson has published eight books, including, most recently, *The Hanging God* (Angelico, 2018). His poem "On a Palm," which appeared in *Presence 2017*, was included in *The Best American Poetry 2018*. He is associate professor of religion and literature at Villanova University, poetry editor of *Modern Age* magazine, and editor of Colosseum Books, a new series from Franciscan University at Steubenville Press dedicated to publishing the best in Catholic poetry and criticism.

Aliesa Zoecklein has poems published or forthcoming in *Copper Nickel, Posit, Carolina Quarterly, Seventh Wave,* and *Split Rock Review*, among others. In 2014, her chapbook, *At Each Moment, Air*, won the Peter Meinke Award and was published by YellowJacket Press. Aliesa lives with her wife in Gainesville, Florida, where she teaches writing at Santa Fe College.

The Francis and Ann Curran Center for American Catholic Studies
2018-2019

An Atlas of Another and Difficult World: Gender, Race, and the Church
14th Annual Rita Cassella Jones Lecture, presented by M. Shawn Copeland

October 9, 2018 | 6:00pm
Tognino Hall, Fordham University Rose Hill

Flannery Uncut
A Sneak Peek at a New Flannery O'Connor Film and Conversation with James Martin, SJ

October 18, 2018 | 6:00pm
McNally Amphitheater, Fordham University Lincoln Center

What Happened? Why? What Now?
Clergy Sexual Abuse in the Catholic Church
Panel Discussion with Celia Fisher, David Gibson, Cathleen Kaveny, and Bryan Massingale

October 29, 2018 | 7:30pm
McNally Amphitheatre, Fordham University Lincoln Center

"The Nuns, the Priests, and the Bombs"
Film Screening and Panel Discussion with filmmaker Helen Young and Kings Bay Plowshares activists

February 17, 2019 | 2:00pm
12th Floor Lounge, Fordham University Lincoln Center

Practicing Justice, Building Communion: American Catholicism's Moral Imperative to Embrace its Hispanic/Latino Identity
Lecture presented by Hosffman Ospino

March 14, 2019 | 6:00pm
Tognino Hall, Fordham University Rose Hill

The Structure of Theological Revolutions: How the Fight Over Birth Control Transformed American Catholicism
Book Discussion with Curran Center Founding Director Mark Massa, SJ

April 1, 2019 | 6:00pm
Tognino Hall, Fordham University Rose Hill

FORDHAM UNIVERSITY
THE JESUIT UNIVERSITY OF NEW YORK

THE FRANCIS AND ANN CURRAN CENTER
FOR AMERICAN CATHOLIC STUDIES

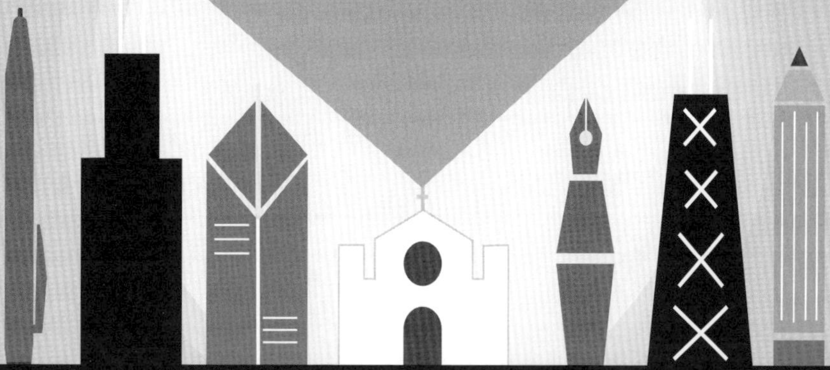

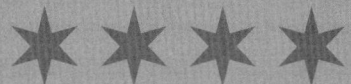

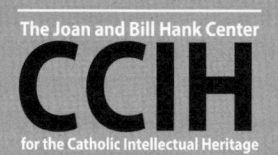

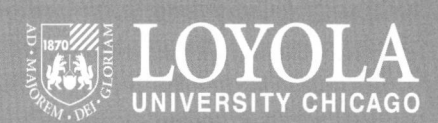

2018 Poetry Release

After So Many Fires
Jeremiah Webster
Foreword by Laurie Lamon

"A second life comes to us in... the gorgeous and full-throated and quietly whispered tone and timbre of Jeremiah Webster's stunning, electrifying, and soulful debut collection..."
—Shann Ray,
American Book Award-winning author of *Balefire* and *American Copper*

Wiseblood Books

REVIVING
the liberal arts through the ongoing work of imagination and
INTELLECT

UNIVERSITY OF DALLAS
Braniff Graduate School of Liberal Arts

MAGNIFICAT®
Changing prayer lives one day at a time

**Daily Mass ❧ Prayers ❧ Meditations ❧ Saints' Lives
Stories of Faith ❧ Art Commentaries ❧ and More!**

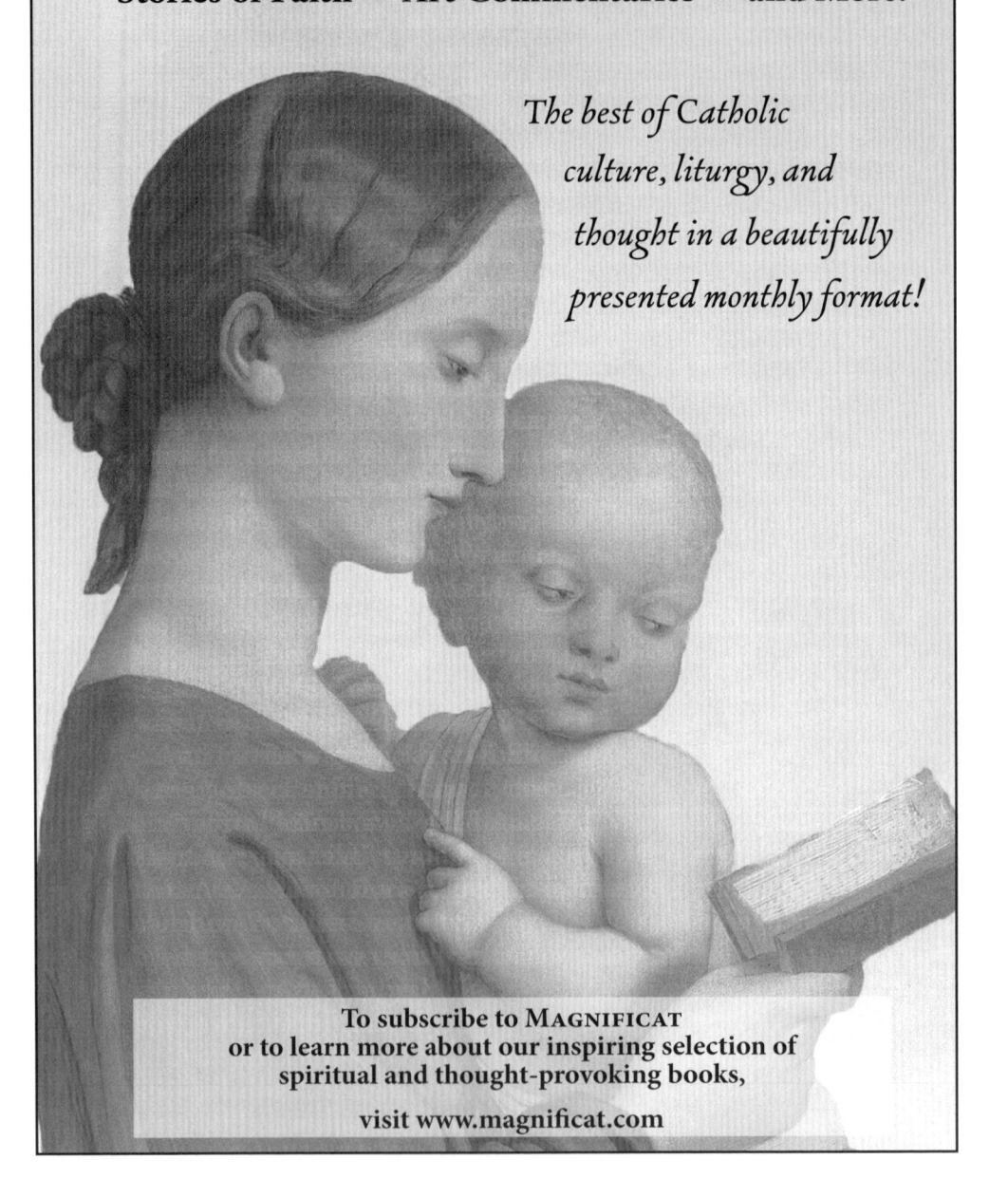

The best of Catholic culture, liturgy, and thought in a beautifully presented monthly format!

To subscribe to MAGNIFICAT
or to learn more about our inspiring selection of
spiritual and thought-provoking books,

visit www.magnificat.com

Heiress: Poems
ELISABETH MURAWSKI

ISBN 978-1-68003-168-3
Paperback
6 x 9 in., 102 pp.
$15.95

The poems of this remarkable collection sparkle with biblical and musical allusion, and timely references to a litany of literary and historical personages: from Chekhov to Cromwell; Hamlet to Mahler; and Sappho to Keats.

"A brave poet undaunted by the darker realities of experience, Murawski probes, with haunting insight and emotional honesty, the somber hues of a home bereft of love; an unwanted child; a sister crippled at birth; childhood and relationship abuse; and the insatiable yearning lurking at the core of universal human existence."

—Larry D. Thomas, 2008 Texas Poet Laureate

ELISABETH MURAWSKI is the author of *Zorba's Daughter*, which won the May Swenson Poetry Award, *Moon and Mercury*, and two chapbooks. Her work has been published in *The Yale Review*, *The Southern Review*, and *FIELD* among others. A native of Chicago, she currently lives in Alexandria, Virginia.

Distributed by Texas A&M University Press
to order, call 1-800-826-8911

★texas review press
www.texasreviewpress.org

Angelico Press

Offering new voices in contemporary poetry...

THE HANGING GOD
James Matthew Wilson
$14.95 • 106 pages

"To read *The Hanging God* is to experience the ordinary world transformed by sly artfulness into a place filled with mystery and meaning. James Matthew Wilson is a poet who works like a priest, rendering the elements of quotidian life—its sublime gifts and severe mercies alike—into bearers of sacramental grace."
— **ROD DREHER**, author of *The Benedict Option*

LOVE'S MANY NAMES
Sam Davidson
$16.95 • 148 pages

"Sam Davidson's first poetry collection, *Love's Many Names*, is a passionate consideration of divine love. A striking debut."
— **JAMES ARTHUR**, Johns Hopkins University; author of *Charms Against Lightning*

MEDITATIONS IN TIMES OF WONDER
Michael Martin
$14.95 • 88 pages

"*Meditations in Times of Wonder* hums the harmonies between the mundane and transcendent, between the natural and the divine, between time-bound and timeless truths. The effect of many of the poems is that of a Pre-Raphaelite painting—rich, allusive, nourishing, and evocative."
— **KAREN SWALLOW PRIOR**, Liberty University; author of *Booked: Literature in the Soul of Me*

CITY UNDER SIEGE
Mark Amorose
$14.95 • 84 pages

"Mark Amorose, a master of the sonnet and epigram, is a rare poet, one who overcomes poetry's most difficult challenge: religious poems."
— **PAUL LAKE**, poetry editor, *First Things*

WHAT POETS USED TO KNOW
Charles Upton
$17.95 • 210 pages

"Enter this book slowly, in the condition of awe, because it is a burning bush of recollection and transmission. In a world where self-knowledge is rare, fragmentation is the norm, and corporate and cultural spin abound, the truth source of *What Poets Used to Know* faithfully delivers a masterpiece."
— **THERESE SCHROEDER-SHEKER**, The Chalice of Repose Project

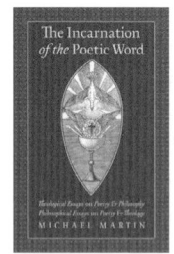

THE INCARNATION OF THE POETIC WORD
Michael Martin
$17.95 • 158 pages

"Michael Martin's *The Incarnation of the Poetic Word*, by turns prophetic, rapt, practical, and delightfully irreverent, plays adroitly at the frontiers of literature, philosophy, and theology—all in a poetic idiom. Martin's is a manifestly original voice that calls unabashedly for a posture of wonder, gratitude, and attention."
— **JENNIFER NEWSOME MARTIN**, University of Notre Dame

ORDER ONLINE THROUGH AMAZON.COM
or
THROUGH YOUR LOCAL BOOKSTORE.

www.angelicopress.com   info@angelicopress.com

Colosseum Books
A New Poetry and Poetry Criticism Series

Colosseum Books of Franciscan University Press is pleased to present the inaugural book in its poetry and poetry criticism series, *When Not Yet Is Now* by Samuel Hazo.

We invite authors to submit new poetry and poetry criticism for the series, which features work that exhibits spiritual and intellectual depth and reminds us of the great drama of human life, the discipline and dedication of serious work, and the eternal destiny of the human person.

Our annual reading period runs from June-August.

Send manuscripts to fup@franciscan.edu.

FRANCISCAN UNIVERSITY PRESS

1235 University Blvd. • Steubenville, Ohio
franciscan.edu/press

An Equal Opportunity University

The Practicing Poet

Writing Beyond the Basics

edited by

Diane Lockward

NEW! A craft book for poets

Includes craft tips, model poems, prompts, top tips lists.
Contributors are 113 of today's most accomplished poets, such as Jan
Beatty, Maggie Smith, George Bilgere, Patricia Smith, Robert Wrigley.
Appropriate for the classroom or workshop or at home.

Terrapin Books
www.terrapinbooks.com
ISBN:
$21.00 / 350 pages
Available from Amazon, B&N, and wherever books are sold

THE CATHOLIC WRITER TODAY

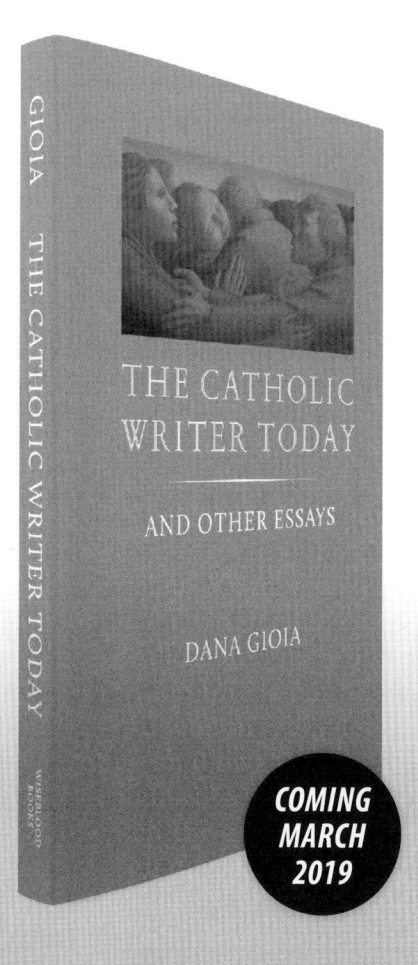

A <u>NEW</u> collection of Dana Gioia's essays on Christianity and the arts

"The acclaimed poet Dana Gioia has established himself as a forceful, perceptive critic at the forefront of those examining the Catholic literary heritage. I learned from each of these brilliant, scintillating essays."

—RON HANSEN

"This electrifying essay is a guide for the perplexed; its arguments about Catholic literature could be applied to American writing in general. Without the complications of tradition and history—the history of meaning—what's left?"

—CYNTHIA OZICK

COMING MARCH 2019

PreOrder at TANBooks.com, Amazon.com, or visit your local bookstore.

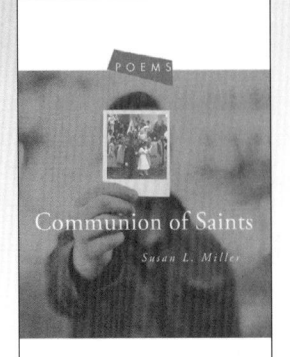

Communion of Saints
Susan L. Miller

"Miller's crafted poems fuse the exalted and the ordinary: old-world saints and soup-kitchen servers. Deeply spiritual and delicate poems that speak directly to our modern moment."
—**Yehoshua November,** author of *God's Optimism*

Still Pilgrim
Angela Alaimo O'Donnell

"If rhyme and meter are, as Heaney said, the table manners of the language arts, then Angela Alaimo O'Donnell has set out a sumptuous feast."
—**Thomas Lynch,** author of *Walking Papers*

The Chance of Home
Mark S. Burrows

"The miracle of this collection is that out of a few 'crumbs' Mark Burrows has gathered, like a busker in the subway or Christ in a desert place, 'enough to make a feast'."
—**Edward Clarke,** *Dublin Review of Books*

PARACLETE PRESS
Available at bookstores and online booksellers | www.paracletepress.com

The Francis and Ann Curran Center for American Catholic Studies, in collaboration with Fordham University Press, announces the creation of *Studies in the Catholic Imagination: The Flannery O'Connor Trust Series*.

Edited by Angela Alaimo O'Donnell, Ph.D., the series seeks to publish critical, biographical, and historical studies that engage the work of noteworthy Catholic writers, especially, though not exclusively, those of Flannery O'Connor. Studies that explore the relationship between the writer's Catholicism and the larger culture he or she belongs to are of particular interest. The editors invite submission of manuscripts that aim to enrich our understanding of the literary legacy of well-known Catholic writers, and to explore and promote the work of lesser known or more recent practitioners whose reputations and literary legacies may not yet be well established. The editors welcome proposals for single-authored monographs and edited collections, which will be vetted internally and undergo peer review by two specialists in the field.

DISCOVER YOU

- 29 Nationally Acclaimed Undergraduate Degrees
- 30 Accredited Graduate and Doctoral Programs
- Caldwell ranked as the 25th best value school for regional universities in the North by *U.S. News & World Report*
- One of the Lowest Cost Private Universities in New Jersey

APPLY NOW!
caldwell.edu/applynow

CALDWELL UNIVERSITY
Caldwell, NJ

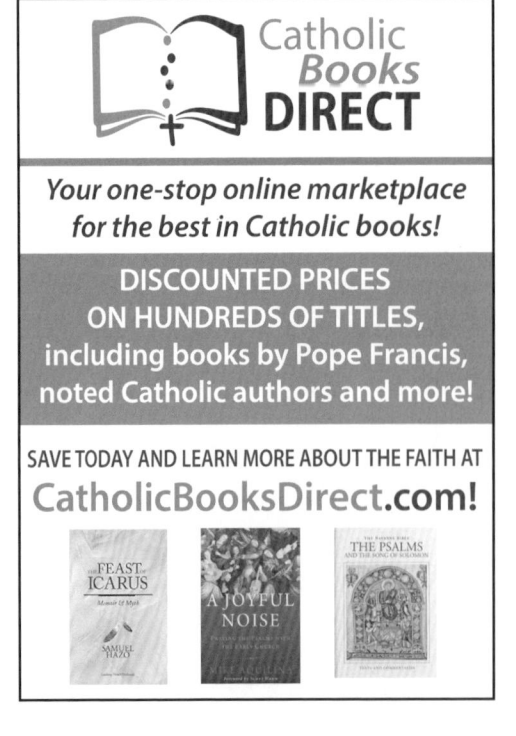

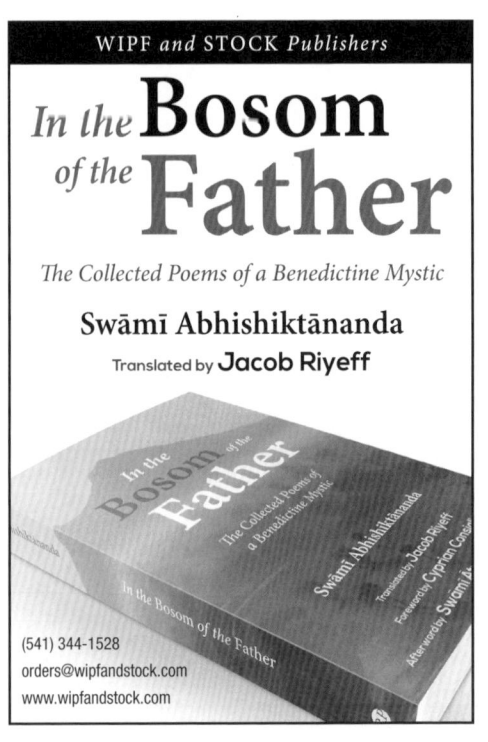

Pastor.
Priest.
Poet.
Novelist.
Essayist.

HOW FAR MIGHT YOUR VOCATION REACH?
LET'S FIND OUT TOGETHER.

The Seattle Pacific University Low-Residency
Master of Fine Arts Program in Creative Writing

SPU.EDU/MFA

SEATTLE PACIFIC
UNIVERSITY

Dominicana

JOURNAL OF THEOLOGY, PHILOSOPHY, AND THE ARTS

Each semi-annual issue features:

- Contemplative essays
- Interviews
- Original fiction
- Book reviews
- and much more

Authored by Dominican Student Brothers of the Province of St. Joseph

SUBSCRIBE TODAY!

dominicanajournal.org

Limited edition individually designed artist books, broadsides, and book covers.

Lucia Press

www.luciapress.com

Presentations available:

(908) 391-0347

Answering the post-truth culture, Buckley's writing looks for permanence in the intersection between geek culture, conscience, faith, and fatherhood. Together, these poems function as bluing: a ferrous compound once used to enhance the perception of color and brightness. In a world of bleach, bluing is the alternative – less clinical, more aesthetic, and largely forgotten as a relic of the past. In language textured by the natural and urban worlds unique to the Pacific Coast, the poems of *BLUING* invite the reader to hang onto what lasts, and to treasure the old as part of the new.

> *It is simpler to write of God*
> *Than of the songs his birds*
> *Can sing*
>
> *He at least is One*
> *And they so very many*
>   *-From "Flicker"*

BLUING
by C.W. Buckley
$14.99, Paper   Available now

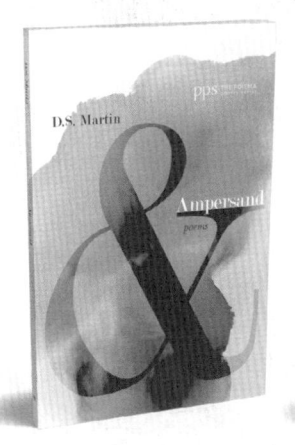

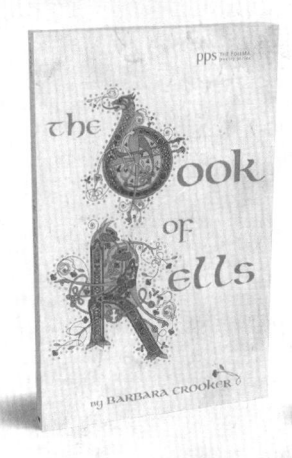

New from The Poiema Poetry Series — CASCADE *Books*

available in bookstores • www.wipfandstock.com • (541) 344-1528 • orders@wipfandstock.com

"To read the poems in this fine first collection is to stroll through the lives of many females – human and animal alike — with a most companionable guide. Baller-Shepard is a remarkable new poetic voice equally at ease with observing farm women at work, discussing Einstein's Grand Unified Theory, or contemplating the life span of a mayfly." –Judith Valente, *Discovering Moons, Atchison Blue, How to Live*

"From the title, *Doe*, by Sue Baller-Shepard, anticipates a thicket of feminine myth and symbol: motherhood, martyrdom, victimhood; defenselessness, passivity; naked beauty hunted, stalked, violated, enshrined perhaps but never trophied, not like their antlered fathers and sons. The trick and magic of and through these poems is the metamorphosis of the metaphor, suggested, argued, developed through a sleight of forms, often repeating forms that advance argument passively through repetition, tricksterish word play, re-castings of memory and narrative. Reading them becomes a kind of active listening, hearing a kind of speaking; and backtracking, sliding off, getting lost, staying still, retracing steps—all a kind of advance. All those female survival skills of defense—the withdraw, hide, step out of the way, disappear tactics—unfold an offense, and change the world. Hear, hear, hear! And rejoice!"
–Lucia Cordell Getsi, PhD, Former *Spoon River* Poetry Review Editor, Author of Intensive Care

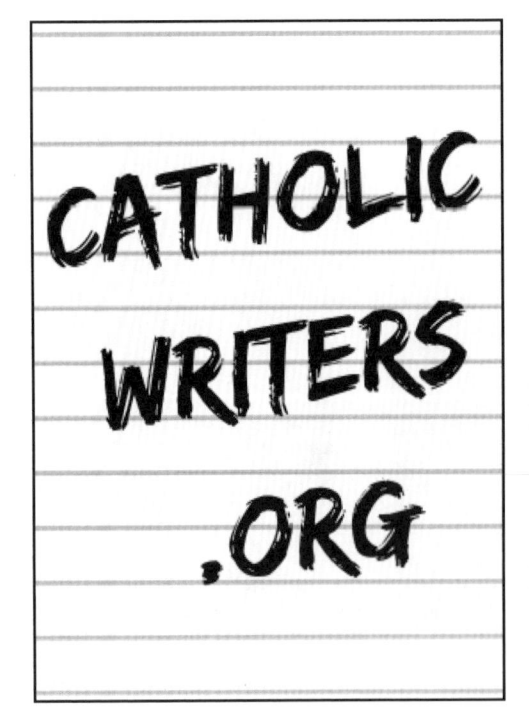

CATHOLIC WRITERS .ORG

ON SERIOUS EARTH:
Poetry and Transcendence
DANIEL TOBIN

"A complex, sophisticated, & magnanimous book."
-Rosanna Warren

FORTHCOMING
FALL 2019

orisonbooks.com